Echoes of Sin

Exploring Biblical Times, Human Choices, and Lasting Consequences

By
Gary E. Risenhoover

Published by Kinetic Digital Publishers

www.kineticdigitalpublishers.com

For permissions, inquiries, or other correspondence, please visit our website.

ISBN eBook: 979-8-90235-120-7
ISBN Paperback: 979-8-90235-121-4
ISBN Hardcover: 979-8-90235-122-1
LCCN: 2026908993

TABLE OF CONTENTS

Preface

There is a certain gravity in the word sin, a term that transcends epochs and cultures, reverberating through millennia as both a personal shadow and a collective burden. The echoes of sin are not distant whispers confined to dusty scrolls or ancient stone tablets; they pulse within the corridors of history, hum beneath the surface of human experience, and resonate acutely in the moral dilemmas of our own lives. This book, *Echoes of Sin: Exploring Biblical Times, Human Choices, and Lasting Consequences*, invites you to journey into that profound landscape, where age-old narratives offer textured insights into the complexities of human frailty and divine justice. These are more than stories preserved in the canon of sacred scripture, they are living dialogues that intertwine with our deepest questions of righteousness, failure, mercy, and hope.

From the moment we peer into the Genesis account, witnessing Adam and Eve's fateful choice, we encounter not just an origin tale but an unfolding drama of ethics and consequences. Sin, in this primal moment, appears not merely as a breach of divine command but as the primordial divergence of human will from its intended harmony. It sets into motion an intricate web of cause and effect, marking the human condition with vulnerability, conflict, and a persistent yearning for redemption. The ensuing chapters of Scripture reveal sin's capacity to fracture relationships between brothers and sisters, leaders and peoples, God and humanity, while simultaneously illuminating pathways back toward restoration. This duality, this tragic beauty, forms the heart of what I hope you will discover within these pages.

Echoes of Sin is structured to guide you through the winding corridors of biblical history, an immersive exploration that traces the footprints of sin from the garden to the flood, from patriarchal tents to the anointed thrones of kings, through prophetic calls to repentance, and culminating in the transformative grace revealed in the life and teachings of Jesus Christ. Throughout this journey, I have sought to strike a delicate balance between narration and reflection, weaving vivid retellings of ancient events with thoughtful theological and cultural analysis. The goal is not only to understand what happened "then" but to uncover why these stories endure, how they function as mirrors reflecting our own moral landscapes, and how the tension between human imperfection and divine expectation continues to shape spiritual and ethical discourse.

One of the most compelling aspects of these biblical narratives is their portrayal of sin as a pervasive, almost living force, rather than isolated lapses or mere rule-breaking. Sin's reach extends beyond individuals; it colors entire communities, disrupts social orders, and challenges the very fabric of covenantal relationships. Yet this pervasive presence of sin is met equally by the steadfast hand of mercy, divine justice tempered by compassion, judgment entwined with forgiveness. This dynamic interplay invites us to reconsider our own understanding of morality not in rigid binaries of good and evil, but as a complex tapestry woven from choices, consequences, repentance, and hope.

As you engage with the stories of Cain and Abel, Noah's flood, Abraham's covenant, Moses' laws, and the triumphs and failures of Israel's kings, you will encounter profound moral conflicts and moments of heart-wrenching failure alongside glimpses of courage, faith, and grace. These human figures are strikingly relatable, they wrestle with doubt, succumb to temptation, confront fear, and yet often rise toward redemption. Their struggles speak across time, inviting us to reflect on the nature and consequences of our own decisions, the societal ripples they create, and the divine possibility for renewal that lies even in the aftermath of error.

This book also embraces the rich theological tensions embedded within these narratives. What does divine justice truly mean in the face of human sinfulness? How do mercy and judgment coexist without contradiction? How do ancient texts, with their cultural and historical particularities, inform individual faith and modern ethical living? Tackling these questions with sensitivity and scholarly respect, *Echoes of Sin* aims to honor the diverse interpretations that readers bring to the text, fostering an inclusive dialogue rather than prescribing rigid conclusions.

Beyond academic reflection, my hope is that this book fosters a transformative reading experience. By connecting the ancient and the contemporary, it seeks to illuminate the continuous presence of sin's echoes in our world today. Whether in personal struggles, societal fractures, or spiritual quests, the fundamental themes of choice, fallibility, justice, and redemption remain profoundly relevant. I invite you not merely to observe these biblical accounts as distant historical curiosities but to engage with them as living narratives that challenge, comfort, and inspire. Let these chapters serve as a mirror reflecting your own moral conscience, a window opening onto the vast divine panorama, and a guide toward navigating the complexity of human existence with wisdom and grace.

Ultimately, the story we encounter through these pages is far from static, it is dynamic and ongoing. Sin's shadow may darken the horizon, but so too does the dawn of hope break relentlessly. Each turning page offers a chance to listen carefully to the voices of ancient prophets, kings, and apostles, to heed their warnings and embrace their hopes. Through their layered experiences, we gain the tools not only to comprehend the historical weight of sin but to participate in the perpetual work of redemption, both within ourselves and in the communities we inhabit.

So, whether you are approaching this book with a thirst for historical understanding, theological insight, or personal growth, I welcome you to this journey. Together, let us explore the echoes of sin, its haunting power and its transformative promise, across biblical times and into the present moment of your own life. In doing so, may we uncover not only the depths of human frailty but also the boundless reach of divine grace.

Genesis of Transgression

The Garden and the Command

In the beginning, before time was measured in days or years, before history unfurled its vast tapestry of kings and empires, a singular moment of divine creativity gave birth to a sanctuary, a garden unlike any other. The Garden of Eden stood as a cosmic jewel cradled in the earth, a place where heaven and earth intertwined seamlessly, where the presence of the divine was not distant or abstract but palpably near. This garden, resplendent with lush foliage, rich and vibrant blossoms, and streams that shimmered like threads of silver under the eternal light of God's watchful gaze, embodied perfect harmony. It was a realm where every leaf whispered the tender care of its Maker, every breeze carried the promise of peace, and every creature moved in accord with the divine design. Here, in this idyllic haven, humanity's story first took root, a story that would echo through time with profound implications for the nature of human freedom, morality, and our relationship with the divine.

Into this garden, God breathed life into Adam, the first man, molding him from the earth's dust and igniting his nostrils with the breath of life, thus transforming inert matter into a living soul. Adam awoke within Eden, his senses immediately captivated by the garden's beauty and the palpable presence of his Creator, who walked with him 'in the cool of the day.' God then fashioned Eve from Adam's side, a companion made of the same substance, equal yet distinct, signifying relationship and community as intrinsic to humanity's design. The human couple, created in the image of God, lived not as solitary beings but as co-regents of creation, called to tend to the garden and to steward the abundance entrusted to them. Their dominion was not one of coercion or exploitation, but a sacred partnership reflecting the Creator's own benevolent authority. In this perfect setting, there was no fear, no pain, no shame, only innocence and the flourishing of life in its purest form.

God's initial instructions to humanity framed this existence with clarity and profound responsibility. The command was both simple and solemn: to freely enjoy from every tree of the garden except one, the tree of the knowledge of good and evil. This prohibition was not an arbitrary restriction nor a capricious test of obedience; it was, rather, a profound invitation to trust. To obey was to acknowledge God's wisdom surpassing human understanding, to live harmoniously within the boundaries of divine intention. The choice to obey or disobey introduced into their world the possibility of freedom, the freedom to love or to reject, to align with divine intention or forge a path of independence. Yet in this initial moment, sin had not yet entered; the garden was a realm without division between Creator and creature, without alienation or fear. The command itself was a marker of humanity's unique status: endowed with the capacity for moral discernment, owners of a will capable of choosing obedience or rebellion.

The nature of this command, "Do not eat of the tree of the knowledge of good and evil", is ripe with theological nuance. It is not merely a prohibition but a boundary between innocence and experiential knowledge; a boundary between life lived under the shelter of divine benevolence and life shaped in the grip of autonomous moral judgment. The knowledge of good and evil, in this sense, suggests a wisdom that is both enthralling and terrifying, a power that is not inherently evil but that, when pursued by human pride and severed from divine guidance, becomes the gateway to destruction. This tree, a symbol of moral autonomy, encapsulates the tension between freedom and dependence, a tension that would forever characterize human existence following the pivotal decision in Eden. The divine command does not diminish human freedom; rather, it imbues it with meaning and consequence, introducing the gravity of choice.

The presence of the divine in Eden also introduced an intimate and ongoing relationship between God and humanity, characterized by dialogue and presence. God's walk in the garden, presumably in a form perceivable and memorable to Adam and Eve, is a compelling image of friendship and vulnerability rarely emphasized in later narratives where God often appears remote. The command to abstain from the forbidden tree bespoke a covenantal relationship based on trust and loving reverence rather than mere obedience. It is within this delicate balance that the heart of the human-divine dynamic is revealed, a dynamic marked by divine generosity and human agency. The full richness of this relationship, however, would soon be tested by temptation.

The serpent, introduced without a detailed origin but imbued with cunning and subversiveness, enters the garden not merely as a creature but as an emblem of temptation and deceit. Its dialogue with Eve unveils the subtleties of sin: it does not overtly command disobedience but sows doubt, questioning God's motives and casting aspersions on the prohibition itself. The serpent's rhetorical skill appeals to Eve's curiosity and desire for wisdom, enticing her with the promise that eating the fruit will grant knowledge and godlike discernment. This encounter reveals the nature of temptation as insidious and manipulative, preying on human desires and insecurities. It also highlights that disobedience often begins with a distortion of truth, a subtle redefinition of good and evil, not with blatant defiance. The serpent's role in this narrative is pivotal, illustrating that sin often emerges through seduction rather than force, through whispers rather than shouts.

Eve's decision to partake of the fruit, followed by Adam's willing acceptance, marks the sacred rupture, the original sin, fracturing the union between humanity and God. This act of disobedience is layered with meaning. It is a transgression born of human freedom, yet one shadowed by tragedy because it corrupts innocence, shatters trust, and invites death into the creation. Consuming the fruit symbolizes a grasping for autonomy, a desire to define 'good and evil' independently of divine revelation. In this moment, humanity strives to escape dependency on God and embrace self-determination, but the cost is immediate and profound. Awareness dawns abruptly: Adam and Eve perceive their nakedness, not merely physical vulnerability but a symbolic exposure of their fractured relationship with both each other and their Creator. The loss of innocence introduces shame, alienation, and fear, emotions previously unknown to them, marking the first time human beings experience the weight of guilt and the pangs of conscience.

The consequences of this act ripple through the narrative with inexorable force. When God confronts Adam and Eve, their responses reveal the beginnings of human culpability, evasion, and blame-shifting. Adam's blame of Eve, and Eve's attribution of deception to the serpent, epitomize human attempts to deflect responsibility, an enduring characteristic of moral failure throughout biblical history. God's judgment is measured yet irrevocable: the serpent is cursed to crawl upon the earth and sow enmity between humans and evil forces; Eve experiences expanded suffering in childbearing and relational complexity; and Adam faces the curse of toil and mortality, the ground itself resisting his labor. These curses are not mere punishments but profound alterations in the created order, transforming the physical and social realms. Death, both physical and spiritual, enters the human experience, severing the previous harmony between the divine, humanity, and creation.

Yet even in this moment of rupture, divine grace is perceptible. God clothes Adam and Eve with garments made from animal skins, an act that foreshadows themes of substitutionary atonement and mercy even in judgment. This tender provision intimates that God's judgment is tempered with compassion and that restoration remains possible despite sin's devastating effects. The expulsion from Eden, while enforcing separation for protection and the eventual possibility of growth, also initiates humanity's journey of moral development and hope, one in which the experience of sin and loss is not final but part of a larger divine narrative aimed at redemption.

The exile from Eden has profound symbolic resonance. It marks humanity's transition from a state of unmediated presence with God to one that must navigate a world marked by hardship, mortality, and moral complexity. The garden's gate, now guarded by cherubim with a flaming sword, closes behind humanity, not as a mere denial but as a safeguard against unrestrained access to the tree of life, which would have eternally fixed humanity in a fallen state. The exile initiates life's pilgrimage, a journey of seeking, repentance, and eventual restoration, where humans must live with the weight of their choices and the hope of divine mercy. It also introduces the profound mystery that defines much of biblical theology: how can a holy God reconcile justice and mercy in the face of human sinfulness? Eden, therefore, stands as both a place of origin and a symbol of lost paradise, a source of yearning that repeatedly calls humanity back to reconciliation.

This initial story casts long shadows over every subsequent narrative in the Bible. The themes of temptation, deception, choice, and the tension between autonomy and divine dependency become recurring motifs that shape biblical history and theology. The Garden and the command establish the framework for understanding sin not merely as a legal infraction but as a rupture in relationship, between humans and their Creator, between humans themselves, and between humanity and the natural world. This rupture introduces conflict, suffering, and mortality, but also invites the possibility of transformation through repentance and grace. The immensity of this foundational moment cannot be overstated, as it defines the human condition in its essential terms: a condition marked by freedom and limitation, by the capacity for both rebellion and redemption, by the poignant interplay between loss and hope.

Moreover, the Garden narrative invites a deep ethical and spiritual reflection on the nature of obedience and the human quest for wisdom. Does true knowledge come from disobedience and self-reliance, or from trust and humility before the divine? The command regarding the tree of the knowledge of good and evil challenges readers across centuries to contemplate the limits of human judgment and the dangers of pride. It exposes the paradox of freedom, that the greatest liberty is found not in lawlessness but in loving submission to the divine will. In this way, the story remains relentlessly relevant, inviting each generation to wrestle with questions about the source of true wisdom and the cost of moral failure.

In exploring this narrative, one cannot overlook the profound empathy embedded within it. The portrayal of Adam and Eve, not as simply guilty sinners but as vulnerable beings confronted by complex choices and the consequences of those choices, invites humility and compassion. Their story is not a simple tale of condemnation but a mirror reflecting the perennial human struggle to live rightly, to resist temptation, and to embrace responsibility. It recognizes the fragility of the human heart and the persistence of divine love even when that heart falters. The Garden and the command, therefore, are not just historical or mythic accounts, they are spiritual truths lived out in the journey of every human soul seeking meaning, belonging, and reconciliation.

Ultimately, the Garden serves as a profound metaphor for the human path. It captures the tension between innocence and experience, divine proximity and separation, freedom and responsibility. It calls humanity to acknowledge the consequences of choice and to live with the awareness that actions have ripple effects beyond immediate gratification. This awareness is a call to ethical maturity, inviting ongoing reflection on the intertwined realities of temptation and obedience, sin and grace, death and life. The echoes of Eden reverberate through the corridors of history and faith, urging each person to engage with the deepest questions about what it means to be human in a world where the divine beckons even as temptation lurks.

Thus, the initial setting, the Garden, and the command provide a foundational lens through which to understand not only the origin of sin but also the possibility of mercy and hope. It sets the stage for the unfolding drama of human history and divine interaction that permeates biblical scripture. It invites readers to contemplate the enduring tension between human frailty and divine expectation, between judgment and forgiveness, and between exile and restoration. In this early encounter between God and humanity, we find the blueprint for all moral and spiritual journeys, the origin of the profound human struggle to walk wisely and gracefully through a world forever marked by the interplay of light and shadow. The Garden of Eden thus remains more than ancient history; it is the perennial landscape of the human heart, the birthplace of free will, and the enduring symbol of God's longing for a relationship with a flawed but beloved creation.

The Serpent's Temptation

In the lush and tranquil expanse of the Garden of Eden, where life unfolded with unblemished harmony under the watchful gaze of the Creator, a singular presence carried with it the quiet weight of disruption, a creature both enigmatic and sinister, the serpent. This serpent, far more than a mere reptile, serves as the fulcrum of the primordial drama that sets the course for the unfolding human narrative. Its role transcends the physical form, becoming a profound symbol of temptation, cunning, and the insidious nature of disobedience that invites humanity into a confrontation with freedom, morality, and the reality of choice. The biblical account, in its brief yet dense description, captures a moment suffused with tension, a moment where the innocence of the first humans, Adam and Eve, encounters the stark challenge of temptation, signaling the inaugural fracture in the relationship between man and God.

The serpent's approach to Eve is not brusque or overtly hostile; rather, it embodies subtlety and craft. It initiates its encounter with a question, sowing doubt about the command given by God. "Did God really say, 'You shall not eat from any tree in the garden'?" This question is masterful in its simplicity and its devastating potential. It invites Eve to reconsider the boundaries set by the divine, boundaries meant to protect, to preserve the sanctity of life, and to maintain the delicate balance of obedience and trust. By framing the command in terms of prohibition and limitation, the serpent plants the seed of suspicion, suggesting that the divine command might be a restriction born not of care but of control. This subtle corroding of trust in the divine word embodies the seductive character of temptation, it is rarely raw coercion but rather a whispered suggestion that fractures certainty and invites rebellion through intellectual and emotional appeal.

Temptation, as portrayed in this encounter, is not simply a desire for the forbidden fruit or a craving for sensory gratification; it is much deeper, more complex. It engages the mind's capacity for reflection, interpretation, and rebellion. The serpent appeals to Eve's reasoning and emotions by promising that the fruit will open her eyes, making her like God, knowing good and evil. Herein lies the profound psychological and theological premise of temptation: the allure of autonomy, the desire to grasp knowledge and power reserved solely for the divine. This moment reflects humanity's perennial struggle with the notion of freedom and the boundaries that define it. How does one balance the God-given freedom to act with the humility to accept divine limitations? The serpent's proposition challenges Eve to transcend her place as a creature beholden to divine command, tempting her with the intoxicating promise of self-empowerment and godlike understanding.

The nature of the serpent's temptation thus reveals a key dimension of human vulnerability: the yearning for dignity, identity, and autonomy that exists alongside the imperative of obedience. In yielding to the serpent's enticement, Eve's response embodies the tragic complexity of human choice, an act that is at once deeply personal, profoundly consequential, and irrevocably communal. The decision to eat the fruit is not taken lightly or absent reflection; it is a deliberate crossing of a threshold toward independence, a rupture in relational obedience. It signifies the moment when the ideal harmony between humanity and God is shattered, inaugurating the epoch of sin, alienation, and mortality.

The serpent's role is not merely that of tempter but also as an emblem of the forces that undermine divine order and corrupt the primordial goodness of creation.

Following Eve's choice, Adam's subsequent participation in eating the fruit further underscores the complex dynamics of temptation and disobedience. Adam's action, taken after Eve had already eaten, may reflect solidarity, complicity, or weakness, an embodiment of how sin's ripples extend beyond the initial choice, affecting relationships and communities. This act of shared transgression precipitates a chain of consequences not only for the individuals but for the entire created order: eyes are opened, awareness of nakedness and vulnerability emerges, and the innocence of unselfconscious existence is lost. The intimate relationship with the divine is severed as fear and shame enter the human experience, signaling the introduction of spiritual and existential suffering.

The aftermath of the serpent's temptation involves profound theological and anthropological implications. The human encounter with sin introduces mortality, toil, and estrangement, marking the transition from a state of paradisiacal innocence to one of fallen reality. God's judgment, while just and inevitable, is also mercifully tempered, clothing is provided to cover nakedness, and the expulsion from Eden serves not only as punishment but also as a protective boundary to prevent humanity from turning irrevocably to death in their disobedience. This dual aspect of divine justice and mercy signals the complexity of God's response to human failure, a tension that courses throughout the biblical narrative and into the New Testament revelations.

Moreover, the serpent itself is cursed, condemned to crawl on its belly and to be in perpetual enmity with humanity. This curse represents the cosmic scope of sin's intrusion into the fabric of creation, not only altering human destiny but disrupting the harmony of the natural world. The persistent enmity between the serpent and humanity embodies the ongoing struggle between good and evil, obedience and rebellion, life and death. This ongoing conflict echoes through biblical history and theology, serving as a foundational motif for understanding sin's pervasive and enduring influence.

The temptation narrative also invites reflection on the nature of freedom and responsibility. Humanity is created in the divine image, endowed with the freedom to choose, but this freedom is not without cost. The choice to obey or to rebel carries profound consequences, underscoring the moral gravity inherent in human agency. The serpent's temptation reveals how freedom can be distorted by deceit and desire, how autonomy without reverence leads to fragmentation, and how the ethical dimensions of choice cannot be separated from their spiritual implications. This episode thus serves as an archetypal moment, illustrating the perennial human predicament, caught between the divine call to faithfulness and the temptation to assert self-will.

Importantly, the serpent's temptation also encapsulates a theological reflection on knowledge and wisdom. The notion of "knowing good and evil" that the serpent tantalizingly offers is a double-edged sword. It suggests an aspiration toward wisdom, yet the means by which it is attained, through disobedience and deception, renders it a corrupted wisdom. True knowledge in biblical thought is inseparable from covenantal faithfulness, humility before the Creator, and righteous living. The serpent tempts Eve with a counterfeit knowledge, one that severs her from these orienting truths and plunges her into confusion and alienation. This invites readers to consider the dangers of knowledge divorced from moral and spiritual grounding, a theme that resonates deeply in contemporary ethical discourse.

The serpent's role is also a reminder of the presence of evil within the created order, a presence that, while not originating from God, exploits freedom and choice to propagate disorder. The biblical text's portrayal dialogues with ancient Near Eastern symbolic traditions yet uniquely frames evil's emergence as a corrosive force that distorts freedom and fractures relationships. The serpent, therefore, is neither a mere beast nor a simple symbol of evil; it is a complex figure embodying deception, temptation, and the existential challenge confronting humanity: the call to embrace divine wisdom versus the allure of self-determined but destructive autonomy.

In sum, the serpent's temptation in the Garden of Eden is not merely a narrative of a first sin but a profound theological and moral tableau that encapsulates the essence of human existence. It reveals the vulnerability and dignity of humanity, the nature of temptation as a subtle and complex force, and the tragic consequences of disobedience. It marks the entrance of sin not simply as an act but as a pervasive condition that shapes the human experience, the divine-human relationship, and the cosmic order. Through this narrative, readers are invited to grapple with the tension between freedom and responsibility, trust and doubt, knowledge and folly, tensions that remain as relevant today as they were in antiquity, echoing through the stories of biblical history and the ethical challenges faced by all who seek to walk in faith and wisdom.

The Fall and Its Fallout

In the serene stillness of the Garden of Eden, where every blade of grass shimmered with morning dew and the air was fragrant with blossoming trees, humanity's first footsteps were unburdened by sorrow or strife. It was an enclave of divine perfection, a place unmarred by the corrosive touch of sin, where the Creator walked in joyous communion with His masterpiece. Yet, beneath the tranquility of this idyllic paradise loomed an invitation of choice, a profound crossroads where free will would meet temptation, setting in motion a cascade of consequences that would echo through the corridors of time. The story of the Fall is as much about the nature of disobedience as it is about the subtle allure of temptation, illustrating the profound rupture that occurs when humanity steps away from divine trust and embraces autonomy at a devastating cost.

Temptation in Eden was neither blatant nor overpowering; rather, it was insidiously entwined with curiosity and the desire for autonomy. The serpent's voice, soft yet persuasive, drew the first humans into a realm of doubt, casting shadows on the simplicity of God's command. "You will not surely die," it whispered, unraveling the fabric of trust that had wrapped Adam and Eve in innocence. This moment foregrounds a deep tension inherent in human nature, the tension between obedience born of faith and the allure of self-determination. It reveals a fundamental aspect of sin: it ensnares not merely through overt defiance but through the distortion of truth, inviting humanity to question the goodness of divine boundaries and promising elevation through self-will. This nuance reshapes our understanding of the Fall, portraying it not simply as transgression but as a tragic reconfiguration of relationship, perception, and identity.

The act of disobedience, the biting into the forbidden fruit, introduces a seismic shift not only in the moral landscape but in the very essence of human existence. The consciousness of nakedness, previously unknown and unneeded, instantly floods Adam and Eve with shame, a raw and painful self-awareness birthed from their severed innocence. This newfound vulnerability is emblematic of the spiritual chasm that sin carves between humanity and God. No longer clothed in the garments of grace, they are exposed to the harsh realities of self-judgment and alienation. The immediate response is flight, from God, from responsibility, and from one another in their mutual recriminations. The intimate dialogue with the Creator fractures under the weight of blame and fear, underscoring that sin's first true consequence is relational rupture: with the divine, with others, and within oneself.

The repercussions of the Fall extend far beyond psychological alienation; they permeate the physical realm and human destiny. Death, previously an abstract possibility, becomes an inevitable reality, shadowing every heartbeat and breath. The introduction of mortality is a stark marker of the cost of disobedience, transforming eternity into a distant promise rather than a present possession. Pain enters the fabric of existence, pain in childbirth, toil in labor, and the finality of dissolution, manifesting as a constant reminder of humanity's fallen state. The world itself shifts, moving from a bountiful garden into a terrain marked by thorns and thistles, symbolic of the broken harmony between creation and its caretaker. This alteration of the natural order encapsulates the broader cosmic implications of sin: disobedience against divine law not only jeopardizes human well-being but disrupts the very ecosystem interconnected with human stewardship.

Crucially, the expulsion from Eden marks a physical and symbolic exile. The cherubim placed to guard the way to the tree of life signify a severing of direct access to divine sustenance, encapsulating the profound estrangement between Creator and creation. This expulsion inaugurates a new existential condition characterized by labor and longing, where humanity must navigate a fractured world without the immediate presence or sufficiency of God's provision. Yet, within this exile, hints of mercy and hope quietly persist. The narrative records that God fashioned garments for Adam and Eve, a poignant gesture indicating ongoing care despite their rebellion. Furthermore, the barred path to the tree of life implies that restoration, while barred temporarily, is not beyond the realm of possibility, foreshadowing future redemption woven throughout biblical history.

As this initial act of disobedience reverberates forward, it establishes a paradigm of choice and consequence that shapes every human encounter with moral reality. The story of the Fall does more than recount ancient mythology; it lays the existential groundwork for understanding the persistent human condition marked by ethical tension, vulnerability to temptation, and the necessity of forgiveness. The psychological aftermath, the shame, fear, and blame, unfold as a mirror to every individual's internal battle with conscience and accountability. Eden's narrative thus invites readers into a reflection on the enduring weight of choices and the cascading effects they engender on personal and collective life.

Furthermore, the introduction of sin into the world creates a complex dynamic between divine justice and mercy, a theme that echoes throughout the biblical text and theological discourse. The pronouncement of judgment is tempered by gestures of grace, situating God's character not solely as a judge but as a compassionate redeemer who mourns the Fall yet works toward restoration. The punitive elements, pain in childbirth, and the curse upon the ground are not merely punitive but pedagogical, teaching the cost of rebellion while leaving room for growth and repentance. In this tension, readers witness a divine economy that balances holiness and love, justice and forgiveness, encapsulating the profound mystery of a God who disciplines desires and reconciliation.

Beyond the immediate family in Eden, the Fall's fallout extends into the fabric of human society and history. It sets the stage for the complex relationship between humanity's aspirations and failings, influencing patterns of sin that emerge in subsequent biblical narratives. The themes of jealousy, violence, and estrangement, so palpable in the stories of Cain and Abel, trace their roots back to this foundational rupture. The archetype of sin as a force that fractures relationships and distorts God's intent provides a lens through which to view the escalating brokenness in human history. By understanding the Fall as the primordial fracture, readers recognize how ancient themes persist, not as relics of a distant past, but as living realities shaping human experience and morality today.

Moreover, the disobedience in Eden invites a profound inquiry into the nature of freedom and responsibility. The gift of free will, a cornerstone of human dignity, is shown to be fraught with peril. The capacity to choose holds within it the possibility for goodness and virtue but inevitably entails the risk of failure and separation from God. This dual potentiality calls readers into a deeper reflection on the meaning of moral agency and the importance of aligning will with divine will. It challenges simplistic notions of sin and righteousness, revealing the complexity of human motives, the seductions of autonomy, and the transformative power of humility and obedience.

In narrative and theological terms, the Fall acts as a pivot point around which the entire biblical drama revolves. It is not only a moment of loss but also the beginning of a redemptive journey that seeks to restore what was broken. The impending hope introduced through subsequent promises, the protoevangelium's glimpse of redemption through the seed of the woman, casts the shadow of grace back upon this dark episode. Such messianic anticipation underscores the enduring tension between sin's grip and the possibility of salvation, reminding readers that the story of humanity's separation from God is not the final chapter. Instead, it sets the stage for the unfolding saga of reconciliation, mercy, and the quest for restoration that defines the biblical witness.

In contemplating the profound consequences of the Fall, one encounters a sweeping vision of human nature and destiny, marked by both fragility and promise. The narrative invites deep empathy for the first humans caught in a moment of frailty and illustrates the complexities of moral decision-making under divine scrutiny. It contextualizes suffering and mortality within a framework of covenantal relationship, a fallen but redeemable world where God remains actively engaged. This perspective challenges readers to see sin not merely as a static defect but as a dynamic power shaping individual lives and societal patterns, demanding continuous vigilance, repentance, and hope.

The story of Eden's loss also prompts an intimate meditation on the human yearning for paradise regained. Across centuries and cultures, this yearning resonates within the spiritual imagination, inspiring quests for wholeness, justice, and peace. The expulsion from Eden thus stands as both a lament and an invitation, a lament for what is lost, for innocence shattered and harmony disrupted, and an invitation to pursue restoration, to seek reconciliation with God and neighbor, and to participate in the divine purpose overall. In a world still shadowed by sin's echo, Eden remains a touchstone of origin and hope, reminding humanity of its capacity to fall yet also to rise anew.

Ultimately, the Fall and its fallout reveal the depths of human vulnerability and the heights of divine compassion. They encapsulate the tension between freedom and obedience, justice and mercy, despair and hope that permeates the human story. Through vivid narrative and profound theological reflection, the Eden story becomes a mirror reflecting the timeless struggle of the human heart, a struggle to live rightly, to choose wisely, and to seek forgiveness when those choices falter. It calls each reader to stand before the ongoing challenge of sin's legacy, to acknowledge the consequences of disobedience, and to embrace the transformative journey toward grace and redemption that continues to unfold in the human saga.

Cain and Abel: The First Fratricide

Sibling Rivalry and Offering

In the dawn of human history as portrayed in the biblical narrative, the story of Cain and Abel unfurls as one of the earliest and most poignant illustrations of human conflict, a raw and primal echo of sin reverberating through the intimate bonds of family. Their tale is more than a mere account of sibling rivalry; it is a profound exploration of how sin escalates from internal discontent and personal choice to rupture relationships and fracture the very fabric of community and divine interaction. This ancient episode, steeped in theological nuance and psychological depth, stands as a cornerstone for understanding the dynamics of jealousy, moral tension, and the consequences born from choices that carry beyond the self to affect society and the sacred covenant between humanity and God.

At the outset, Cain and Abel emerge as the first offspring of Adam and Eve in a world just introduced to the shadow of disobedience. They represent the initial generation struggling to navigate the complexities of human existence forged in the aftermath of the primordial fall. Cain, the elder, is a tiller of the ground, his life entwined with the soil and labor, while Abel, a keeper of sheep, tends to his flocks with a seemingly gentler vocation. Their respective offerings to God, the fruits of Cain's agricultural toil and the best portions of Abel's flock, are not mere acts of ritual but symbolic gestures reflecting their hearts, intentions, and relationship to divine command. It is here, at the altar of offering, that the first fissure appears, exposing the vulnerability of human judgment and the volatile interplay of pride, worthiness, and acceptance that seeds discord.

The narrative reveals that the Lord looked with favor upon Abel and his offering, but not upon Cain and his. This divine preference is rarely explained directly, yet it invites thoughtful reflection on the nature of the offerings and the attitudes behind them. Abel's sacrifice is often interpreted as representing a heart aligned with God's will, marked by reverence and sincerity, offering the best of his flock with faith and humility. Cain's offering, conversely, may be viewed as lacking in such qualities, perhaps offered perfunctorily or without genuine devotion, revealing a discordant heart. The tension here transcends mere ritual propriety; it is a divine mirror held up to human motivation and spiritual authenticity. The rejection of Cain's offering becomes the catalyst for his surging emotions, resentment, anger, and jealousy, an internal tempest that soon spills over into external violence.

As Cain's demeanor shifts, God's response is both a warning and an invitation to self-reflection. In a dialogue fraught with pathos, God cautions Cain that sin is crouching at his door, eager to overtake him, yet beckons him to mastery over it. This profound moment underscores the theological gravity of choice in human life. Sin is not a passive condition but an active force, poised to claim agency over heart and behavior unless consciously resisted. Cain's failure to heed this warning signals a critical juncture where personal sin mutates into relational destruction. The ensuing act of murder, where Cain kills Abel, is unprecedented, marking the first bloodshed in human history and setting a dark precedent for violence borne out of envy and rejection.

This act of fratricide resonates far beyond the immediate family. Cain's crime fractures the integrity of the nascent community borne from Adam and Eve, introducing fear, alienation, and the erosion of trust. The blood of Abel cries out from the ground, symbolizing not only the loss of innocent life but the breaking of humanity's communion with God and with one another. The earth itself, once a source of sustenance and blessing, becomes a silent witness to sin's destructive power, emphasizing the broader communal and even cosmic consequences of individual transgressions. Cain's subsequent punishment, exile and the mark placed upon him, reflects divine justice tempered with mercy, a complex response that balances retribution with protection and an ongoing opportunity for repentance.

Exploring this ancient narrative opens a window into the profound psychological and spiritual dimensions of human relationships under the strain of sin. Cain's reaction to rejection and perceived favoritism models a human tendency to interpret situations through the lens of self-worth and envy, fueling bitterness that, if left unchecked, escalates into anger and aggression. Abel's role, though less detailed, invites contemplation of innocence and the vulnerability of goodness in a broken world. Together, their story confronts readers with foundational questions about how individuals negotiate rivalry, acceptance, and identity within families and communities, and how these dynamics inevitably intertwine with divine expectations of justice and righteousness.

Furthermore, the Cain and Abel narrative serves as a theological reflection on the nature of sin's contagious and escalating quality. Sin begins as an internal inclination, resentment, jealousy, and pride, that festers when unattended. It then manifests in concrete actions that inflict harm upon others and destabilize social harmony. The story demonstrates that sin is not contained within the individual but radiates outward, unsettling relationships and calling into question humanity's status as God's image-bearers entrusted with stewardship over creation and each other. It poses an enduring moral challenge: to recognize the danger of allowing such impulses to govern hearts and to cultivate vigilance and humility in the face of personal and communal temptation.

The implications for divine-human interaction are equally profound. God's engagement with Cain, his invitation to confront sin, his response to the murder, and the installation of the protective mark, illustrate a divine posture that encompasses accountability without annihilation. This dual movement reveals the depth of God's justice alongside divine mercy, offering a nuanced perspective on punishment as a corrective and protective measure rather than mere retribution. It signals that while sin fractures relationships and has profound consequences, the door remains open for restoration and transformation, a theme that will echo throughout biblical history and into the New Testament revelation.

In addition, the narrative's emphasis on offering and worship elucidates early biblical theology regarding human-divine communication and the demand for sincere devotion. The story subtly critiques superficial adherence to ritual devoid of heartfelt obedience and integrity, a motif that recurs across Scripture. Cain's offering, rejected by God, becomes emblematic of a worshiper's inward disposition rather than the external formality of religious acts. This insight challenges readers to examine their own motives and the authenticity of their spiritual expressions, warning against complacency and spiritual pride that obscure the heart's true alignment with divine will.

Moreover, the story of Cain and Abel, while singular in its details, resonates universally with human experience. The tensions of sibling rivalry, the pain of rejection, the corrosive power of jealousy, and the devastating consequences of unresolved anger are as contemporary as they are ancient. By grounding these themes in a primordial context, the narrative emphasizes that these struggles are intrinsic to human nature, intertwined with sin's pervasive influence. It invites empathy for the fragility of human relationships and calls for a vigilant cultivation of love, forgiveness, and reconciliation to counteract the destructive impulses sown by envy and pride.

As readers reflect on this episode, the story compels a reckoning with the ways in which interpersonal conflicts mirror larger moral and spiritual battles. Cain's tragedy is not merely a family dispute but a microcosm of the human struggle against sin's encroachment. It challenges individuals and communities alike to confront the consequences of their choices in promoting justice, mercy, and peace. The motif of offering also sets a paradigm for how faith communities understand worship and relationship with God, highlighting the necessity of sincerity, humility, and a heart oriented toward divine goodness.

In sum, the origins of conflict between Cain and Abel encapsulate a profound theological and moral lesson about the nature of sin as a corrosive force within human relationships and communal life. Their story, though ancient, pulses with vivid life, illustrating how personal choices rooted in pride and jealousy can unleash devastating consequences that ripple across family, society, and the sacred bond between humanity and God. It reveals sin not as an abstract concept but as a dynamic, escalating reality that challenges every generation to wrestle with the tension between fallibility and grace. By illuminating this earliest human conflict, the narrative lays a foundational understanding of sin's enduring impact and invites an ongoing dialogue about repentance, reconciliation, and hope in the face of human frailty. Through this exploration, readers gain a deeper appreciation of the delicate interplay between human emotion, divine expectation, and the possibilities for redemption that flicker even in the darkest moments of estrangement and loss.

The Act of Violence

In the lush and untamed world where the first humans walked, the narrative of Cain and Abel stands out as a chilling echo of the profound moral rupture occasioned by sin's escalation. The act of violence Cain commits against his brother Abel is not merely a tragic fratricide but a pivotal moment that reveals the deepening perversion of human relations under the influence of sin. This grievous act, the first homicide recorded in the biblical narrative, symbolizes a catastrophic breach with not only familial trust but the very fabric of community life and the divine-human covenant. The gravity of Cain's sin lies not only in the physical destruction of Abel's life but in how such violence amplifies the consequences of the primordial disobedience of Adam and Eve, illustrating that the corrupting power of sin extends from individual rebellion to the disruption of societal harmony and spiritual communion with God.

Cain and Abel, as the sons of the first human couple, represent the nascent human community, a fragile assembly shaped by divine blessing yet vulnerable to the internal rot of envy, anger, and rejection. Their offerings to God, which set the stage for conflict, are laden with symbolism and theological undercurrents. Abel's gift of the firstborn of his flock, offered with genuine faith and devotion, contrasts starkly with Cain's offering of the fruits of the soil, which the text suggests was ultimately not accepted by God. This divine preference is not about the intrinsic value of the offerings but the attitude and heart behind them, intimating the profound spiritual truth that God desires sincerity, repentance, and humility rather than mere ritual compliance. Cain's reaction reveals the darkening human heart under sin's influence: jealousy festers into bitterness, which quickly morphs into rage. His inability to master these emotions unleashes a violent eruption that culminates in Abel's murder. This progression illuminates the swift and deadly escalation of sin's grip on human relationships, where unchecked emotions lead to the destruction of life itself.

The murder of Abel by Cain is profoundly unsettling, not only as an act of brutality but as a manifestation of the breakdown of what it means to be human in God's image. This act severs the bond between the two brothers, destroying the potential for reconciliation and community that should have defined their relationship. Instead of nurturing his sibling, Cain turns into a stranger and a threat, marking the emergence of alienation and distrust within humanity. This fracturing of fraternal bonds signifies a larger cosmic disorder introduced through sin, where the harmony of creation, intended to reflect divine love and justice, becomes marred by suspicion, fear, and violence. The weight of Cain's action is also theological; it challenges the very notion of creation as 'good' and invites reflection on the disturbing question of human agency in amplifying sin's consequences. His crime is an affront not only to Abel but to God, who cherishes human life and commands respect for the image borne by every individual.

Moreover, Cain's violent act introduces critical themes about justice and mercy that resonate throughout sacred history. When God confronts Cain with the piercing question, "Where is your brother Abel?" it is not a mere inquiry but an invitation to accountability and confession. Cain's evasive and defiant reply, "Am I my brother's keeper?" embodies the denial of responsibility that undergirds much of human sinfulness. His refusal to own his wrongdoing testifies to the moral blindness engendered by pride and rebellion, which insulates the sinner from repentance and prolongs estrangement from the divine. Yet, even in the aftermath of this grievous sin, God's interaction with Cain reflects a complex interplay of justice and mercy. God pronounces a punishment that isolates Cain, marks him for protection against retaliation, and sends him into a restless exile. This punishment both acknowledges the seriousness of the crime and limits retributive violence, signaling divine concern for the preservation of life and the prevention of further bloodshed within a community already destabilized by sin.

The ripple effects of Cain's act of violence extend far beyond the immediate tragedy, foreshadowing the ongoing cycle of sin and its ramifications within human society. The narrative implicitly warns that unchecked bitterness and hatred can escalate into destructive patterns that threaten not only individuals but the entire social order. The story presages the biblical theme of communal responsibility and the necessity of maintaining ethical vigilance against the seeds of violence sown in the human heart. Sin's corrosive power did not simply manifest in an isolated murder but unfolded as a contagion capable of infecting communities, eroding trust, and fomenting fear. The distrust Cain experiences after his crime, coupled with his exile into the land of wandering, portrays the alienation and displacement that sin imposes on the human soul, disrupting one's sense of belonging and communion with others, and ultimately distancing the sinner from God's protective presence.

At its core, Cain's murder of Abel challenges readers to confront essential moral questions about choice, consequence, and the nature of responsibility. The tragedy exposes how sin provides fertile ground for human relationships to degrade, revealing the potential for even the closest bonds to become arenas of conflict and destruction when selfishness and envy prevail. This moment inscribes a somber warning that sin's consequences are not confined to the individual but echo across communities, destabilizing social and spiritual structures. Cain's defiant posture and ensuing punishment offer a sobering insight into the limits of human freedom distorted by sin and the necessity of divine intervention to arrest its deadly trajectory. God's protective mark on Cain paradoxically serves as a reminder that justice must be tempered by mercy even amid judgment, reflecting a God who grieves human violence yet refuses to abandon the sinner completely.

The story's moral significance is amplified by its placement early in the biblical timeline, suggesting that violence and moral failure are inherent dangers from the inception of human society. The act of violence committed by Cain thus becomes emblematic of the profound struggle between human fallibility and divine intention, a struggle that recurs throughout scripture and human history. It underscores the biblical assertion that sin is not merely an external transgression but an internal corruption that distorts the very essence of humanity created in God's image. The narrative invites readers to examine their own lives in light of this ancient conflict, recognizing the potential for hatred, pride, and envy to harm relationships and estrange them from God's grace. It calls for vigilance and humility, urging an embrace of responsibility for one another and a commitment to rebuilding fractured bonds through repentance and love.

Furthermore, Cain's story introduces an important dimension to the theology of sin and redemption by portraying sin not as a steady descent into despair but as a condition interwoven with the potential for grace. The dialogue between God and Cain, harsh yet measured, reveals a divine posture that allows space for transformation even after grave sin. Cain's exile is a form of both punishment and protection, reinforcing the possibility that even those who have fallen deeply may yet find a path toward restoration. This notion resonates with later biblical themes that picture sin and forgiveness as dynamic forces within the human-divine relation, where judgment aims not only to punish but to redirect toward redemption. The narrative's tragic climax does not signal the end of the human story but opens a space for reflection on the power of mercy to interrupt the destructive patterns sown by sin.

The psychological depth of Cain's violence also speaks to the human condition in profound ways. His initial reaction, anger turned murderous rage, illustrates how emotions left unchecked can overwhelm reason and moral conscience. The story therefore functions as a cautionary tale about the perils of allowing negative emotions to fester unchecked, ultimately consuming the individual and undermining communal peace. Cain's failure to master his impulses and acknowledge his sin results in catastrophic suffering for his family and, by extension, for all of humanity. This insight into human nature underlines the biblical wisdom that sin's escalation is often intimate and relational, weaving through the fabric of everyday life in subtle but life-altering ways. It exposes the vulnerability inherent in freedom, our capacity to choose good or evil, and the devastating consequences of choices veiled by pride and self-centeredness.

In the broader biblical context, Cain's violent act also serves as a foundational motif for interpreting subsequent narratives of sin and divine response. His story becomes a lens through which we understand the persistent human struggle with violence, jealousy, and moral failure. It sets a pattern echoed in the stories of kings, prophets, and communities throughout scripture, where the tension between human frailty and divine expectation continually unfolds. The biblical authors, by including this grim episode so early in the religious canon, underscore the need for constant moral vigilance and the search for divine guidance in navigating the complexities of human relationships. In this way, Cain's story remains timeless, speaking across millennia about the dangers of turning away from God's law and the devastating effects that follow.

Moreover, the social implications of this violence cannot be overstated, for it illustrates the initial rupture in the social fabric that God intended to be marked by peace, cooperation, and mutual responsibility. Cain's refusal to care for his brother signals a rejection of the communal ethic that sustains human society. This dissolution of fraternity portends the difficulties later communities face in maintaining justice and cohesion when individual sin threatens collective well-being. The biblical narrative, therefore, situates Cain's violence within the broader human experience of ethical failure and its consequences, highlighting that personal sin inevitably becomes communal crisis. This truth remains deeply relevant, challenging readers to reflect on how their actions affect not only themselves but the wider community to which they belong.

Theologically, the story also critically engages with the notion of divine justice in a world marred by sin. God's judgment upon Cain is severe yet merciful, embodying a justice that neither trivializes sin nor condemns without hope. The divine mark placed upon Cain, serving as both a warning to others and a means of protection for the offender, exemplifies this delicate balance between punishment and grace. This dual aspect of justice is central to the biblical understanding of how God interacts with sinners, as one who disciplines but also redeems, who holds people accountable but desires restoration. The narrative, thus, becomes a profound meditation on the complexities of divine righteousness in the midst of human failing, inviting readers to see beyond retributive justice toward a vision suffused with mercy and the possibility of renewal.

In reflecting on this ancient story, modern readers are invited into a dialogue about the nature of sin and its insidious progression from envy to hatred to lethal action. The narrative insists that sin's escalation is not a distant myth but a present reality that manifests in broken relationships, fractured families, and conflicted communities today. It challenges individuals to consider their own responses to anger and resentment, emphasizing the necessity of accountability, confession, and healing. Importantly, it insists that moral failure in personal life invariably ripples outward, emphasizing that "being one's brother's keeper" is a foundational ethical imperative. This story, therefore, is not an isolated moralistic tale but a vital lens for understanding ongoing human struggle with sin and the urgent need for divine grace to transform hearts and societies.

Ultimately, the act of violence carried out by Cain against Abel emerges from the narrative as a somber parable of shame and warning woven into the early human story. It stands as the first dark echo of sin's destructive power reverberating through the corridors of biblical history, an echo that challenges each generation to confront the destructive potential within the human heart. It is a call to vigilance against the corrosive forces of envy and pride and a plea for the cultivation of compassion, accountability, and forgiveness. Through this prism, Cain's story transcends its ancient setting to become a mirror reflecting the moral complexities and vulnerabilities still faced today. The enduring power of this narrative lies in its capacity to awaken ethical consciousness, deepen spiritual awareness, and prompt a humble recognition that the path to peace and reconciliation begins with facing the shadows within ourselves and extending mercy to others.

Divine Judgment and Mercy

The story of Cain and Abel occupies a pivotal space within the biblical narrative, a profound and deeply unsettling portrayal of sin's rapid escalation in the human condition. At its core, this account illuminates the complex and often paradoxical nature of divine judgment and mercy, revealing the intricate ways God engages with humanity in the aftermath of sin's first tragic outbreak beyond Eden. The response to Cain's fratricide, a heinous act born not only of jealousy but of a deeper moral rupture, provides a stark window into how sin ruptures relational bonds and reverberates through both personal identity and communal life. It is within this charged tension between condemnation and compassion that we encounter powerful lessons about the character of God and the enduring struggle of humankind with its own brokenness.

The initial context is critical to grasp: Cain, the elder son of Adam and Eve, commits the world's first recorded murder by killing his brother Abel. This act is not merely a crime of passion or rivalry; it reflects an alarming internal decay, envy festering into rage, resulting in irreversible violence. The narrative leaves us with a haunting question: what propels one human being to extinguish the life of another, especially when both share the intimacy of family? More importantly, how does God, the ultimate moral arbiter, respond to such profound sin, and what does this response reveal about divine justice and mercy?

God's reaction to Cain is multifaceted, both decisive and compassionate, judicial and protective. Upon confronting Cain, God asks, "Where is your brother Abel?" and, upon learning of the murder, pronounces a judgment: Cain is cursed and condemned to be a "fugitive and wanderer on the earth." This sentence fundamentally alters Cain's existence, severing his ties to the land he once cultivated and to the community that could have supported him. The land itself, once fertile and a source of blessing, becomes a place of hardship and alienation. This divine decree is harsh, underscoring the seriousness of human sin and its capacity to estrange individuals not only from each other but from the very earth itself, the life-sustaining creation that God intended to be stable and bountiful.

However, the narrative does not end with unmitigated condemnation. Herein lies the paradox of divine judgment and mercy: although Cain receives a severe punishment, God also marks him with a protective sign, a divine guarantee that no one shall kill him. This enigmatic mark has sparked myriad interpretations but centrally expresses God's commitment to preserving life, even that of a murderer. Rather than answering violence with violence, God interposes a measure of grace, preventing Cain from being destroyed by others and thus further perpetuating the cycle of bloodshed. This protective sign symbolizes an extension of divine mercy amid judgment, a profound assertion that even sinful humans are precious and guarded within the fabric of creation.

The effect of this dual response, punishment mingled with protection, resonates deeply within the human psyche and society. Cain's exile signifies more than mere removal from a physical homeland; it speaks to the fragmentation of human relationships following sin. His wandering life becomes a metaphor for the restless condition of humankind after transgression: alienated, disconnected, searching for belonging yet barred from it due to moral failure. The consequences extend beyond Cain himself, reflecting on communal dynamics as the burgeoning human family must now grapple with the reality of violence from within. The legacy of Cain's sin threatens the social fabric, foreshadowing cycles of retaliation, fear, and disunity that will characterize much of biblical and human history.

This tension between judgment and mercy, then, serves as a theological fulcrum, embodying the complex interplay between divine justice, which demands accountability, and divine grace, which offers restoration. God's response to Cain is not a simple punitive act but a nuanced engagement that preserves the possibility of repentance and change. Despite Cain's failure to master sin internally and externally, God's protection offers a window for transformation, underscoring that judgment is not final annihilation but a call to recognize the gravity of sin and its dangers to both self and society.

Furthermore, the narrative implicitly addresses human responsibility in the face of sin. Before delivering judgment, God warns Cain that sin "is crouching at your door; it desires to have you, but you must rule over it." This admonition reveals that sin is not merely an external force punishable by divine decree but a lurking presence within the heart and will of every individual. The call to mastery over sin introduces a moral imperative, emphasizing free will and personal accountability. It suggests that, though sin escalates and carries consequences, humans are invited, and expected, to exercise moral agency, to confront and overcome their darker impulses.

The escalating nature of sin within human relationships also finds profound commentary in Cain's subsequent life after his banishment. Exiled, he builds a city and establishes a lineage. This act of creating a city is paradoxical: it is both a constructive human effort, signaling civilization's growth, and a marker of separation from God's original harmony and blessing. In this way, human society begins to evolve amid sin's shadow, wrestling constantly between creativity and corruption. The city, a symbol of human culture and achievement, is thus also a place where sin resides, reminding readers that human communities invariably bear the marks of moral failure.

At the same time, the story casts a sobering light on the enduring effects of sin beyond the individual. Cain's crime fractures not only brotherly bonds but the nascent human community itself, introducing cycles of fear and vengeance. The divine protection imposed on Cain, while merciful, also instills fear in others, suggesting the fragile nature of human trust once broken by violence. The social implications are severe: sin disrupts not only individual lives but the collective peace necessary for community to flourish. The human family, envisioned initially as united and whole, becomes a landscape marked by suspicion, conflict, and estrangement, where divine-human interaction is complicated by moral ruptures.

Beyond the immediate story, the echoes of God's judgment and mercy resonate throughout biblical theology and ethics, informing understandings of justice, forgiveness, and human dignity. The narrative sets a precedent for the ways God deals with sin across the ages: sin must be confronted, it carries consequences, yet it does not elude divine compassion. This dialectic challenges simplistic notions of a God who punishes without mercy or forgives without justice. Instead, it portrays a divine love that encompasses both, refusing to abandon the sinner while upholding the moral order. It reveals a God deeply invested in human freedom and transformation, operating with a balance that invites reflection on the complexities of moral existence.

Moreover, the story of Cain and God's response invites readers into a deeper meditation on human vulnerability and the ever-present risk of succumbing to destructive impulses. Sin, here personified as a crouching beast at the door, embodies an existential threat that humankind cannot casually dismiss. The warning and subsequent judgment illustrate how sin, left unchecked, leads to ruin, not only for the sinner but for the entire community. It calls forth urgent ethical introspection about how individuals govern not only their own lives but also their relationships with others, highlighting the fragile interdependence of human society and divine order.

God's merciful act of protecting Cain further introduces a critical narrative thread about the potential for redemption and the persistence of hope even amid judgment. This divine safeguard preserves the possibility of reconciliation and return, hinting at grace's transformative power that can interrupt cycles of sin and violence. It foreshadows later biblical themes where divine mercy breaks into human history, offering new beginnings and restoration. The tension between punishment and mercy found here thus becomes a lens through which to view the broader biblical witness to God's redemptive purposes, an early example of the divine commitment to healing what sin has wounded.

In considering the broader implications of God's dual response to Cain, one recognizes the story's richness as a theological reflection on the human condition. It captures the profound tragedy of sin's spread from individual disobedience to communal disintegration and illuminates the enduring hope that divine mercy never abandons creation to its worst impulses. Cain's narrative reveals how divine judgment acts not merely as retribution but as a wake-up call, a form of tough love that confronts sin while still upholding the dignity and value of the sinner.

Thus, the episode stands as a timeless meditation on the balance between justice and compassion, law and grace, punishment and protection. It invites readers to grapple with their own moral failures and the ways these affect relationships and communities, challenging them to recognize both the seriousness of sin and the boundless nature of divine mercy. It encourages a vision of justice that is restorative rather than merely punitive, one that seeks to transform rather than destroy.

In sum, God's response to Cain encapsulates a profound theological principle: sin bears destructive consequences that must be acknowledged and faced with honesty, but divine mercy intervenes to preserve life and inspire transformation. This interplay deeply informs biblical understandings of human sinfulness and divine-human interaction. It challenges individuals and communities to reflect on their ethical choices, to seek mastery over sin's persistent presence, and to embrace the hope found in God's compassionate justice. Through the story of Cain, the ancient Scriptures thus speak powerfully into contemporary reflections on morality, justice, and the possibility of redemption amid a world marked by brokenness.

The Flood: Judgment and Renewal

Wickedness on Earth

In the days when the world was still young, and humanity's footprints had barely marked the vastness of the earth, a slow, insidious darkness began to spread. What started as isolated missteps and individual failings soon escalated into a widespread contagion of wickedness that permeated society itself. The initial whispers of disobedience, born from the choices of the earliest humans, grew unchecked, weaving through the fabric of humanity as a potent and corrupting force. This was not merely the frail missteps of a few but a pervasive defilement of the human heart and spirit that would draw the firm hand of divine judgment upon the earth. It was a period when the shadows deepened, and the echoes of sin intensified, disturbing the order intended for creation.

Humanity's moral compass seemed broken, as people's desires twisted from simple needs into rampant selfishness, cruelty, and rebellion against the divine order. The original harmony between humans and their Creator, the balance of responsibility, freedom, and love, was shattered by incessant defiance. Wickedness had become a flood within, swelling and overflowing into societal structures. The narrative captures an ecosystem of moral decay where violence flourishes, and corruption becomes endemic. People turned away from justice, kindness, and truth, choosing instead domination, exploitation, and deceit as their tools. The earth, once described as good and thriving under divine stewardship, now bore the scars of humanity's spiritual rot: filled with lawlessness, greed, and a heart bent on evil continually. This was not a mere fall from innocence but a collective plunge into moral ruin.

The depth of this corruption is almost unimaginable; the biblical account tells us that every inclination of human hearts was only evil all the time, a haunting phrase that captures the totality of moral collapse. Where once there had been communal life guided by shared reverence and mutual care, now there existed a chaotic struggle for power and survival. Violence overwhelmed the land. Brothers turned against brothers; communities warred within themselves. The sacred bond to the Creator had been broken, replaced by idols of pride, wealth, and fleeting pleasure. The earth groaned beneath the weight of human acts that defied the intention of creation. It was not simply the disobedience of individuals that cried out for reckoning but the structural unraveling of society, where morality was no longer a guiding light but a forgotten relic, drowned beneath waves of corruption.

At this pivotal juncture in the biblical story, God's response arises not from caprice but from deep justice mixed with enduring mercy. Observing the utter devastation wrought by unchecked sin, the narrative describes a divine heart burdened by sorrow. The Creator, who had breathed life into the dust to form humanity, now found that covenantal relationship broken and tarnished by persistent rebellion. In the profound silence before judgment, a decision was reached: a great and devastating flood would cleanse the earth, purging the wickedness that had poisoned its soil and souls. Yet even in this act of cosmic justice, there was an undeniable grace woven into the divine decree. A plan to preserve a remnant, a hope for renewal, was set in motion.

Noah, described as a righteous man and blameless in his generation, was chosen to embody this hope. Amidst the widespread corruption, he alone obediently heeded the divine call to prepare an ark that would preserve life amid the coming deluge. His story stands as a compelling counterpoint to the mass rejection around him, an individual whose faithfulness contrasted starkly with societal decay. The arduous task of building the ark, met often with skepticism and hostility from those around him, symbolized the challenge and cost of living righteously in a world engulfed by sin. Through Noah's unwavering obedience, we witness the tension between human frailty and divine expectation, a tension visible throughout biblical history.

As the waters began to rise, the boundary between judgment and mercy blurred. The flood narrative is suffused with vivid imagery: torrential rains falling unceasingly, the earth submerged beneath waters that wiped away the old order, and the ark as a sanctuary of salvation amid chaos. This catastrophe was both an ending and a commencement, an act of divine wrath that nevertheless bore the seeds of regeneration. The devastation served as a tangible reality of sin's consequences, a sober illustration of how far human wickedness could plunge the world. Yet, the covenant with Noah following the flood announced a new beginning, a solemn promise that such destruction would never again befall the earth. This covenant, exuberantly marked by the rainbow, signified divine commitment to mercy and preservation despite human failings.

The flood story encapsulates a profound and complex theological statement that sin's societal consequences are vast and demand accountability, but that divine grace always offers restoration and hope. It challenges readers to reflect on the balance between justice and mercy, between human responsibility and divine compassion. The narrative raises difficult questions about the nature of judgment, the reasons suffering must sometimes intervene in moral decline, and the enduring possibility of redemption even when failure seems overwhelming. These themes resonate deeply with contemporary readers, who recognize the patterns of corruption and renewal echoed in our own world.

Moreover, the story underscores the interconnectedness of human choices and their ripple effects. The moral degeneration of one generation bore consequences not only for that period but for all ensuing humanity, reflecting the collective dimension of sin. Likewise, Noah's faithfulness not only saved his family but also set a foundation for reestablishing humanity's relationship with God. This dynamic interplay of judgment, grace, destruction, and hope forms a timeless motif, the echo of sin and redemption reverberating through history.

In the grand sweep of biblical narrative, the flood serves as a poignant reminder of the dangers of unchecked wickedness and the possibilities of divine mercy. It vividly illustrates that sin is never a private matter but a force that shapes societies and history itself, calling for both personal integrity and communal responsibility. At the same time, it reveals the heart of God, a God who, while intolerant of wickedness, remains steadfastly committed to restoring creation. The flood's aftermath, with its establishment of a covenantal relationship, points to the enduring promise that, despite humanity's flaws, restoration and new beginnings are always possible.

This story beckons readers into a deeper meditation on the nature of their own choices and their place within the continuum of human morality. It challenges us to recognize the societal impact of our actions, to confront the persistent shadows of sin prevalent in our world, and to embrace the hope offered through fidelity and grace. In doing so, it transforms the flood from a distant historical account into an intimate mirror, reflecting human frailty but also the incredible potential for renewal entrusted to us. Through Noah's example and the covenant wrought in the flood's wake, we glimpse the profound truth that even amid overwhelming darkness, the light of divine mercy endures, calling humanity forward into a path of righteousness and life.

Noah's Obedience and the Ark

In the vast tableau of biblical history, the story of Noah stands as a monumental testament to the intertwining of divine judgment and mercy, a complex interplay that challenges our understanding of sin's reach and the profound possibilities of redemption. Noah emerges not simply as a solitary figure constructing a colossal vessel, but as the embodiment of obedience amid a world unraveled by transgression and moral collapse. His role is pivotal, offering a window into how one man's faithfulness intersects with the wider consequences of human injustice, inviting us to grapple with the nature of salvation, responsibility, and covenant in a broken world.

The narrative of Noah unfolds against a backdrop of escalating wickedness, one where the human condition has deteriorated so deeply that the earth itself weeps under the weight of its inhabitants' corruption. Scripture paints a harrowing portrait: mankind's thoughts and actions are persistently evil, and violence saturates the social fabric. This pervasive sin does not exist in isolation, it is an all-consuming force that corrupts communities, devastates relationships, and distances humanity from the Creator's original intent. The moral decay is so profound that the divine decision to cleanse the earth with a flood is both a severance and a stark reckoning. It is not merely punitive; embedded within this narrative is a sorrowful recognition that creation itself suffers and requires renewal.

Noah's character emerges in sharp contrast to the chaotic milieu around him. Described as a righteous man, blameless in his generation, and one who walked with God, Noah is the counterpoint to his contemporaries' depravity. His righteousness is not a passive attribute but an active stance, a conscious, continuous alignment with divine will despite prevailing societal norms that increasingly embraced sin. The narrative doesn't present Noah's obedience as an isolated act of heroism but as a relational dynamic, one where communion with God informs his choices. This relationship positions him not simply to observe the corruption but to act decisively within it, embodying the possibility of human fidelity in the face of overwhelming opposition.

The command to build the ark is at once practical and symbolic. God's instruction details dimensions and materials, a blueprint for salvation tailored to withstand the impending deluge. Yet, the ark is more than a vessel; it is a sanctuary, a mobile covenantal space that embodies divine protection amid judgment. The scale of the task Noah undertakes is staggering, both physically and socially. Constructing the ark demands unwavering commitment across years, perhaps decades, an enduring testament to faith in an invisible yet imminent divine plan. As Noah labors, he becomes a beacon amidst a scoffing society, a living testament to the reality of divine warning and the seriousness of sin's consequences.

The ark's construction itself invites reflection on obedience's nature and endurance. It is a tangible expression of trust, where every plank and beam is imbued with anticipation and hope. In the face of societal mockery and isolation, Noah's determination reveals obedience not as mere compliance but as an active partnership with God's redemptive intentions. His work transcends the physical, encompassing prayer, hope, and resilience. This intricate process also evokes a broader theological motif: salvation prepared and enacted through human cooperation with divine initiative, underscoring the delicate balance between divine sovereignty and human agency.

As the floodwaters rise, the narrative shifts into a sobering meditation on judgment. The deluge is both cataclysmic and transformative, eradicating a corrupted world while preserving the seeds of future restoration through Noah, his family, and the animals aboard the ark. This moment encapsulates the devastating cost of sin, revealing how deeply human actions echo through creation. The flood is simultaneous destruction and rebirth, a divine reset button that underscores the necessity of divine justice in the face of unchecked depravity. In this, the story challenges readers to consider the societal consequences of sin not as abstract moral failings but as forces capable of dismantling communities, ecosystems, and the very fabric of human life.

Within the ark's confines, there is a profound intimacy and tension. Noah's family, preserved from the widespread destruction, represents a microcosm of humanity's potential to transcend sin through obedience and covenant faithfulness. The cramped quarters and long duration of their confinement create an atmosphere thick with hope, anxiety, and trust. This juxtaposition reflects spiritual realities: the narrow path of righteousness amid a broader world succumbing to judgment, the fragile yet enduring promise of renewal through covenant relationship. The ark becomes a symbol of refuge and the necessity of separation from corrupting influences, emphasizing that salvation involves both deliverance and transformation.

The covenant God makes with Noah after the flood introduces a rich theological dimension that reverberates through biblical history. The rainbow, set in the sky as a sign of this covenant, signifies divine promise and mercy, an assurance that while sin holds great power, it does not have the final word. This pledge not to destroy the earth again by flood establishes a cosmic trust, unveiling God's commitment to creation despite humanity's frequent failures. It simultaneously affirms human responsibility within this divine framework; the covenant is not merely about protection but about participation in the ongoing task of stewardship and moral accountability.

Noah's story, thus, is a profound meditation on interactions between divine justice and mercy. The flood is an act of judgment against pervasive sin, yet it is interlaced with grace, preservation, and a forward-looking hope. His obedience exemplifies a model of faithful response that anticipates redemption even amid devastation. This dynamic interplay invites readers to reflect on the complex nature of sin's consequences, how it isolates and destroys, yet also how steadfast faith can carve out spaces for renewal. Furthermore, it highlights the essential reciprocity between divine initiative and human cooperation in the unfolding drama of salvation.

The societal implications of the flood narrative extend beyond ancient Israel's worldview, challenging contemporary readers to grapple with the enduring consequences of collective sin and the urgent need for faithful witness. The story underscores how sin is not merely a personal failing but a force with expansive social and ecological ramifications. It highlights how judgments, whether divine or natural, often follow patterns of moral decay, yet always leave open the possibility for transformation through grace and obedience. In this sense, Noah's obedience is not only historical but emblematic; it calls communities in every age to cultivate righteousness amid cultural currents that often promote compromise or complacency.

Moreover, Noah's role prompts a deeper exploration of what it means to be righteous "in one's generation." His blamelessness is contextual, inviting considerations of integrity as measured not by perfection but by faithfulness within a particular social milieu. This perspective challenges modern readers to reflect on the standards by which they judge themselves and others, especially within societies marked by moral flux. It gently nudges toward a recognition that obedience and righteousness often require countercultural courage, a willingness to stand apart from prevailing norms in pursuit of divine ideals.

Equally integral to the narrative is the tension between judgment as a corrective mechanism and mercy as a restorative force, a dialectic that runs throughout biblical literature. The flood story vividly illustrates this tension: sin's reach necessitates judgment to curb its destructive impact, yet the provision of the ark and the subsequent covenant affirm God's desire to restore and redeem rather than merely condemn. This tension enriches theological reflection, revealing a God who is just yet compassionate, whose actions are driven by both holiness and love. Noah's obedience exemplifies the human willingness to participate in this divine economy, accepting responsibility for both judgment's reality and mercy's promise.

In conclusion, the tale of Noah's obedience and the ark operates on multiple levels, historical, theological, moral, and existential, making it a rich subject for contemplation. It confronts us with the stark consequences of sin's societal corrosion, the necessity of standing firm in faith amid widespread corruption, and the enduring hope embedded within divine covenants. Noah's journey from faithful builder to covenant recipient encapsulates the transformative power of obedience as a conduit for divine grace, reminding us that even in the depths of judgment, the chance for renewal and redemption persists. His story echoes through time as a clarion call for integrity, resilience, and hope, inviting every generation to navigate the complex dance of sin and salvation with courage and trust.

The Deluge and Aftermath

The narrative of the great flood, known universally as the Deluge, stands as one of the most profound and compelling stories within the tapestry of biblical history. It shines a piercing light on the devastating consequences of humanity's descent into pervasive sin and the complex interplay between divine judgment and mercy. As the story unfolds in Genesis, we are drawn into a world so suffused with moral decay and violence that it grieves the heart of God, compelling Him to enact a sweeping course correction that would reset the trajectory of human existence. It is a moment heavy with both dread and hope, tragedy and new beginnings, embodying a divine response that refuses to abandon creation despite its failings.

In the era before the flood, the ancient world, as depicted through Scripture, was marked by a proliferation of evil. Human hearts, once created good and in harmony with their Maker, had grown darkened with corruption, deceit, and bloodshed. The text insists on the pervasiveness of wickedness, it was not merely isolated incidents that human society suffered, but a deep-rooted, systemic rot that infected the social fabric. This collective moral unraveling strained the divine-human relationship to its breaking point. The Scripture states that "the wickedness of man was great in the earth, and every intention of the thoughts of his heart was only evil continually." Such a capacity for evil, unchecked and widespread, invoked divine grief, revealing God's profound sorrow over what humanity had become and signaling not the abandonment of God's creation but a critical moment of intervention.

Into this atmosphere of decay enters Noah, a man described as righteous, blameless among his contemporaries, who "walked with God." His character serves as a brilliant contrast to the rampant depravity that surrounded him. Noah's righteousness was not simply a matter of external compliance but a faithful alignment with divine will, an enduring trust that set him apart. He became the vessel through which God would preserve the potential for redemption amidst ruin. The commissioning of Noah to build the ark was more than a practical mandate for survival; it was a profound act of grace, a divine invitation to participate in the restoration of a broken world.

The flood itself is depicted with overwhelming imagery, its waters symbolizing not only physical destruction but the rinsing force of divine judgment. The ark, a massive wooden sanctuary, floated amidst relentless rainfall and increasing chaos, symbolizing both refuge and judgment. As the waters rose and the old world was submerged beneath this deluge, the scope of humanity's rebellion and its consequences were laid bare. This cataclysm wiped away the generation steeped in violence but simultaneously opened the possibility of renewal through those who entered the ark. The narrative does not shy away from the harsh realities of judgment, but curiously, it is suffused with a tone of hope and salvation through the survival of a faithful remnant.

The aftermath of the flood carries rich theological and moral significance. When the storm subsided and land reemerged, Noah and his family stepped onto a cleansed earth, bearing the daunting task of beginning anew. In this new covenantal moment, God promised to never again destroy the earth by floodwaters, setting the rainbow as both a visible sign and a perpetual reminder of this oath. This covenant is a testament to divine mercy that transcends human fallibility, an eternal pledge of grace that promises hope even after catastrophic judgment. It marks a delicate balance in divine justice, while sin demanded consequence, mercy was extended to ensure continuity, restoration, and the possibility of human transformation.

Beyond the immediate narrative, the flood's ripples spread into the social and theological consciousness of biblical communities. It served as a stark illustration of sin's societal consequences, a powerful reminder that when righteousness slips away, chaos and destruction follow in its wake. Simultaneously, it empowered future generations with the assurance that divine grace remains accessible, even amidst human failure. The ark and the flood symbolized not only punishment but also deliverance, merging the themes of justice and mercy into a complex dialectic that continues to resonate deeply through centuries.

As the post-flood world unfolded, the story reflects on human frailty anew. The narrative reveals that sin's shadows were far from vanquished; patterns of human error and moral failure would reemerge. Yet, the flood story also affirmed God's enduring commitment to creation, highlighting a divine patience that would weave itself intricately through the unfolding drama of human history. It is a tale that holds both a mirror up to human brokenness and a window open to the possibility of redemption. The covenant with Noah thus becomes a foundational Scripture, echoing through time as a symbol of hope that persists despite humanity's propensity for sin.

In the broader theological dialogue, the flood serves as a profound meditation on the consequences of collective sin and the role of divine intervention. It illustrates a God who is not indifferent to human morality but deeply invested in the outcome of human choices. This investment is not punitive alone; it is a redemptive engagement that seeks to restore order and relationship. The covenantal promise thus affirms that grace tempers judgment, offering humanity a path forward from the ruins of their own making.

The story of the deluge also invites reflection on the tension between destruction and mercy, a theme woven intricately into the fabric of biblical theology. The watery judgment that swept over the earth was total, yet not absolute, as God's decision to save Noah and his family reveals a divine reluctance to end creation altogether. Instead, the flood is a profound expression of divine discipline aimed at awakening humanity to the consequences of their actions while simultaneously opening a new chapter marked by forgiveness and hope.

Moreover, the ark itself becomes a powerful symbol, predating and foreshadowing later biblical themes of salvation and refuge. Its construction, survival, and aftermath serve as poignant metaphors for the sanctuary God provides amid chaos and sin, an emblem of the possibility for renewal even after devastating consequences. This narrative invites readers to consider how human choices not only provoke destruction but also elicit divine responses that blend justice with mercy, punishment with promise.

The flood story's enduring resonance lies also in its capacity to foster empathy and spiritual introspection. It challenges readers to consider the depth of human sin and its ripple effects across society while simultaneously reminding them of the possibility for divine forgiveness and new beginnings. The covenant with Noah rekindles hope that no matter how fractured human existence becomes, restoration remains within the realm of divine possibility.

Finally, the impact of the flood narrative extends beyond theological reflection into contemporary ethical considerations. It echoes a timeless warning about the societal consequences of moral failure and the urgent need for responsibility, righteousness, and repentance. Yet it also offers an inspiring example of faithfulness and divine grace, encouraging modern readers to embrace a path where mercy tempers judgment and where human decisions carry profound spiritual weight. The flood thus emerges not merely as an ancient story but as a living echo of sin's destructive power and divine redemptive potential, bridging biblical times and today's moral journey with enduring relevance.

God's Covenant with Noah

The deluge that swept across the earth was more than a cataclysmic event; it was the divine reckoning against an age steeped in profound moral decay. Society had descended into such depths of corruption and violence that the very breath of life seemed poisoned by sin's pervasive grip. In the swirling turbulence of a world unhinged by human transgression, Noah emerged not merely as a survivor but as the embodiment of divine favor and obedience. His unwavering faith and righteousness set him apart, a solitary beacon of hope amid the engulfing darkness. The flood's waters, as relentless as the consequences of sin itself, washed away the old world, erasing the shadow of pervasive wickedness that had clouded the earth like an unrelenting storm. Yet, intertwined with the cataclysm was a profound narrative of grace, a promise whispered through the tempest and etched into the earthly covenant that God made with Noah and every living creature thereafter.

This covenant stands as one of the most significant gestures of divine mercy in biblical history, a bridge stretching from judgment to redemption, from destruction to hope. After the waters receded and the ark rested upon the mountains of Ararat, lengthy silence gave way to a divine proclamation that reverberated with solemn assurance. God spoke not only to Noah but also established an eternal bond with all creation, a sacred pledge that the earth would never again be consumed by a flood of such devastating proportions. This promise was profound, not merely in its content but in its cosmic scope, addressing the entirety of creation, affirming life's endurance beyond human failure. The covenant is a testament to the intricate balance between justice and mercy threaded throughout the biblical narrative. Sin had demanded its toll, yet mercy emerged not as a mere reprieve but as a new covenantal order designed to restore and preserve.

At the heart of this covenant lay the rainbow, a breathtaking spectacle of colors arcing across the firmament, infused with both symbolic depth and profound theological significance. The rainbow, shimmering in its fragile yet resplendent beauty, was decreed as the visible sign of this sacred agreement, an everlasting reminder emblazoned in the sky to be witnessed by generations yet unborn. It was a divine emblem that encapsulated the tension between wrath and grace, a luminous promise that the destructive floodwaters that once cleansed the earth in judgment would never return to that degree. The rainbow served as an irrefutable sign, not merely of God's power but of God's enduring commitment to creation, an eternal marker of divine patience in the face of human frailty.

To grasp the full meaning of this covenant and its symbol requires immersion into the flood narrative's profound layers, where sin's societal consequences are displayed with stark clarity. The people of Noah's generation had become consumed by pervasive violence, cruelty, greed, and moral anarchy. Their hearts, hard and rebellious, rejected the divine order intended to sustain harmony between humans, creation, and the Creator. The flood was thus not inflicted capriciously but was the catastrophic outcome of a society that had severed its intrinsic link to righteousness. The ark, in contrast, symbolizes God's refuge for those who preserved fidelity amidst collapse. Through Noah's obedience in building the ark according to divine instruction, an act of faith against overwhelming societal skepticism, the story underscores personal responsibility amidst collective sin. Noah's covenant is inseparable from his role as a righteous remnant, his survival emblematic of the wider possibility of restoration and hope despite overwhelming human brokenness.

Yet the covenant is not solely about the past or a promise fixed in ancient times. It is a dynamic, living testament to the continuous human story, inviting reflection on how sin's consequences ripple across generations and societies. The rainbow transcends its immediate historical moment, inviting all who behold it to consider the interplay between divine justice and mercy in their own lives and communities. It is a symbol that issues a call to ethical introspection; to recognize the potential for ruin that unchecked sin creates, and simultaneously, to embrace the boundless grace that God extends even in the face of failure. The covenant with Noah urges a deeper contemplation of humanity's role as caretakers of the earth, stewards of life's fragile beauty highlighted by the rainbow's arc. Each appearance of this celestial sign draws attention to God's enduring presence and fidelity, affirming that while human sin can devastate, divine mercy persistently offers renewal.

Reflecting on the rainbow's significance leads to a meditation on the paradox of sin and grace woven throughout biblical history. The devastation wrought by the flood reveals sin's capacity to fracture the divine-human relationship, to corrupt the social fabric, and to imperil the very future of creation. Yet God's covenant, marked by the rainbow's gentle glow, illuminates the possibility of healing and restoration. It portrays a God who, with relentless compassion, chooses to make a fresh beginning rather than abandon creation to destruction. This duality reverberates through subsequent biblical epochs, echoing in every moral decision and spiritual trial. From the flood onward, the rainbow becomes a cosmic signpost pointing to the interdependence of divine judgment and loving forgiveness, a tension inviting believers to navigate their own moral landscapes with humility and hope.

Noah's covenant invites us also to consider the communal dimensions of sin's consequences and divine grace. The flood narrative communicates that while sin often manifests through individual choices, it ultimately inflicts societal and environmental upheavals that demand collective responsibility and response. The covenant issued to all flesh signifies a universal concern, transcending ethnic, cultural, or personal boundaries. Here, the biblical text asserts the sacredness of all life forms and the interconnectedness of existence, a visionary ecological vision centuries ahead of its time. The rainbow, therefore, is not merely a sign between God and humanity but an emblem encompassing the entire created order, a reminder that sin's rupture and God's reconciliation affect the whole web of life. As such, the covenant presses contemporary readers to reflect on how modern societies handle sin's fallout, from environmental degradation to social injustice, highlighting the ongoing relevance of Noah's story.

The flood and its aftermath reveal a profound divine pedagogy at work, a teaching method that uses both judgment and promise to educate humanity. The judgment flushes away the accumulated corruption that suffocated righteousness, while the covenant brings forth a new paradigm rooted in fidelity and hope. The rainbow's ethereal shimmer serves as a visual curriculum in the heavens, instructing generations to come about the necessity of recognizing the consequences of their choices while trusting in God's capacity to forgive and renew. In this light, the covenant can be read as an invitation to enter a covenantal relationship with God that is not static but evolving, one requiring continual repentance, ethical vigilance, and openness to divine mercy.

Furthermore, the covenant with Noah introduces a foundational theological motif of promise that unfolds richly across the biblical canon. It anticipates later covenants, such as those with Abraham, Moses, and ultimately the New Testament revelation centered on Jesus Christ. Each subsequent covenant carries echoes of this primal promise, an assurance that God's commitment to humanity endures despite frailty and failure. The rainbow's presence in the flood narrative is the mother-image of hope, the original emblem of a God who does not abandon a world scarred by sin but rather invites it into healing and wholeness. Consequently, understanding this moment allows readers to trace a spiritual trajectory that moves from cataclysmic judgment to the redemptive grace that culminates in Christ's incarnation.

Beyond theological reflection, the covenant calls for deep personal engagement. It challenges individuals to contemplate their own experiences of sin, judgment, mercy, and redemption. The rainbow becomes a mirror reflecting the human condition, fractured yet hopeful, culpable yet beloved. It invites each person to embody the covenant's spirit, embracing accountability for their actions while leaning into the hope of divine grace. In a world increasingly marked by division and despair, this ancient promise offers a timeless source of spiritual renewal and moral compass. It softens hearts hardened by failure and emboldens souls wearied by guilt, offering a path to reconciliation that is as relevant today as it was in Noah's time.

In this unfolding tapestry, the flood and the rainbow covenant stand not only as historical-theological markers but as catalysts for transformative dialogue between past and present. They compel us to wrestle with sin's persistent echoes that shape collective and individual destinies, to acknowledge the depth of human fallibility that calls for humility, and to celebrate the boundless grace that enables redemption. The rainbow arcs across the sky as a silent sermon, a gentle yet inexplicable phenomenon bridging earth and heaven, reminding us of a God who both judges and loves relentlessly. In its colors, there is a promise inscribed in the very fabric of creation, a promise that despite sin's darkness, the dawn of mercy always breaks through, offering light to guide humanity's journey forward.

Thus, the covenant made with Noah symbolizes much more than the cessation of divine wrath upon an ancient world or the reassurance against another flood. It represents a profound theological statement about the nature of God's relationship with creation, encapsulating the tension and continuity between sin's ruin and God's restorative grace. The rainbow is a perpetual invitation to trust in the possibility of new beginnings, a covenant that stretches across history inviting both nations and individuals to live with conscience, courage, and hope. In embracing the legacy of Noah's covenant, readers are called to hear once again the echoes of sin not as a final condemnation but as the prelude to divine mercy, a mercy that, like the rainbow's fragile arc, spans the heavens with the unyielding promise of grace.

Patriarchal Challenges: Abraham's Test

Call and Covenant

In the quiet vastness of ancient Mesopotamia, amid the fertile crescent cradled by shifting rivers and endless skies, a profound summons echoed, a divine call that would ripple through history, forever altering the course of a people and the fabric of faith itself. Abraham, originally Abram, stood at the crossroads of destiny, a figure both remarkable and ordinary, called out from the familiar to embrace a journey fraught with uncertainty, promise, and the weighty burden of covenant. This moment was not merely a summons to relocate or to assume a new identity; it was an invitation into a sacred relationship that would intertwine human frailty with divine purpose. To understand the depth of Abraham's call and covenant is to enter a narrative realm where faith and fallibility intersect, where promises gleam amidst the shadows of doubt, and where moral complexity abounds, offering a mirror to the timeless struggles of the human spirit.

God's call to Abraham was radical in its nature and comprehensive in its reach. "Go from your country, your people and your father's household to the land I will show you," the divine command resounded, blending firmness with mystery, setting Abraham on a path whose destination was as unknown as it was consequential. This was not a call to a place alone but to a way of life defined by trust and obedience. Abraham's story had already begun in the bustling city of Ur, a place rife with its own religious and social constructs, where he likely participated in established customs and inherited traditions. To respond to God's summons was to uproot not just physical ties but also to confront internal landscapes shaped by generations. The call demanded not only displacement but transformation, challenging Abraham to relinquish the security of legacy and cultural norms. At this juncture, it becomes clear that the call itself was a test of faith, an initial step into a relational covenant that would not only demand loyalty but also expose the fragile human assumptions about security, identity, and divine fidelity.

The covenant that emerged from this call was as unprecedented as it was binding. It was not simply a contract but a sacred bond characterized by promises that transcended time and circumstance. God promised Abraham that he would become the father of a great nation, a bearer of blessing to all families on earth. Such a promise echoed through the ancient world's prevailing ethos, where lineage, land, and legacy formed the foundation of identity and survival. Yet, this promise was counterintuitive, especially given Abraham's age and the barrenness of Sarah, his wife. The grand vision laid before him was therefore imbued with seeming impossibility, a seed sown in dry soil, inviting faith to bloom against all odds. It was this tension between promise and circumstance that would define much of Abraham's journey: the interplay of divine assurance and human doubt, of patient waiting and occasional impatience.

Abraham's covenant was also deeply relational, reflecting a dialogue rather than dictatorship. Throughout his life, Abraham conversed with God, questioned Him, and sometimes bargained on behalf of others. His famous intercession for the cities of Sodom and Gomorrah reveals a man acquainted with God's justice and mercy, wrestling not only with the fate of others but with the moral weight of divine judgment itself. This dynamic relationship illuminates the covenant as more than a mere promise; it was a lived experience, a dance of faith and moral engagement that invited Abraham into partnership with divine will. This nuanced interaction challenges simplistic views of ancient piety, revealing instead a complex spiritual landscape where obedience coexists with struggle, and where the human voice finds space to question and entreat.

Yet, faith for Abraham was no unbroken stream; it was punctuated with moments of profound fallibility. The journey into the unknown was fraught with fear, misunderstanding, and ethical dilemmas that tested the limits of his trust in God's promises. At times, Abraham's responses reveal a man striving to navigate the chasm between divine fidelity and life's stark realities. When confronted with threats in foreign lands, he at times resorted to deception, such as when he presented Sarah as his sister, hoping to protect himself through subterfuge. This moral ambiguity displays the human tendency to blur ethical lines in the exigencies of survival, highlighting that even patriarchs are not immune to frailty. These episodes complicate the portrait of Abraham as merely a paragon of faith; rather, they render him deeply relatable, a figure wrestling authentically with fear and hope.

One of the most poignant episodes reflecting Abraham's faith and fallibility is the command to sacrifice his son Isaac, a test that reverberates with psychological and theological intensity. This moment forces Abraham to confront the highest stakes: the potential loss of the very promise God had made. The narrative plunges into the heart of obedience, trust, and anguish, revealing a man willing to surrender all, even what seemed most sacred. Yet, the intervention of God at the crucial moment spares Isaac, affirming divine mercy alongside justice and reinforcing the covenantal theme of redemptive promise. This story remains hauntingly complex, inviting reflection on the nature of faith under pressure, sacrificial love, and the paradox of divine demand and divine provision. It encapsulates the fullness of Abraham's spiritual journey, a journey not into certainty but into trust amid doubt and sacrifice.

Beyond the individual experiences of Abraham, the call and covenant resonate deeply within the broader theological and cultural context of the ancient world. These narratives were not isolated religious anecdotes; they functioned as foundational myths shaping Israelite identity and worldview. The covenant framed the relationship between God and a chosen people, establishing ethical norms and social responsibilities, tethering divine blessing to fidelity and justice. It underscored the principle that divine-human interaction was active and ongoing, that morality was not a static code but a dynamic journey shaped by history, character, and circumstance. Abraham's story thereby becomes a microcosm of the human quest for meaning and belonging, offering a paradigm for navigating the tensions between divine sovereignty and human agency, between destiny and choice.

At the heart of this covenantal relationship is the enduring tension between divine grace and human responsibility. God's initiative in calling Abraham invites a response, but that response is fraught with limitations and hesitations inherent in human nature. The covenant demands fidelity, yet acknowledges human weakness, suggesting a divine patience that accommodates struggle without abandoning promise. This duality opens rich avenues for ethical reflection, particularly in understanding sin, not merely as broken law but as failure to live fully into the covenant relationship. Abraham's life exemplifies this dynamic interplay, fostering empathy for the complexities of faith in an imperfect world, while also uplifting the hope embedded in divine commitment to restoration and blessing.

As the narrative unfolds, the symbolic acts performed by Abraham further crystallize the covenant's dimensions. The sacrificial rituals, the marking of circumcision, represent tangible signs of an intangible promise, a physical covenant marking the body that serves as a permanent reminder of God's presence and claim on Abraham's descendants. These rituals provide continuity through generations, embedding the covenant not only in narratives but in lived practice. Such practices serve to bridge the ancient with the contemporary, linking past commitments with ongoing communal and spiritual identity. They remind readers that covenant is not a static historical event but a covenantal way of being, continually reenacted in trust, repentance, and hope.

The call to Abraham and the covenant established with him thus operate on multiple levels, historical, theological, and existential. Historically, they anchor the genesis of a people and their understanding of God as a faithful, demanding, yet merciful deity. Theologically, they invite deep questions about the nature of God's promises, the human condition, and the meaning of obedience. Existentially, they mirror the timeless human experience of making commitments, facing uncertainties, and living with the weight of both promise and fallibility. Abraham's story encourages readers not only to admire an ancient patriarch but to wrestle alongside him, to recognize echoes of their own spiritual dilemmas and moral complexities in his journey.

Ultimately, Abraham's call and covenant reveal a world where divine invitation meets human vulnerability, where greatness is forged not in perfection but in perseverance and fragile faith. The narrative radiates with the paradox of a God who calls imperfect people into holy partnership, who institutes covenants not on flawless obedience but on enduring love and grace. Abraham emerges not simply as a historical figure but as an archetype, a symbol of the human journey toward covenantal faith, a journey punctuated by hope, doubt, fear, and the ceaseless quest for meaning amid the unfolding tapestry of divine-human encounter. As readers trace these threads, they are invited into their own reflections on faith's callings, the covenants they embody, and the ever-present possibility of transformation that lies within the interstices of promise and fallibility.

The Testing of Faith

Abraham's narrative is, undeniably, one of the most profound and challenging stories within the biblical corpus, serving as a focal point for deep theological reflection and ethical inquiry. Central to this remarkable account is the episode often referred to as "The Testing of Faith," wherein Abraham's obedience is pushed to its extreme when God commands him to offer his son Isaac as a sacrifice. This moment unravels layers of tension between divine command and human moral consciousness, faith and doubt, obedience and ethical struggle, creating a tableau that has stirred interpreters and seekers for millennia. To understand the profound depths of this event, one must approach the story within the broader context of Abraham's journey, a journey marked by divine promises, personal trust, and recurring moral dilemmas that illuminate both the strength and fallibility inherent in human faith.

At the outset, Abraham's life is rooted in a covenantal relationship with God, one underscored by promises that seem paradoxically both grand and fragile. God declares to Abraham that he will become the father of a great nation, that his descendants will be as numerous as the stars of the heavens and the sands on the seashore. Yet, this promise is shadowed by the stark reality of Abraham and Sarah's childlessness. This gap between divine proclamation and human experience seeds a tension that colors the unfolding of Abraham's faith. It is within this crucible of hope and uncertainty that the testing arises. When Abraham is commanded to sacrifice Isaac, the son through whom the promises are to be fulfilled, the stakes elevate to a celestial and earthly crisis, one encapsulating faith's paradox: obedience in the face of a seemingly incomprehensible demand.

In contemplating Abraham's internal landscape at this juncture, we glimpse a man wrestling with profound cognitive dissonance. The request to sacrifice Isaac is not merely about surrendering a life; it challenges the very foundations of trust in God's faithfulness and justice. Abraham's response cannot be simplistically reduced to blind obedience; rather, it is a complex interplay of submission, doubt, and moral negotiation. As he ascends Mount Moriah with Isaac, each step embodies a tangible, visceral confrontation with the gravity of the command. There is evidence, when we consider the narrative's subtle cues, that Abraham is not devoid of inner turmoil. His silence, Isaac's questions, and the presence of the ram caught in the thicket, all these narrative elements suggest a landscape rich with emotional and ethical texture rather than mechanical compliance.

The moral implications of Abraham's willingness to sacrifice Isaac reverberate far beyond the event itself. On one hand, the story is often cited as the epitome of unwavering faith and ultimate devotion to the divine will. Abraham's readiness to part with his beloved son demonstrates an extraordinary level of trust, trust that God's promises are not null despite the apparent obliteration of their immediate fulfillment. This perspective rightly emphasizes faith as a dynamic relationship involving unwavering commitment even in the face of severe trial. On the other hand, the episode unnervingly probes the boundaries of moral discernment. How can obedience to a command which, if taken at face value, entails an act we would today classify as morally abhorrent be reconciled with the broader biblical ethos of justice, mercy, and respect for life? Is Abraham to be seen as transcending ordinary moral constraints due to his unique covenantal status, or is this narrative an invitation for readers to wrestle with the complexities inherent in absolute faith?

The tension between obedience and morality embodied in Abraham's trial reflects a profound theological dialectic, one that touches on the nature of divine authority and human ethical responsibility. Abraham is caught in a paradox where divine command suspends, or even subverts, human moral intuition. This paradox challenges simplistic notions of divine will as unconditionally good in human terms, revealing instead that faithfulness may demand navigating ambiguous terrain where right and wrong are not always transparent. The story invites a nuanced reflection on the limits of human understanding and the willingness to embrace uncertainty within a faith framework. Abraham's example is not so much a call to unquestioning submission but rather an invitation into the arduous path of carrying faith through moral quandaries and holding trust even when clarity falters.

Furthermore, the narrative serves as a lens through which to examine the theme of testing itself, both divine and human. God's testing of Abraham is not gratuitous; it appears designed to shape and deepen Abraham's faith, to move him from simple acceptance of promises to a lived experience of trust that persists despite the erosion of all apparent guarantees. From the divine perspective, the test is a means of revealing the quality of Abraham's trust and his capacity to align his will with God's purpose, which remains inscrutable. From Abraham's perspective, it is a moment of existential risk involving ultimate sacrifice but also profound potential for transformation. This dialectical process makes faith an act of courage and vulnerability, a terrain where risk and grace intersect.

In the broader scope of biblical tradition and moral theology, Abraham's test becomes emblematic of the human experience of encountering divine commands that disrupt settled moral calculations. It underscores the reality that faith is not a static acquisition but an evolving practice involving continual re-engagement with divine mystery and human conscience. The episode has given rise to diverse interpretive paths, some emphasizing the spiritual heroism of Abraham, others questioning the morality of divine demands, still others drawing out the symbolic dimensions related to covenant, sacrifice, and divine-human relationship. For instance, the near-sacrifice serves as a typology for later redemptive themes in the New Testament, where the notion of sacrifice and obedience reaches new theological horizons. This reflects the story's layered richness, where historical events resonate with ever-expanding spiritual meanings.

The human element of Abraham's experience, the fear, confusion, hope, and resignation, is critical to appreciating the depth of this story. Abraham's journey to the mountain, Isaac's silent accompaniment, the building of the altar, and the raising of the knife evoke a narrative charged with palpable emotional tension. This tension invites readers into empathetic engagement, recognizing that faith journeys are seldom neat or untroubled. Rather, they are marked by struggles to reconcile personal affections, communal norms, and divine imperatives. Abraham's ability to withhold final action until the decisive intervention of the angel highlights an openness to divine mercy that reframes the ordeal as not a ruthless test but a dialogic encounter. This nuance points toward the relational dynamics characterizing biblical faith, not mere submission but responsive communication.

The episode also raises enduring questions about authority and obedience in religious life. When confronted with a divine command that appears morally perplexing, how should one respond? Is obedience an absolute, or are there conditions under which moral conscience must assert itself? Abraham's story neither fully resolves this tension nor offers a simple formula, instead modeling a path where obedience is suffused with faith, reflection, and, ultimately, submission to divine providence. This ambiguity has generated abundant theological discourse, emphasizing that authentic faith does not bypass moral reflection but wrestles with it deeply.

Moreover, the testing highlights the relationship between faith and sacrifice in human spirituality. Abraham's willingness to sacrifice Isaac symbolizes the surrender of personal desires, plans, and attachments in the pursuit of a higher calling. It dramatizes a universal spiritual motif where growth often comes through letting go, sometimes of what is most precious. This motif resonates across religious traditions and human experiences, making Abraham's story not only an ancient historical narrative but a timeless psychological and spiritual archetype. The story thus invites readers to contemplate what it means to trust beyond sight, to embrace vulnerability, and to open oneself to transformation amidst uncertainty.

Importantly, this episode does not end with the act of near sacrifice; its aftermath is infused with rich symbolism and theological affirmation. The appearance of the ram caught in the thicket, offered as a substitute for Isaac, introduces themes of divine provision, mercy, and substitutionary redemption. This moment has profound theological significance, echoing through later biblical texts and religious thought. The provision of the ram announces that divine demands for faithfulness do not override divine compassion, pointing toward a harmonious interplay between justice and mercy. For the reader, it affirms that faith involves not only sacrifice but also hope, that the divine presence can turn moments of distress into occasions of grace.

As a whole, the story of Abraham's testing holds a mirror to the perennial human experience of wrestling with faith and morality. It encapsulates the strains of trusting a transcendent will that is not always clear or palatable, while also nurturing the possibility of communion with that will in ways that transcend human limitations. Abraham's journey is both a personal saga and a universal paradigm demonstrating that faith is a pilgrimage through uncertainty, frailty, and grace. His example neither sanctifies unquestioning compliance nor condemns moral questioning but situates faith within the dynamic ebb and flow of trust and doubt, obedience and reflection, sacrifice and redemption.

The richness and complexity of this narrative invite readers today to reflect on their own moral dilemmas and faith journeys. In a world where ethical choices often involve competing claims and ambiguous outcomes, Abraham's story reassures that wrestling with these tensions is integral to authentic spiritual life. It encourages embracing doubt and vulnerability while maintaining openness to divine guidance and mercy. In this light, "The Testing of Faith" is less about the heroic act of sacrifice and more about the ongoing, often painful relationship between humanity and the divine, a relationship marked by trust made possible through grace and sustained amidst uncertainty.

Ultimately, Abraham's encounter with the command to sacrifice Isaac stands as a monumental testament to the intricacies and challenges of faith. It transcends simple moral binaries and ventures into the realm where narrative, theology, and human experience intertwine. Through it, the biblical text offers a textured, profoundly human account of faith confronted by the limits of understanding and the demands of obedience, inviting each generation to engage with the echoes of this ancient text and to find within it a source of both humility and hope.

Intercession and Mercy

In the wilderness of ancient promises, where the pillars of faith and judgment rise in uneasy harmony, Abraham stands not only as a patriarch but as an emblem of intercession and mercy, forever etched in the tapestry of divine-human interaction. His journey, already heavy with covenantal assurances and human frailty, reaches a critical juncture in the shadow of impending judgment against Sodom and Gomorrah. This moment lingers in the sacred memory because it reveals a profound dialogue, not merely of words exchanged but of hearts laid bare, of justice and compassion wrestled within the divine council itself, and the enduring human task of approaching God with both reverence and boldness.

Abraham arrives at a crossroads where the promise of descendants and possessions merges with the stark reality of human depravity incarnate in the cities destined for destruction. The narrative, so tender and turbulent, exposes the intimate tension between divine holiness and human sinfulness. The cities of Sodom and Gomorrah, steeped in violent outrage and moral decay, have become symbols of extreme transgression, prompting God's declaration of intention to destroy. It is here that Abraham assumes the role of mediator, a role that demands not only unwavering faith in God's justice but also an audacious hope that mercy might temper judgment. The story unfolds with Abraham's initial incredulous questioning, which is deceptive in its simplicity but profound in theological implication. "Will you sweep away the righteous along with the wicked?" he asks, not out of defiance but deep concern, wrestling with the enormity of divine judgment and hope for human righteousness within the doomed cities.

This negotiation is remarkable because it peels back layers of theological complexity and exposes a God who is not distant or detached but deeply engaged with human beings. Abraham's approach is neither presumptuous nor timid; it is bold yet respectful, a delicate dance in the shadow of divine wrath. His request is incremental, beginning with fifty righteous souls and descending in careful steps, forty-five, forty, thirty, twenty, until the perilously low number of ten is reached. Each step illustrates not only Abraham's hopeful advocacy but also the merciful character of God, who listens intently without compromising divine justice. This exchange echoes a divine openness to intercession, challenging simplistic views of God as a rigid dispenser of punishment and instead emphasizing a relational God eager to engage with human pleas, to balance righteousness with compassion.

In the midst of this dialogue, the character of Abraham reveals layers of spiritual complexity, emblematic of human frailty intertwined with sacred trust. Abraham is not presented as flawless; rather, he models a faith that questions and petitions, a faith that dares to speak into the unseen realm with humility and persistence. This is a faith that acknowledges the tension between divine omniscience and human agency, a faith that neither demands nor dictates but pleads for mercy grounded in the innocent amidst the guilty. The negotiation serves as a vivid illustration of the human role in divine justice, suggesting that prayer and intercession are not passive acts but active participation in the divine economy, a co-working in the unfolding of mercy and judgment.

As the dialogue unfolds, its implications ripple beyond the immediate narrative, inviting reflection on the nature of righteousness and justice in community life. Abraham's advocacy foregrounds the importance of even a few righteous individuals in society, suggesting that the presence of goodness can influence, delay, or even alter the course of collective fate. This tension with the harsh reality of widespread sinfulness in Sodom and Gomorrah, urging readers to consider how individual and communal morality are intertwined, and how divine judgment is never impersonal but filtered through relational realities. The intercession becomes an ethical mirror, prompting contemplation about the power of righteousness, not just in isolation but as a force with potential to challenge and transform societal corruption.

The theological resonance in this encounter is profound. It reveals that divine justice is both serious and supple, a justice that cannot be reduced to mechanical retribution but one that is permeated with mercy and openness to repentance. The narrative suggests that even at the precipice of catastrophe, the door of dialogue remains open between God and humanity, where negotiation is possible, and where mercy remains a hopeful counterpoint to judgment. This interplay of justice and mercy shapes much of the unfolding Biblical narrative and frames a fundamental dilemma that has haunted believers across centuries: how to reconcile the holiness of God with His love, and how to approach divine patience without taking it for granted.

Within this unfolding drama, the personalities involved are richly human. Abraham's role is dynamic and nuanced, showing a leader deeply committed not just to his own household's destiny but to the fate of broader humanity. His concern for Sodom and Gomorrah transcends tribal or familial interest, marking a significant shift from earlier chapters when the focus was narrowly on covenantal promise, to an embrace of a wider ethical responsibility. This development aligns Abraham closer to the prophetic voice, emphasizing advocacy as a sacred duty. His interaction with God illustrates how, in the biblical worldview, human intercession can influence divine actions, an impetus toward humanitarian concern rooted deeply in faith.

Meanwhile, God's responses portray a tension between justice's necessity and mercy's possibility. God does not dismiss Abraham's requests but engages with them, carefully, sincerely, and with a certain dramatic restraint. The divine willingness to "listen" and "respond" suggests a model of divine-human interaction marked not only by command and obedience but by partnership and negotiation. This scenario complicates simplistic notions of divine sovereignty and instead portrays a God who respects human voice and agency. It also implies a divine pedagogy that educates humans in the mysteries of judgment and mercy, inviting reflection and participation rather than dictating unilateral decrees.

The outcome of the negotiation, while ultimately resulting in the destruction of Sodom and Gomorrah due to insufficient righteousness, is rich with theological and ethical import. It highlights the limits of intercession and the reality of consequence, yet it also ensures that mercy had every opportunity to manifest. The failure of the cities to find even ten righteous people is framed as a tragic reminder of the cost of sin, but not as a condemnation of intercessory hope. Instead, the narrative elevates intercession as a sacred, courageous act, essential to the divine drama and to human spiritual life.

Furthermore, Abraham's intercession sets a theological precedent extended throughout later biblical texts: the figure of the intercessor, the one who stands in the breach between divine wrath and human sinfulness. This motif deepens with the prophets and finds its ultimate expression in the New Testament with Christ's sacrificial mediation, connecting the threads of mercy in the grand tapestry of redemption. Abraham's negotiation is thus not a mere story from antiquity but a foundational episode illustrating how divine judgment and mercy are forever interwoven, and how human voices can echo into eternity, shaping the course of salvation history.

From a moral perspective, the exchange raises profound questions about responsibility, advocacy, and the nature of grace. It challenges readers to consider the power and limits of pleading on behalf of others, the courage required to confront divine justice, and the humility necessary to trust in a mercy that is never guaranteed but always possible. Abraham's role as an intercessor models a form of deep relational courage, an ethical stance that dares to believe in the transformative power of prayer and petition while accepting the precariousness of human fate when confronted by divine holiness.

The story also invites contemporary reflection on the dynamics between law, justice, and compassion in community and personal life. It suggests that intercession is not just an ancient theological concept but a living practice requiring empathy, persistence, and the willingness to engage uncomfortable realities for the sake of others. It compels readers to confront their own responses to human sin, suffering, and societal collapse, pushing beyond passive judgment toward active compassion and advocacy. The narrative thereby transcends its historical moment and becomes a mirror for modern ethical decision-making, inviting an ongoing engagement with divine mercy in a broken world.

Moreover, this dialogue between Abraham and God unfolds within a larger narrative movement that intertwines divine promises with human ethical obligations. Abraham's faith is inseparable from his moral responsibility; the covenant relationship is not merely about blessings and promises but about living faithfully in recognition of divine holiness and justice. The intercession episode underscores that faith involves wresting honestly with difficult questions, approaching God candidly, and embracing the complexity of divine-human partnership. This partnership is dynamic and fraught but ultimately transformative, revealing the depth with which biblical texts address human struggle in relation to the divine.

The richness of this narrative also resides in its emotional texture, where urgency and hope mingle with awe and fear. Abraham's voice, rising in measured increments from fifty to ten, conveys a restless hope that refuses to capitulate even before the full weight of impending destruction. His willingness to engage in this risky dialogue reflects not lukewarm mediation but a passionate love for justice and mercy. This emotional investment humanizes both the patriarch and the divine response, reminding readers that theology is lived in the arena of struggle, vulnerability, and relational courage.

In sum, Abraham's negotiation with God over Sodom and Gomorrah offers a profound exploration of the intersection between divine judgment and mercy, authority and advocacy, faith and fallibility. It reveals a God who listens, a human who intercedes, and a world where sin carries devastating consequences but never closes the door on hope. This ancient dialogue continues to echo across millennia, inviting every reader into a space where they might wrestle with the same questions about justice, mercy, and the power of prayerful intercession. It models a faith deeply engaged with moral complexity, reminding us that in the face of sin's threatening shadow, the earnest plea for mercy remains a sacred and necessary act, one that shapes destinies and invites us into the transformative dance of grace.

Egyptian Bondage and Liberation

Oppression in Egypt

The story of Israel's suffering under Pharaoh in Egypt stands as one of the most poignant illustrations of sin manifesting not merely as individual moral failure but as a systemic force, oppression, that dehumanizes and distorts the very fabric of society. The narrative, deeply entrenched in the biblical tradition, is a powerful testimonial to the enduring consequences of human sinfulness when multiplied and institutionalized. In Egypt, the Israelites, once welcomed and prosperous sojourners, became a subjugated people, crushed beneath the heavy hand of a foreign ruler whose fear and insecurity breed cruelty and dominion. This period of bondage is a sprawling chapter in the biblical saga, rich with themes of injustice, endurance, divine justice, and the promise of deliverance, all underscored by the complex interplay between human sin and divine action.

The oppression in Egypt did not arise in a vacuum; it emerged from Pharaoh's sin, a sin compounded by pride, fear, and a thirst for power that refused to recognize the sanctity and dignity of the Israelite people. Pharaoh's initial generosity had turned into suspicion as the Israelite population grew numerous and strong, a demographic shift that stirred anxiety in the heart of a ruler whose authority rested on control and dominance. This fear morphed into a crescendo of oppression, driven by a desire not just to contain but to crush any possibility of Israelite ascendancy. Thus, the sin of Pharaoh was fundamentally one of injustice, rooted in the devaluation of human life and the aggressive maintenance of power through brutality. To oppress another, whether an individual or an entire nation, is to invert the divine order of creation where every human being is made in the image of God, worthy of respect, freedom, and flourishing.

As the narrative unfolds, the plight of the Israelites under Pharaoh's iron rule serves as an embodied illustration of sin's corrosive effect on community and morality. The Egyptians impose harsh labor, forcing the Israelites into grueling toil that wears down bodies and spirits alike. Yet, it is not merely physical suffering that defines the experience but the erosion of hope and identity under the weight of relentless oppression. The sin here transcends individual acts of cruelty and becomes a systemic evil, an apparatus designed to extinguish dreams and silence the voices of the oppressed. The Hebrew slaves are subjected to backbreaking work, tasked with brick-making and forced into fields, denied even the simplest reprieve, a reality that reflects how sin rooted in domination destabilizes social bonds and perpetuates cycles of violence and dehumanization.

Oppression, as the narrative portrays it, is a sin that festers because it equates another's suffering with acceptable collateral in the pursuit of one's own security or prosperity. Pharaoh's policies reflect this, prioritizing the preservation of his dominion over the basic human rights of an entire people. In essence, this sin mirrors a spiritual blindness, a refusal to see the oppressed as equals deserving of justice. This blindness is amplified by the political structures that enable and normalize cruelty. Pharaoh's sin is exacerbated by courtiers and officials who implement his decrees, bureaucratic agents in a machinery dedicated to perpetuating cruelty. The story reveals how sin can become embedded not only in personal hearts but also within the political and social institutions that shape human life.

Yet, amidst this grim landscape of suffering, the narrative weaves a profound testimony to the possibility of divine intervention and the power of hope as an antidote to the sin of oppression. The story pivots on the divine call of Moses, whose life and mission are intimately bound to that of his oppressed people. Moses emerges from within the very context of Egyptian oppression, a child saved from death, nurtured in the house of Pharaoh, yet deeply connected to his Israelite heritage. His journey is emblematic of the tension between living within a sinful world and being called to enact divine justice. Moses' eventual confrontation with Pharaoh is not merely a clash of wills but a cosmic battle between divine righteousness and human iniquity. Through Moses, God reveals that sin, even when institutionalized and deeply entrenched, is neither unchallenged nor unredeemable.

The biblical story underscores the notion that sin as oppression summons a divine response that is both just and merciful. The plagues that afflict Egypt serve as divine rebukes, hardening Pharaoh's heart yet progressively dismantling the structures of sin he embodies. Each plague peels back the layers of Egypt's false security, exposing the fragility of sin attained through oppression and pride. This divine judgment is imbued with patience; the plagues are not arbitrary acts of punishment but invitations to repentance, opportunities for Pharaoh to relent and choose justice over cruelty. The theological tension here is profound. It reveals a God who is sovereign yet patient, just yet merciful, responding to human sin not merely with retribution but with an ongoing call to transformation.

It is important to recognize that the narrative is not solely a tale of divine wrath but also one of steadfast covenantal love. The bondage of Egypt becomes the backdrop against which God's covenant with Israel is tested and ultimately reaffirmed. This covenantal dimension highlights that God's actions in delivering the Israelites are not only acts of judgment upon sin but expressions of divine faithfulness and commitment to human dignity. The Exodus, therefore, is not just a physical liberation but a spiritual redefinition of what it means to live in relationship with God and one another. It symbolizes hope amid despair and the possibility of renewal where sin seems insurmountable.

The story also invites readers into contemplation of the enduring nature of sin's echoes. Oppression is not confined to ancient Egypt; the dynamics that fueled Pharaoh's cruelty continue to manifest in countless forms throughout history, systems of slavery, racism, exploitation, and tyranny. The biblical account thus speaks into contemporary realities, challenging readers to recognize how sin as systemic violence still pervades societies and calls each generation to resist complicity and work for justice. Moses' call to leadership, his courage in confronting power, and the eventual liberation of the Israelites become archetypes of moral resistance, showing how faithfulness to divine justice can break the chains of oppression.

At the heart of this narrative lies a profound theological reflection on the nature of sin itself. Sin is not only about individual failings but about the structures that perpetuate injustice and bind communities in cycles of suffering. The Egypt story confronts readers with the reality that sin is an active force, one that demands vigilance, repentance, and divine grace. It also portrays the interplay between human agency and divine sovereignty. While Pharaoh exercises free will in choosing oppression, God orchestrates deliverance, crafting a redemptive path that challenges and overturns human sinfulness. This dynamic tension invites readers to grapple with questions about power, responsibility, and the ways divine grace intersects with human history.

Moreover, the narrative's rich symbolism enhances its theological depth. Egypt itself stands for more than just a geographical location; it becomes a metaphor for bondage in all its forms, physical, spiritual, and moral. The harsh labor, the cries of the oppressed, and the stubborn refusal to acknowledge the wrongs inflicted all paint a vivid picture of sin's impact on creation. Against this backdrop, the deliverance through Moses is not just an act of rescue but a profound spiritual awakening, marking the dawn of a new relationship between God and humanity. The journey from oppression to freedom echoes the broader human quest for meaning, justice, and reconciliation with the divine.

In revisiting this ancient story, readers are invited into a profound meditation on the cost of sin and the power of deliverance. The Israelites' suffering in Egypt illustrates how sin, when left unchecked, diminishes and destroys, but it also reveals the eternal promise that no sin is beyond the reach of divine mercy. The Exodus is a testament to hope, a hope that inspires courage, creativity, and faith in the face of overwhelming odds. It challenges each person to consider how the echoes of sin manifest in their own lives and communities and calls them to participate in the ongoing work of liberation and healing.

In this light, oppression under Pharaoh transcends historical narrative and enters the realm of moral allegory, teaching enduring lessons about the consequences of sin and the transformative potential of divine love. It beckons modern readers to confront injustices in their own contexts and to embrace the call to resist sin's dehumanizing effects with the resilient faith exemplified by Moses and his people. In so doing, the story affirms a timeless truth: while sin may echo across generations, so too does the promise of redemption, inviting all to journey from bondage into freedom, from despair into hope.

God's Call to Moses

The moment Moses encountered God's call transformed the story of a singular man into the monumental narrative of a nation's liberation, a divine intervention born out of an acute recognition of injustice and human suffering. God's call to Moses was not merely a summons for leadership; it was a profound indictment of systemic sin manifesting in the cruel oppression of the Israelites in Egypt. Their bondage was no ordinary hardship but a pervasive evil that enslaved bodies and fractured spirits, weaving sin into the very fabric of their daily existence. This sin was not only personal disobedience but had become institutionalized, an entrenched power structure that dehumanized an entire people. To understand the weight of God's call to Moses is to delve deeply into the nature of sin as oppression and the role divine deliverance plays not just as rescue, but as profound moral reckoning and restoration.

Moses' life before the call attests to layered complexity. Born an Israelite but raised as Egyptian royalty, he inhabited an ambiguous identity caught between worlds. His flight to Midian after killing an Egyptian slave driver was not just an act of rebellion but a moment of failure and exile, a personal tragedy steeped in the very oppression he sought to challenge. For decades, he lived as a shepherd, distant from his people and destiny, until the flame from the burning bush interrupted this quiet obscurity. This fiery theophany was no ordinary encounter with the divine; it symbolized purification and illumination, a sacred moment where holiness touched the earth without consuming it. Here, Moses was invited into a covenantal mission that transcended personal ambition and narrative, it was an invitation to partner in God's redemptive purpose against the sin that enslaved a nation.

The sin of Egypt was multifaceted: it was sin as domination, sin as injustice, and sin as the systematic erasure of the vulnerable. The Pharaoh's hardened heart became the emblem of resistance not only to God's command but to the possibility of liberation itself. This obstinacy underscored the far-reaching implications of sin, it was not confined to individual choices but had social and political consequences that perpetuated suffering. Moses' call thus became a direct confrontation with power corrupted by pride and cruelty. Divine justice demanded the liberation of those shackled by human cruelty, and God's call carried the authority that was both divine and prophetic. It declared that sin's dominion, no matter how entrenched, was ultimately subject to divine disruption and judgment.

Moses, however, did not step into this calling without hesitation or doubt. His response highlights the complexity of human frailty when faced with divine purpose. From questioning his own adequacy to negotiating for authentication of God's presence, Moses' wavering reflects the natural tension between fear and faith. His reluctance humanizes the encounter, it reminds readers that liberation, whether personal or communal, often begins with uncertainty and the need for reassurance. Sin's grip is not easily loosened, and the pathway to deliverance invariably challenges the leader to confront internal doubts as much as external adversaries. God's patience and provision of signs testify to a compassionate partnership that sustains weary leaders while calling them beyond their limitations.

In the grander theological vision, Moses' call exemplifies the interplay between human agency and divine sovereignty. It affirms that while sin disrupts creation's harmony, divine grace initiates restoration through chosen instruments. Moses embodies this dynamic tension; his mission to free Israel is not just a political revolt but a sacred task charged with reconciling a fractured relationship between God and humanity. The liberation narrative enfolds ethical imperatives; freedom is not merely the absence of bondage but an invitation to covenantal living rooted in justice, mercy, and reverence for God. This vision confronts readers with enduring moral questions about complicity in systems of oppression and the courage required to answer God's call for justice.

God's commissioning of Moses also sets in motion a transformational journey that exposes sin's consequences in their most visceral form, plagues, wilderness wandering, and rebellion within Israel itself. These episodes underscore that liberation is rarely swift or simple; it is a pilgrimage of repentance, testing, and growth. The narrative acknowledges that sin's echoes persist even among the delivered, necessitating continual grace and the ongoing work of sanctification. Moses, as mediator, intercedes between a nation prone to forgetfulness and a holy God who demands faithfulness. The call is thus not only about emancipation from physical captivity but about cultivating a people capable of living into divine promises that transcend freedom from oppression to embody covenantal holiness.

Viewed through the lens of liberation theology, Moses' call resonates powerfully across centuries and cultures. It challenges communities today to confront the sin of oppression wherever it exists, be it racial injustice, economic exploitation, or systemic violence. The divine call does not recede into antiquity; it persists as an urgent summons to participate in redemptive action that dismantles structures of sin and restores dignity to the oppressed. Moses' hesitant yet faithful response offers a paradigm for contemporary readers who grapple with their own callings amid complex realities of injustice, urging them to trust in divine accompaniment amid uncertainty.

Furthermore, the invitation to Moses unveils the intimate relationship between suffering and divine mission. It reveals how God's awareness and compassion intersect deeply with human pain, aligning the divine will with liberation rather than mere survival. This alignment transforms suffering from arbitrary tragedy into a crucible where faith is forged and destiny is shaped. The call exemplifies a God who actively confronts evil rather than passively observing it, thus redefining divine power in terms of deliverance, justice, and life-giving restoration. This contrasts sharply with common perceptions of divine detachment, offering a refreshing theological insight that God's holiness compels engagement with brokenness rather than aloofness.

The narrative of God's call to Moses also invites reflection on the nature and effects of obedience. Moses' eventual acceptance of this daunting task illustrates how obedience to divine will is not about effortless compliance but involves ongoing struggle, perseverance, and trust. Obedience becomes an active stance against sin's encroachment, a form of resistance that enacts God's justice in tangible ways. It also carries the paradox of power and vulnerability, Moses is empowered by God's presence but remains a mortal subject to failure and human limitation. This paradox enriches the narrative, presenting leadership not as infallibility but as responsible dependence on divine strength amidst human weakness.

Delving deeply into the imagery of the burning bush enriches this exploration of sin and deliverance. The bush that burned without being consumed mirrors the paradox of Israel's suffering, it undergoes intense trial but is not destroyed, sustained by divine presence amid affliction. This vivid imagery encapsulates the hope embedded within the call: although sin's oppression seems overwhelming, it cannot extinguish the covenantal promise. The bush's fire also symbolizes purifying transformation, suggesting that liberation involves a refining process that purges sin and prepares the people for covenantal fidelity. Such symbolism offers profound theological insight about endurance and sanctification, portraying deliverance as both a dramatic rescue and a gradual shaping into God's holy community.

Moreover, the narrative tension in God's call to Moses challenges simplistic understandings of sin as merely individual guilt. It reveals sin's structural dimensions, the way systems and powers perpetuate injustice and defy divine order. Moses' mission unveils sin as a communal reality that requires collective response and transformation, not just personal repentance. The story invites readers to consider their own social contexts and the systemic sins embedded within them, recognizing that divine deliverance may call for courageous confrontation with entrenched powers and the unsettling work of societal reform.

Integral to this call is also the theme of covenant and promise. God's commissioning of Moses reiterates that the liberation of Israel is an act of fidelity to a covenant relationship established with their ancestors. This act of deliverance is not accidental but a continuation of God's steadfast commitment to God's people, despite their repeated failings. The call to Moses thus serves to remind readers that divine grace is a persistent and patient response to sin's disruption, offering hope that redemption is always within reach. It frames history within a divine narrative that moves from fallenness toward restoration, underscoring that no sin, however pervasive, ultimately thwarts God's redemptive purposes.

Even as Moses embarks on this divine mission, the narrative does not gloss over the deep costs and struggles entwined in the road ahead. The impending confrontation with Pharaoh is fraught with danger, the potential for failure, and immense pressure. Through Moses, the text conveys a profound vulnerability that respects the difficulty of answering God's call in the face of overwhelming opposition. This emphasizes that liberation is never guaranteed or easy; it requires courage, perseverance, and an ever-renewed trust in divine guidance. The reality of sin's resistance is raw and consequential, reminding readers that the journey from bondage to freedom is marked by conflict and costly perseverance.

At the heart of God's call to Moses lies an enduring spiritual principle: that sin's hold can be broken not by human power alone but by divine intervention working through human hearts willing to be instruments of justice. This principle carries profound implications for faith communities today, encouraging them to seek divine partnership in confronting injustice and embodying mercy. The call invites an ongoing reflection on how God's liberating work continues in the present age, through acts of courage, advocacy, and steadfast faith. It encourages believers to see their struggles against oppression as part of a larger sacred narrative, where human suffering and divine purpose intersect in the ongoing unfolding of redemption.

In sum, the call of God to Moses is a deeply layered and evocative encounter that illuminates the nature of sin as oppression and divine deliverance as both rescue and moral summons. It portrays liberation as a complex, transformative journey rooted in covenantal faithfulness and suffused with divine presence amid human frailty. Moses' hesitant yet obedient response encapsulates the tension between fear and faith that defines all meaningful engagement with God's call to confront sin in whatever forms it takes. This episode encourages readers to recognize the enduring relevance of biblical liberation theology, inspiring them to participate courageously in the ongoing work of justice and grace amid the echoing shadows of sin. Through this profound narrative, we glimpse a

God who calls out from the midst of suffering, inviting broken humanity into a transformative partnership that reshapes history, restores dignity, and embodies hope.

Plagues and Exodus

In the vast tapestry of biblical history, the narrative of the plagues and the Exodus stands as one of the most compelling and poignant illustrations of sin's oppressive reach and the divine response to human suffering. Within the unfolding drama of ancient Egypt, we find a profound exploration of sin not simply as personal failings or isolated moral lapses but as a systemic force of oppression, one that crushes the spirit of a people and threatens to extinguish hope itself. The story of the plagues and the Exodus, therefore, emerges not only as a historical account or theological assertion but as a vivid meditation on freedom, justice, and the consequences of hardened hearts.

At the core of this narrative lies the figure of Pharaoh, whose stubborn refusal to heed the divine command to release the Israelites from bondage encapsulates the tragic dynamics of sin as pride, intransigence, and abuse of power. Pharaoh's hardness is not a mere character flaw; it is a manifestation of a deeper spiritual blindness and a deliberate choice to perpetuate oppression rather than respond to an ethical summons. This refusal sets into motion a dramatic confrontation between human will and divine authority, justice and tyranny, deliverance and captivity. Each plague, while devastating in its scope and effect, functions as a deliberate act of judgment designed to expose the impotence of Pharaoh's gods and the perilous consequences of refusing to submit to a higher moral law.

The oppression endured by the Israelites in Egypt exemplifies sin's social dimension, how systemic evil can become entrenched in political institutions and cultural practices, distorting relationships and enslaving whole communities. As slaves, the Israelites were reduced to mere property, their dignity stolen, their hopes suppressed beneath the heavy yoke of forced labor and cruel governance. This collective suffering is the backdrop against which the divine drama unfolds, underscoring the theological truth that sin's reach extends beyond individual transgressions to the fabric of societies and the structures that govern them. This is a sin not of isolated acts but of an institutionalized system that dehumanizes and devalues life itself.

Moses emerges in this context as the divinely appointed agent of liberation, a figure whose own journey from prince of Egypt to shepherd in the wilderness and finally to leader of Israel mirrors the transformative power of grace and the call to righteous action. His encounter with God at the burning bush is not a mere mystical episode but a theophany charged with ethical implications, a summons to confront injustices and to participate in God's redemptive work in the world. Moses' mission is fraught with difficulty, for he must navigate not only the intransigence of Pharaoh but also the doubts and fears of the people he is called to lead. Through his leadership, we see that deliverance is never simple or immediate; it is a process that demands courage, perseverance, and trust in divine providence amidst uncertainty.

The plagues themselves, each increasing in their intensity and scope, function symbolically as acts of divine judgment against the brokenness of Egypt's society and the vaunted powers it worshiped. They represent a systematic dismantling of the false security upon which Pharaoh clung: the Nile, the lifeblood of Egypt, turned to blood in a dramatic display of vulnerability; the fertility of the land and its creatures were subjected to pestilence and death; darkness engulfed the land, a metaphor for the spiritual blindness that accompanied Pharaoh's pride and stubbornness. These calamities illustrate sin's disruptive power, not only in the physical realm but as a spiritual and moral bankruptcy that pervades a nation's very identity.

Yet, even amid the devastation wrought by the plagues, the narrative does not lose sight of God's mercy and the opportunity for repentance.

The recurring refrain of God's command to Pharaoh to "Let my people go" offers a pattern of judgment tempered by grace, allowing room for a change of heart. Pharaoh's repeated refusals, however, reveal how sin can harden the human heart to the point of self-destruction. This hardness is not mere obstinacy but a profound spiritual pathology where self-interest blinds one to justice and compassion, leading inevitably toward ruin.

The climax of this harrowing saga is the final and most devastating plague, the death of the firstborn, a tragic event that brings the house of Egypt to its knees but also marks the pivotal moment of Israel's liberation. It is a stark reminder of the high cost of sin, the suffering inflicted not only on oppressors but also, tragically, on innocents caught in the tidal wave of judgment. This event demands from the Israelites a deep ethical reckoning as well, as they are called to leave behind Egypt and embark on a journey toward a new identity grounded in freedom, covenant, and obedience to God's law.

The institution of Passover, which follows, encapsulates the dual themes of judgment and salvation, becoming a ritual that commemorates both the tragic consequences of sin and the hope of divine deliverance. The blood of the lamb on the doorposts signifies protection and grace, a mystical boundary between death and life, bondage and freedom, despair and hope. The Passover thus becomes a foundational symbol of redemption that resonates across generations, pointing forward to the ultimate liberation promised in the unfolding biblical story.

As the Israelites embark on their journey out of Egypt, across the wilderness toward the Promised Land, the narrative continues to explore themes of faith, obedience, and human frailty. The experience of liberation is fraught with challenges that test the community's resolve and trust. The wilderness itself becomes a crucible where the people confront their dependence on God and grapple with the lingering effects of their years in bondage, the echoes of sin that still cling to their hearts and social structures. Sin, after all, is not easily overcome; the journey toward freedom requires a transformation that touches every aspect of life.

In analyzing the plagues and the Exodus through a theological lens, one cannot help but see the broader implications for understanding sin as a force that distorts human relationships at every level, from individual hearts to entire nations. The oppression of the Israelites is a mirror reflecting the ways in which sin enslaves and diminishes, and the divine deliverance enacted through Moses reveals God's steadfast commitment to justice and mercy. This interplay challenges readers to consider the various forms of bondage and oppression in their own contexts, how sin remains a present force that demands confrontation and offers the possibility of redemption.

The Exodus narrative, therefore, invites an ongoing reflection on moral responsibility and the dynamics of freedom. It raises profound questions about the nature of power and leadership, the costs of resistance, and the possibilities for transformation. Pharaoh's stubbornness serves as a cautionary tale about the dangers of pride and the futility of opposing divine justice. Conversely, Moses embodies the potential for faithful mediation between God and humanity, calling forth courage and obedience in the face of overwhelming odds.

This story's enduring significance lies not only in its historical and religious meaning but also in its existential resonance. The struggle for liberation from Egypt becomes a metaphor for the spiritual journey each person undertakes, a movement from the bondage of sin toward the freedom of grace. It is a narrative that speaks across millennia, reminding readers that the battles against oppression and injustice are perennial, that sin's echoes reverberate still, and that divine deliverance remains a beacon of hope. Through this lens, the plagues and Exodus emerge as a profound reflection on human fallibility, divine faithfulness, and the transformative power of redemption, urging us to consider the ways in which we, too,

might confront the sins of our own times with courage, compassion, and
faith.

85

Gary E. Risenhoover

The Giving of the Law and Covenant

Encounter at Sinai

The moment at Sinai stands as one of the most profound encounters recorded in the story of Israel and its unfolding relationship with the Divine. It is here, on that rugged mountain etched by fire and cloud, that God reveals Himself not as a distant force but as an intimate lawgiver who desires not only obedience but a transformation of a people into a covenant community. The air was thick with anticipation and fear, a palpable tension as the Israelites, still fresh from their deliverance from Egypt, gathered at the foot of the mountain. This gathering was not merely a crowd; it was the nascent nation, poised on the brink of defining its identity and destiny. God's voice thundered across the wilderness, beckoning them into a new moral order through the proclamation of the Ten Commandments. These commandments, etched into stone tablets, were more than mere rules; they were the heartbeat of a community ethic designed to harmonize the individual's relationship with God and with fellow human beings.

The initial commandments establish a profound paradigm: the centrality of a divine, exclusive relationship. The prohibition of other gods, the call to reject idolatry, the mandate to honor the sacred name, and the establishment of the Sabbath as a consecrated time all underscore a covenantal framework that begins by orienting the community around its Creator. This orientation shapes not only spiritual allegiance but daily rhythms and priorities. It draws a sharp line between the chaos of former bondage and the order of freedom grounded in divine hospitality and sanctity. The exclusivity demanded was not just a theological claim; it was a call to fidelity that would unite a fractured people into a cohesive body whose identity was inseparable from their devotion. The covenant revealed at Sinai served as an anchor, a compass for ethical living amidst a wandering journey through deserts both physical and moral.

Beyond these foundational religious commands, the subsequent laws delineate the social and ethical fabric of the community. They integrate the imperative of justice into the daily lives of the Israelites, demanding respect for life, truthfulness in speech, and the sanctity of marriage and family. The prohibition against murder, adultery, theft, false testimony, and covetousness were not arbitrary prohibitions but essential safeguards ensuring the integrity and flourishing of the community. Each commandment signals a break from the selfish impulses that led humanity into disorder, a refusal to let jealousy, deceit, and violence fracture the fragile bond between neighbors. These laws resound with an acute awareness of human frailty and the consequences that arise when social trust erodes. They envision a society in which the dignity of each person is protected because all bear the divine image, and where harmony is cultivated not by force but by shared commitment to justice and holiness.

The encounter at Sinai also reveals an intentional, communal dimension of sin and righteousness. God's speech, delivered not privately but before the entire assembly, establishes accountability not merely as an individual matter but as a corporate responsibility. The people's unanimous declaration of "We will do and hear" captures both eagerness and apprehension, showing that ethical commitment demands a readiness to obey without complete foresight, an act of faith itself. This moment is charged with paradox: divine authority imposing limits on human freedom, yet simultaneously granting freedom through the gift of law. The commandments serve not to constrict but to liberate, structuring a space in which individual lives can flourish within a framework of mutual respect and divine guidance. The community that emerges is marked by covenantal solidarity, in which each person's moral choices ripple outward, affecting the whole.

The thunder, lightning, smoke, and trumpet blast that shrouded Sinai emphasize the awe-inspiring nature of this revelation, signaling divine transcendence and immanence. The sensory intensity disrupts ordinary experience, drawing the Israelites into a liminal moment where heaven and earth intersect. This theophany, a visible and audible manifestation of God's presence, impresses upon the people the seriousness of their calling and the holiness required to approach the Divine. The mountain itself becomes a sacred symbol, both a place of divine encounter and a reminder of the weight of covenantal promises. Yet, even amidst this grandeur, the encounter imparts a message of nearness; God is not remote but accessible to a people willing to listen and live according to the law given. This dynamic tension between majesty and intimacy undergirds the entire ethical system, framing the commandments as invitations into a lived relationship rather than mere obligations.

The broader context of this revelation is critical. Israel stands at a crossroads between its past as enslaved and its future as a people marked by holiness. The law given at Sinai is, in many ways, a bridge spanning this transition. It confronts deep-rooted patterns of behavior nurtured under oppression and reorients the community toward dignity, justice, and faithfulness. The covenant encapsulated by the Ten Commandments lays the groundwork for a society distinct from its neighbors, governed not by the arbitrary whims of kings or the chaos of tribal conflict, but by a theologically grounded ethic that commands love for God and neighbor. This ethic becomes a visible banner under which the people can rally their scattered hopes for peace, stability, and divine blessing. The Sinai encounter thus initiates a sacred story, one in which human choices matter profoundly, bearing consequences that echo across generations.

The communal aspect shines in the insistence that these laws apply to all members of Israel without exception. The lawmaker's vision resists any form of elitism or moral exceptionalism, seeking instead an inclusive ethical framework that protects the vulnerable and promotes equitable treatment. This is evident in the concern for property, reputation, and even desire, recognizing that justice extends into the depths of the human heart and into the fabric of everyday social interactions. By establishing boundaries on covetousness and falsehood, the Sinai revelation anticipates the social disintegration that unchecked desires and deceit can cause. The law is thus preventive and corrective, aiming to cultivate a community where trust and respect act as the bedrock for collective well-being.

The reverberations of this encounter transcend immediate legality, opening pathways to theological contemplation and spiritual transformation. The Sinai event frames sin not just as failure or disobedience but as alienation from the covenantal source of life. It defines righteousness as the right ordering of relationships with God and others, inviting ongoing reflection on what it means to live faithfully in a world fraught with temptation and moral complexity. The commandments spill beyond their historical moment, becoming touchstones for communal identity and spiritual aspiration across the centuries. They embody a dialogue between divine holiness and human imperfection, a tension that compels a perpetual quest for renewal and repentance.

Furthermore, the Sinai revelation embodies a vision of divine justice suffused with mercy. While the thunderous proclamation warns of consequences and demands obedience, it also invites Israel into a covenant of grace, where turning back from transgression can restore relationships. The law thus functions within a redemptive framework, acknowledging human weakness while offering a way toward reconciliation and wholeness. This balance between justice and mercy is central to the narrative of sin's consequences and God's responses throughout biblical history. It paints a picture of a God who does not abandon flawed humanity but engages deeply with its struggles, providing guidelines that lead toward life rather than death.

One cannot overlook how this moment at Sinai influenced the social and spiritual identity beyond Israel's immediate context. The Ten Commandments resonate as a foundational ethical code influencing subsequent religious traditions and secular moral philosophy alike. Their principles echo the universal quest for justice, fidelity, and respect among diverse peoples and throughout time. The Sinai encounter invites humanity into a profound realization: moral order is rooted not merely in human consensus but in a divine mandate that transcends culture and epoch. This revelation continues to challenge contemporary readers to examine the terms of their own covenantal commitments, to God, to community, and to conscience.

The narrative situation at Sinai also highlights the interplay between fear and trust, law and freedom, judgment and mercy, revealing a layered texture to the human experience of the divine. The trembling fear inspired by the mountain's fire contrasts with the inner peace promised by living according to God's will. This juxtaposition underscores the transformative journey that obedience to the commandments entails, moving from dread toward maturity in faith. The encounter thus does not end with the giving of the laws but sets in motion a lifelong process of learning to live within their demands, a dynamic engagement whose consequences ripple across individual and communal destinies.

In the broader tapestry of biblical history, the Sinai episode marks a decisive moment when the abstract idea of God becomes concretized in a community's lived experience. The commandments create a structure through which the Israelites can embody holiness, imbued not only with fear but with hope, not only with obligation but with the possibility of grace. This encounter insists that divine revelation is not static but dialogical, inviting continual interpretation, application, and renewal. It crafts a legacy whereby each generation inherits not mere rules, but an invitation into a covenantal journey, one in which every ethical choice contributes to the unfolding story of sin, judgment, mercy, and redemption.

Ultimately, the revelation at Sinai reveals a God deeply invested in human freedom and responsibility, calling forth a people capable of reflecting divine justice and mercy in the world. The commandments serve as a tangible manifestation of this call, shaping the moral contours of a community whose very existence depends upon honoring the God who delivered them and upholding the ethical standards that sustain life together. The echo of Sinai continues to reverberate through time, challenging every reader to engage with the vibrant tension between human fallibility and divine grace that defines the moral landscape of Israel and, indeed, the human condition itself.

The Ten Commandments

In the vast desert wilderness where the Israelites wandered, a pivotal moment arose that would forever shape not only the destiny of a fledgling nation but also the moral compass of countless generations to come. Amidst the solitude of Mount Sinai's rugged slopes, Moses ascended to commune with the divine, returning with an unprecedented covenant inscribed on stone tablets, those sacred decrees known humbly yet profoundly as the Ten Commandments. These commandments were far more than a mere legal code; they represented a foundational moral architecture, a bridge between humanity and the divine, encapsulating fundamental expectations that transcend time and culture. Each commandment, etched with deliberate clarity and gravitas, spoke directly to the heart of communal life, individual character, and spiritual allegiance, setting forth an ethical framework designed not only to govern behaviors but to cultivate a holistic understanding of righteousness within society.

The first commandment laid the cornerstone of monotheistic faith: "You shall have no other gods before me." This directive profoundly emphasized exclusivity in devotion, forging an intimate relationship with an unseen yet omnipotent God. It was a radical call in a world rife with polytheistic beliefs, demanding undivided loyalty and trust. This was not a mere prohibition against idolatry; it was an invitation into a covenantal partnership characterized by fidelity, reverence, and an acknowledgment of divine sovereignty. Embedded within this mandate is a poignant recognition that moral order stems from divine authority, serving both as a spiritual anchor and a societal stabilizer. To put God first was to affirm a source of ultimate justice and mercy that would govern human affairs with wisdom beyond mortal limitations.

Closely linked was the second commandment, forbidding the making of carved images or idols. This prohibition safeguarded the ineffable transcendence of the divine, warning against the reduction of the infinite to finite representations. More than an act of religious observance, this rule reinforced an ethical principle: humans are called to relate to the divine authentically, recognizing God's essence rather than attempting to bind divinity to material objects or personal whims. It discouraged idolatry in its many forms, from statues to corrupt practices that elevate false values above truth and integrity. The implications extended to societal ethics, forbidding distractions from higher purposes and preventing the distortion of community values by superficial or misleading symbols.

The third commandment, instructing not to misuse the name of the LORD, underscored the sanctity of language and the power words hold within social and spiritual spheres. To wield God's name carelessly or deceitfully was more than irreverence; it was a violation that eroded trust and moral authority. In a culture where oaths and pronouncements shaped social contracts and personal honor, respecting the divine name reinforced a reality where speech carried weight, demanding honesty, integrity, and responsibility. This commandment invited a deep awareness of how language intersects with morality, nurturing a community where truthfulness and respect for sacred things were paramount.

The fourth commandment introduced a rhythm of sacred rest by mandating the observance of the Sabbath day, setting it apart as holy. This injunction was revolutionary, distinguishing the Israelites with a weekly temporal sanctuary devoted to cessation from labor, reflection, and worship. Beyond physical rest, the Sabbath cultivated spiritual renewal and communal cohesion, providing space for both individual restoration and collective identity centered on divine provision and care. It implicitly critiqued exploitative labor systems and social neglect by valuing rest and dignity for all, including servants and even animals. This commandment wove holiness into time itself, sanctifying cycles that nurtured ethical awareness and humanity's dependence on God and each other.

Transitioning into interpersonal ethics, the fifth commandment demanded honor toward one's father and mother. This directive went beyond mere obedience, emphasizing respect for family bonds as the foundational unit of society. It recognized that the stability and transmission of ethical values largely depend on nurturing familial relationships grounded in honor, care, and reverence. By elevating parental roles, this commandment secured social continuity and intergenerational responsibility, mirroring divine care through human respect. Moreover, this respect anchored a broader societal order, as the family constituted the primary context for moral formation and communal engagement.

Interwoven with social ethics were the commandments prohibiting murder, adultery, and theft, which formed a triad guarding the sanctity of life, fidelity, and property. The sixth commandment's prohibition of murder reaffirmed the sacredness of human life, asserting that life is a divine gift not subject to human caprice or vengeance. This sanctity demanded justice and protection for the vulnerable, rejecting violence and cruelty that fracture community and degrade human dignity. In parallel, the seventh commandment forbade adultery, safeguarding the integrity of marital commitments. Here, fidelity became emblematic of trustworthiness, mutual respect, and the moral fabric that sustains family and community stability. The sacredness of covenantal relationships symbolized broader ideals of loyalty and purity essential to social cohesion. The eighth commandment denounced theft, reinforcing respect for the possessions and livelihoods of others, underpinning fairness and justice in economic interactions. Resisting theft was both a moral imperative and a practical necessity for peaceful coexistence, highlighting awareness of neighborly rights and responsibilities.

The ninth commandment, forbidding bearing false witness, captured the importance of truthfulness within judicial and social contexts. This imperative safeguarded justice from corruption and deceit, ensuring that community decisions emerged from integrity rather than manipulation. Truth-telling was not merely a personal virtue but a collective safeguard, maintaining trust in institutions and relationships. Its violation spawned cascading consequences, sowing discord and injustice that could unravel the social fabric. Thus, this commandment elevated honesty to a public virtue critical for sustaining communal life rooted in fairness and transparency.

Finally, the tenth commandment addressed the internal moral landscape by prohibiting covetousness, the yearning to possess what belonged to others. This subtle command penetrated deeper than outward actions, interrogating desires and intentions that often lay hidden yet drove sinful behaviors. By calling for contentment and restraint, the commandment aimed to curb envy and greed, sources of social strife and personal dissatisfaction. It recognized that true righteousness entails transformation of the heart, fostering generosity and trust rather than jealousy and competition. This focus on inner motives complements external commandments, illustrating the comprehensive nature of the biblical moral vision.

Together, these ten proclamations sculpted a comprehensive ethical framework, intertwining spiritual devotion with communal responsibility, individual character with collective well-being. They embodied more than rigid legalism; they reflected divine pedagogy aimed at forming a people shaped by holiness, justice, and mercy. The Ten

Commandments established parameters within which freedom flourished, not as license to do as one pleased but as boundaries within which human dignity, relationships, and society could thrive. This balance between restriction and liberation illuminated the human condition, recognizing frailty while offering a path toward flourishing rooted in covenantal trust.

The impact of these commandments extended beyond their immediate context, echoing through biblical history as a benchmark against which kings, prophets, and ordinary people measured their conduct. They served as a mirror revealing human tendency to fall short, a standard calling forth repentance and renewal. The prophets would frequently invoke these laws, not as cold statutes but as vibrant calls to authentic worship and justice. By embodying ethical and spiritual values, the Ten Commandments became a living testament to God's desire for human alignment with divine will, inviting ongoing reflection on the interplay between law, grace, and personal responsibility.

Moreover, the communal dimension of the commandments underscored that morality is not solely individualistic but deeply social. The ethical life articulated by these decrees necessitates active engagement with neighbors, family, and society, promoting harmony, equity, and peace. The shared observance of these principles fostered a distinctive identity among the Israelites, uniting them through common covenantal commitments that transcended mere survival to embrace a vision of flourishing under divine guidance.

In contemporary reflection, the Ten Commandments continue to resonate profoundly, informing legal, ethical, and spiritual discussions worldwide. Their compelling blend of spiritual reverence and practical ethics challenges individuals and communities to examine personal integrity and social justice, prompting questions about the nature of authority, the balance between freedom and responsibility, and the call to holiness amid human complexity. Far from antiquated relics, these ancient words carry echoes that reverberate within the modern quest for meaning, justice, and moral clarity.

As we contemplate the moral foundation laid down at Sinai, we glimpse the intricate tapestry woven by divine expectation and human response, where accountability and mercy are partners in a dance of covenant. The Ten Commandments stand not merely as historical artifacts but as enduring invitations, calls to examine our deepest loyalties, to honor the sacredness of life and community, and to pursue a path of righteousness that transcends time, culture, and circumstance. They challenge us to confront the echoes of sin within our own hearts and societies, yet also illuminate the possibilities of grace and transformation when we embrace the covenantal call to live with wisdom and grace.

Community and Covenant

Within the ancient framework of Israelite society, the establishment of law was not merely a code of conduct but the very foundation upon which community cohesion and identity were built. The giving of the Ten Commandments, etched into stone tablets atop Mount Sinai, represented a radical departure from the norms of surrounding cultures. It was a moment where divine instruction penetrated the social fabric, transforming disparate tribes and clans into a unified people bound not only by blood and geography but by covenantal obligation. This moment is pivotal in biblical history, for it signals the introduction of a divine moral order that sought to regulate the intimate interactions of daily life, thereby fostering a sense of collective responsibility and shared destiny.

The social implications of these commandments extend far beyond rigid legalism; they touch upon the very essence of human relationships in a communal setting. The commandments addressed fundamental aspects of social interaction: honoring parents underscored the centrality of family and respect across generations; prohibitions against murder, adultery, theft, and false witness safeguarded personal safety, trust, and property; while the injunction to keep the Sabbath offered a sacred rhythm that united the community in shared rest and worship. Such laws were not imposed as abstract ideals but as pragmatic guidelines aimed at nurturing harmony and preventing the corrosive effects of sin from unraveling the social fabric. With these rules in place, the community was not only protected from external threats and internal chaos but was encouraged to cultivate virtues that reflect divine justice and mercy.

The concept of covenant, integral to understanding these laws, illuminated a profound theological dimension of social ethics. It was not simply a contract between individuals or a legalistic framework; it was an agreement forged between God and the people of Israel, one that defined their identity and purpose. This covenant implied that obedience to the law was inseparable from loyalty to a divine relationship. Social ethics were thus grounded in spiritual commitment, where every act of justice or injustice reverberated within the sacred bond between the community and its God. Sin, therefore, was not a private failing but a communal breach, threatening the very electrochemical currents that sustained the covenantal heart. The community was called to embody holiness, reflecting God's character in their interpersonal dealings and collective life, making obedience to the commandments a shared endeavor to sanctify society itself.

Embedded within this divine-social contract was a profound insistence on justice, especially for the vulnerable and marginalized. The commandments and broader laws that surrounded them addressed inequalities and sought to protect the widow, the orphan, the stranger, and the poor, groups consistently vulnerable in ancient Near Eastern societies. This inclusivity embedded in the law was a moral revolution; justice was no longer a privilege of the powerful but a divine mandate to create equitable social structures. The repercussions of ignoring such commandments were not merely temporal penalties but disruptions to the communal covenant, inviting divine judgment that would cascade through societal institutions and relationships. Conversely, adherence promised flourishing, not simply economic prosperity but social stability, peace, and favor in the sight of God.

Beyond the direct legal prescriptions, the community ethics implied by the Ten Commandments catalyzed an ongoing ethical dialogue within the Israelite religious imagination. These laws functioned as a moral compass, orienting the people toward a vision of society that balanced individual freedom with collective responsibility. Their practical application often intersected with broader biblical narratives, where leaders, prophets, and ordinary people grappled with the tension between human fallibility and divine expectation. The prophetic literature in particular frequently returned to the themes encapsulated by the commandments, lamenting societal neglect or perversion of justice and calling the people back to covenantal faithfulness. These prophetic voices underscored that community well-being hinged on sustained ethical vigilance and repentance, emphasizing that sin had far-reaching consequences not only for individuals but for the entire nation.

The communal dimension of the law also reshaped concepts of punishment and restitution within Israelite society, revealing a justice system deeply intertwined with mercy and restoration. Unlike purely punitive models, biblical justice emphasized repairing relationships and restoring communal harmony. For example, offenses required compensations and acts that acknowledged wrongdoing, catalyzing processes of reconciliation rather than alienation. This approach anticipated modern restorative justice principles, highlighting how legal frameworks underpinned by divine covenant sought holistic well-being. In this light, the law functioned as a dynamic social tool designed not to scapegoat but to redeem, fostering a resilient community capable of confronting and healing its moral fractures.

Moreover, the Ten Commandments and the surrounding legal corpus positioned the community's relationship with God as the ultimate metric of ethical living. The commandments opened and closed with directives that recognized God's sovereignty: "You shall have no other gods before me" and "You shall not covet your neighbor's house, wife, or possessions." This framing elevated morality from mere social contract to divine allegiance, signaling that true community ethic stemmed from recognition of a higher authority. As a consequence, ethical lapses were more than social infractions, they were acts of rebellion that disrupted the divine-human nexus. This theological grounding added gravity and urgency to community ethics, where every act of faithfulness contributed to a sacred social order reflecting heaven's justice and peace.

The social implications extended into the very rhythms of communal worship and daily life, where the law punctuated time and space with sacred markers. Observance of the Sabbath functioned as a communal pause that transcended individual will, aligning society with divine rest and holiness. Beyond religious devotion, this observance had tangible social benefits: it institutionalized rest for laborers and animals alike, mitigated exploitation, and reinforced social equality by leveling the daily hierarchies through collective observance. This practical intertwining of holiness and justice exemplified the law's holistic vision, ethical living involved every dimension of human experience, integrating spirituality with social well-being.

The laws surrounding relationships, property, and speech echoed deeply within the community's social ethos. Prohibitions against bearing false witness and coveting were not mere legal proscriptions but recognition of the fragility of trust that sustains communal life. Falsehoods erode confidence and fuel conflict; covetous desires ignite envy and division. Hence, these commandments promoted a culture where truth and contentment functioned as social glue, fostering mutual respect and preventing discord. When the community internalized these values, the law matured from external impositions into internalized virtues, cultivating individuals who acted justly and compassionately not out of fear but from ethical conviction.

The impact of the law on community extended to its influence on formal leadership and governance structures, vital for maintaining order and justice. Israelite leaders, from judges to kings, were expected to uphold the covenantal statutes, serving as guardians of divine justice within society. Failure to do so often precipitated spiritual and political crisis, as the people saw leadership as accountable not only to human constituents but to God. This expectation injected a powerful ethical imperative into governance, underscoring that political authority was ultimately servant leadership bound by covenantal loyalty. Lessons from the reigns of Saul and David, for instance, vividly illustrate tensions where royal ambitions conflicted with covenantal demands, serving as cautionary tales about the consequences of leadership departures from divine law.

The communal ethos formed by the Ten Commandments and related laws also shaped Israel's interactions with external peoples, informing both boundaries and hospitality. Maintaining religious and moral distinctiveness was paramount to preserving covenant identity, yet the law also enshrined principles of fairness and kindness toward strangers and neighbors. This tension between boundary maintenance and openness underscored the community's complex role as a covenant people called to model divine holiness amid a pluralistic and often hostile environment. The laws thus served as markers of identity that simultaneously protected and challenged Israel's social and moral coherence, reflecting a community in dynamic engagement with a broader world.

Importantly, the social implications of the law anticipated future theological developments that would emphasize internal transformation alongside external obedience. While the commandments enforced behavior, the biblical trajectory revealed an increasing emphasis on heart and intention, culminating in prophetic calls for justice to "roll on like a river" and for internalized law written upon hearts. Such developments acknowledged that true community ethics arise not from mere rule-following but from deep spiritual renewal. This shift does not diminish the social importance of the law but rather enriches it, framing the commandments as invitations into a transformative relationship where communal well-being is inseparable from spiritual vitality.

In contemplating the social dimensions of the Ten Commandments and covenant law, it becomes clear that the biblical vision of community ethics is both timeless and profoundly relevant. The principles embedded within these ancient statutes continue to challenge modern societies to balance individual rights with communal responsibilities, justice with mercy, order with freedom. The social order envisioned by the law is a tapestry woven from threads of holiness, justice, compassion, and accountability, an ethic that demands constant vigilance and humility in the face of human frailty. By embodying these principles, a community participates in a sacred narrative that transcends time, echoing divine intentions for human flourishing amid the ever-present challenges of sin and redemption.

Thus, the social implications of the law illustrate a profound understanding that human beings are not isolated agents but members of an interconnected moral community. The commandments do not merely delineate what is forbidden or required; they shape a social imagination rooted in covenantal loyalty, communal dignity, and divine justice. The resonance of these laws continues to ripple through history, affirming that authentic community life can only thrive when grounded in a shared commitment to ethical principles that honor both God and neighbor. In this light, the Ten Commandments stand not only as ancient relics but as living echoes, inviting each generation to embrace the responsibilities and blessings of covenantal community.

Gary E. Risenhoover

Wandering and Rebellion in the Wilderness

Complaints and Murmuring

The wilderness experience of the Israelites after their dramatic escape from Egypt emerges as one of the most vivid portraits of human struggle and divine forbearance in biblical history. It is a narrative heavily laden with episodes of complaints and murmuring, those plaintive voices that rise from mortal hearts weighed down by fear, uncertainty, and longing for the familiarity of what they once knew, even if that past was a landscape of oppression. The murmuring of the people is not merely a litany of grievances or petty complaints; it is a profound human response to the unknown, a collective expression of doubt toward the promises made by God. It is in these moments of rebellion against divine providence that the tension between human frailty and divine patience unfolds, revealing the complex dynamics of faith and fear, obedience and resistance.

As the Israelites journey through the barren wilderness, their complaints begin almost immediately. The transition from the oppression of Egypt, where survival was marked by harsh labor and servitude, to the harshness of desert life, where survival demands trust and resilience, is more than a physical challenge, it is a radical psychological upheaval. The people, having witnessed astounding signs of divine intervention in their liberation, plagues that toppled the mighty Pharaoh, the miraculous crossing of the Red Sea, nonetheless find their faith quickly wavering. Their dissatisfaction with manna, the mysterious sustenance that appears each morning, and their cries for meat instead of "this miserable food" reflect a deep-seated insecurity that shadows the entire exodus narrative. This is a spiritual crossroads where the Israelites wrestle intensely with the limits of their belief, caught between the certainty of past suffering and the uncertainty of promised freedom.

The complaints surface as a natural human response to the discomfort of the present and the anxiety of the future. They are a manifestation of the internal conflict between remembrance and expectation, between trusting an unseen covenant and yearning for tangible assurance. The people repeatedly question, "Why did you bring us out of Egypt to die here in the wilderness?" Their voices echo not just dissatisfaction with their immediate circumstances but a profound doubt about the nature of divine justice and care. This question reveals a deeper theological struggle: if God is truly their protector and provider, then why do they suffer? Why does divine providence appear so inscrutably intertwined with hardship?

Through these murmurs, the narrative invites readers to explore the essence of human faith. Faith is not presented as an unshakable fortress but as a dynamic engagement fraught with struggle, doubt, and intermittent rebellion. The Israelites' resistance, manifested in their grumbling, challenges readers to reflect on how doubt can coexist with belief. What does it mean to maintain hope when the promises of God feel distant or delayed? This tension between faith and despair, between trust and mutiny, is foundational to understanding the biblical portrayal of human nature. It acknowledges that spiritual journeys are seldom linear or free of struggle; they are marked by cycles of falling away and returning, of questioning and reaffirming.

Yet, even as the Israelites' complaints multiply, so does the narrative's portrayal of divine patience and mercy. God's response to the murmuring is not merely one of judgment, but also of instruction, provision, and gentle correction. Despite their unwillingness to trust fully, God continues to provide manna and water, sustains them through the trials, and repeatedly offers reassurance through prophets and direct communication. This divine forbearance reveals a God who understands the complexities of human weakness and does not abandon the people to their waywardness. Instead, there is a persistent invitation to trust and a miraculous provision that defies human expectation.

This interplay between human resistance and divine patience bears profound implications for broader theological reflection. The narrative challenges readers to reconsider how divine justice operates in the midst of human failure. The wilderness complaints are not punished with immediate, irrevocable condemnation but met with an ongoing opportunity for repentance and renewed faith. This underscores a key biblical theme: divine justice is tempered by mercy, and judgment is always accompanied by the possibility of restoration. It depicts a God who is relational rather than distant, engaging with human vulnerability and inviting partnership in the unfolding story of redemption.

Moreover, the complaints reflect a collective psyche wrestling not only with physical deprivation but also with spiritual disorientation. The Israelites' identity as God's chosen people is in flux; their memories of slavery compel a longing for security, while their newfound freedom demands courage and trust in an unseen future. Their murmuring illustrates the tension between the pull of the past and the call of divine promise. It serves as a poignant reminder that faith is not merely a personal act of devotion but a communal journey that can be as fraught with tension as it is rich with hope.

In this light, the wilderness murmurs also represent a formative stage in the development of Israelite identity. The repeated episodes of complaint and divine response serve as lessons in dependence and obedience, shaping a people prepared to receive the Torah and embrace their covenantal calling. Their struggles expose the imperfections and shortcomings from which growth emerges. This process, though arduous and marked by setbacks, is crucial for the maturation of faith. It reflects a universal human experience: the path toward spiritual maturity is often marked by resistance and failure before reconciliation and acceptance.

This ancient saga invites contemporary readers to see their own doubts and struggles as part of an ongoing dialogue between human vulnerability and divine fidelity. Just as the Israelites were tested in the wilderness, modern believers encounter their own deserts, times of uncertainty, dissatisfaction, and yearning for deeper meaning. In these moments, the biblical narrative offers a mirror and a guide, illuminating how faith can endure through the presence of complaints and the persistence of divine grace. The story encourages an honest acknowledgement of the messiness of faith, revealing that lament and questioning need not be barriers to spiritual growth but can instead be gateways to deeper understanding.

As the narrative unfolds, it becomes clear that the complaints are not mere expressions of ungratefulness but a reflection of the profound alienation and fear felt by a people uprooted from familiar structures and thrust into unfamiliar realities. The human tendency to resist change and cling to the known, even if it was a life of bondage, speaks to the powerful hold of fear and the struggle inherent in trusting a promise yet to be fulfilled. This dynamic invites readers to contemplate their own responses to uncertainty and change, recognizing how easily complacency can masquerade as faith, and how courage in the face of the unknown requires continual renewal.

The narrative's power lies in its nuanced portrayal of both human weakness and divine endurance. While the people falter, the divine presence remains steadfast, revealing a God who is intimately involved in the trials of human existence. The murmuring voice of Israel becomes a symbolic echo of all who wrestle with faith amid hardship, reminding readers that divine mercy is available not despite our doubts and struggles, but through them. This profound patience bids worshippers to lean not on their own understanding but to embrace trust as a courageous, ongoing act.

In this prolonged encounter with the wilderness, the Israelites confront not only external hardships but also internal spiritual battles.

Their murmuring exposes the struggle to reconcile lived experience with divine promise, a tension that echoes throughout biblical history and continues to resonate in contemporary spiritual lives. The interplay of complaint and grace invites a reconsideration of pilgrimage itself, not simply as a physical journey, but as an existential voyage of the heart, where faith is forged in the crucible of endurance and hope.

The wilderness murmuring, therefore, stands as a testament to the complexities of the human condition, a condition marked by contradiction, longing, and imperfection. It challenges simplistic readings of biblical faith as merely obedience to divine command, instead portraying a richly textured relationship between God and humanity. This relationship is characterized by dialogue, even dissonance, yet ultimately grounded in a divine commitment to restoration and hope. In this ongoing conversation between divine expectation and human limitation, the book invites readers to find resonance in their own spiritual paths and to appreciate the depth and breadth of divine patience as an enduring source of strength.

Ultimately, the complaints and murmuring of Israel become more than historical episodes; they serve as invitations to embrace vulnerability, acknowledge doubts, and remain open to transformation. They reveal that faith is not absence of difficulty or questioning but the perseverance to keep moving forward despite them. Divine patience emerges not as passive tolerance but as active, sustaining love that nurtures growth even amid resistance. In this discovery, the ancient voices that murmur through the wilderness become living echoes within the modern soul, calling each of us into a deeper journey of trust, hope, and grace.

Moses' Leadership Challenges

Moses' leadership, forged in the crucible of overwhelming challenges, presents a compelling portrait of human frailty entwined with divine purpose. This pivotal figure in biblical history led a people burdened by centuries of oppression out of Egyptian bondage, navigating not only the external pressures imposed by their formidable adversaries but also the turbulent currents of internal discord and rebellion. The story of Moses is as much about guiding a resistant community as it is about steadfast faithfulness to a divine covenant, revealing multifaceted aspects of leadership fraught with tension, doubt, and perseverance. Amid the expansive wilderness where the Children of Israel wandered, Moses confronted the raw realities of human nature in its vulnerability and obstinance, traits that tested his endurance and the patience of the God he served.

The challenges Moses encountered were not limited to the physical hardships of the journey but extended deeply into the social and spiritual fabric of his people. Time and again, the Israelites queasily confronted scarcity, water, food, certainty, and their unease erupted into rebellion and complaints. These moments were not mere grumblings but seismic upheavals against authority and faith, evident in episodes such as the golden calf incident, where idolatry violently ruptured the fragile trust between God and His chosen nation, and Korah's insurrection, which threatened to dismantle the very hierarchy established to guide them toward the Promised Land. These rebellions were manifestations of a broader human condition, fear leading to skepticism, impatience spiraling into defiance, and hope warped by the desperation to reclaim control. Moses, situated at the crossroads of divine command and human frailty, bore the heavy mantle of mediator and intercessor, navigating the complex terrain where divine justice and mercy intersect.

His leadership style was forged in constant dialogue with God, whose instructions he relayed and whose judgments he implored to temper. This dynamic reveals profound insights into the nature of divine patience; despite repeated infractions that could have warranted immediate and irrevocable punishment, God chose prolonged engagement, offering opportunities for repentance and renewal. Moses, at times overwhelmed and anguished, pleaded on behalf of the people, demonstrating a leadership rooted not in authoritarian dominance but in sacrificial advocacy. This tension between authority and compassion characterizes the biblical narrative of Moses as a leader uniquely human yet uniquely sustained by a transcendent call. The prophetic encounter at Sinai, where Moses received the law, symbolizes this intersection of divine expectation and human responsibility, a covenant with stringent demands yet broad mercy, challenging Moses to embody obedience while preserving hope amid rebellion.

The psychological and emotional landscape Moses traversed cannot be understated. His leadership entailed moments of profound isolation, as the weight of national destiny rested on his shoulders amidst a persistent undercurrent of distrust. When the people murmured against him or questioned his guidance, Moses faced the paradox of leading those who doubted. His resolve, however, did not fragilize; instead, it evolved, tempered through encounters with divine reassurance and visions affirming the ultimate fulfillment of God's promises. Moses' appeal to the people to remain faithful was not rhetorical but drawn from an intimate awareness of their vulnerabilities and the spiritual consequences of their choices. His leadership reveals authenticity in grappling with the limitations of human resolve while exemplifying unwavering commitment to a higher purpose.

An essential dimension of Moses' leadership challenges lies in his dealings with the tension between justice and mercy. He witnessed firsthand the consequences of sin, the fracturing of community, the rise of fear, and the alienation from God's presence, and was entrusted with administering discipline while advocating for forgiveness. The intercessory role he played places him among the profound examples of leaders who bear the burdens of their people's failures yet refuse to abandon them to despair. His prayers, laments, and petitions to God encapsulate a leadership style deeply relational and spiritual, one that acknowledges the gravity of rebellion but longs for restoration. This interplay between divine justice and mercy is a recurring motif throughout Moses' experiences, underscoring the complexity of leadership within a covenantal framework where sin disrupts yet grace endures.

Moses' leadership also offers a nuanced exploration of human resistance. The Israelites' continual wavering between trust and rebellion reflects the universal struggle to reconcile freedom with obedience, hope with skepticism. Each challenge Moses faced symbolizes broader moral and existential dilemmas, the tension between immediate tangible assurances and intangible faith, between autonomy and submission. His ability to maintain faith under siege was a beacon for the people, yet also a reminder of the fragility of belief. The wilderness itself, as a backdrop, serves as a character in this drama, embodying both desolation and potential, hardship and transformation. In this liminal space, Moses' role transcended mere governance; he became a spiritual guide navigating the collective soul of a nation, confronting the echoes of sin that threatened to derail their destiny.

The narrative of Moses' challenges invites reflection on leadership beyond the immediate biblical context, probing the dynamics of authority challenged by dissent, the necessity of perseverance amid setbacks, and the power of faith to sustain vision. Moses did not lead from a position of unchecked power but from an enduring relationship with God, whose presence both empowered and disciplined him. The story confronts readers with questions of how leaders balance firmness with empathy, how communities wrestle with trust and disappointment, and how the journey through rebellion can lead to deeper transformation. Moses' leadership is a study in resilience and dependence on divine guidance, revealing that true authority encompasses humility, patience, and the willingness to bear the burdens of others.

Through an intricate tapestry of events and emotions, Moses' leadership journey maps the contours of human imperfection and divine fidelity. His experience reflects the profound truth that the path of leadership, especially within contexts shaped by moral and spiritual demands, is neither linear nor untroubled. Instead, it is marked by cycles of hope and despair, obedience and rebellion, punishment and forgiveness. The echoes of these dynamics resonate throughout biblical history, shaping not only ancient Israel's destiny but also providing enduring paradigms for understanding the complexities of human nature, communal responsibility, and spiritual perseverance.

In the end, Moses stands as a testament to the possibility of leadership shaped by transparency, vulnerability, and unwavering faith. His ability to confront rebellion not with retributive finality but with intercession and guidance highlights the transformative potential embedded in divine patience and human endurance. The interplay of human resistance and divine forbearance manifested in his story illuminates the persistent challenges faced by leaders and communities alike, while offering a hopeful vision of redemption and renewal that transcends time. Moses' legacy prompts continual reflection on how leaders today might embody such a delicate balance, cultivating communities resilient in faith, steadfast in hope, and open to the redemptive possibilities of grace amid human fallibility.

Judgment and Mercy

In the vast tapestry of biblical history, the themes of judgment and mercy weave a complex and profound narrative thread that reveals the depth of divine character and the persistent nature of human frailty. This intricate interplay between human rebellion and divine response is neither simplistic nor static; rather, it unfolds as a dynamic drama of consequences and hope that reverberates through generations. As we immerse ourselves in the biblical accounts, we witness the persistent defiance of human beings, a resistance born from freedom and frailty alike, counterpointed by divine patience that continually offers the possibility of restoration. This duality challenges the reader to confront the gravity of sin and the remarkable breadth of divine grace, inviting a nuanced understanding of how judgment functions not as mere punishment but as both a corrective and a pathway to renewal.

From the earliest chapters of Scripture, the narrative presents a striking portrait of humanity's propensity toward rebellion. The primordial disobedience of Adam and Eve in Eden sets a precedent filled with profound consequences, as the act of defiance fractures the original harmony between Creator and creation. The consequence is immediate and far-reaching: alienation, suffering, and mortality enter the human experience. Yet intriguingly, this judgment is not solely retributive; it is also simultaneously a merciful boundary-setting, an expression of divine wisdom seeking to restrain further harm. The expulsion from Eden, while devastating, is also an act of preservation, a painful yet purposeful separation intended to protect humanity from consuming the very fruit of eternal life in their fallen state. In this paradox, judgment and mercy are shown as intricately intertwined, embodying the balance of divine justice tempered by compassion.

This foundational tension is echoed and elaborated upon in subsequent narratives, where human resistance to divine authority often erupts into flagrant acts of rebellion with dire repercussions. Consider the story of Cain, who, despite a divine warning, succumbs to jealousy and murders his brother Abel. Cain's punishment is severe; he becomes a wanderer, marked and alienated from community, a living symbol of sin's isolating consequences. Yet even in this judgment, mercy appears. God marks Cain, not for further destruction, but for protection, ensuring that his life remains spared from vengeance by others. This paradoxical gesture reflects a divine reluctance to abandon even the sinful, offering them space for repentance and transformation. Thus, the biblical text portrays judgment not as final annihilation but as a stage in a larger divine economy aimed at awakening conscience and prompting change.

The flood narrative, monumental in its scale and symbolism, further amplifies the themes of judgment and mercy by portraying divine judgment as a response to pervasive human wickedness yet simultaneously highlighting divine mercy through the preservation of Noah and his family. In this cataclysmic event, the rebellion of humanity reaches a climactic low point, warranting a reset of creation itself. The waters of destruction signify both cleansing and condemnation, the severity of divine judgment cannot be overstated. However, intertwined with this is the beacon of hope embodied in the ark. Noah's obedience and righteousness grant him an opportunity not only to escape destruction but to initiate a new covenantal relationship with God. The flood thus embodies judgment's severity tempered by mercy's provision, illustrating the coexistence of justice and compassion within divine action.

Human history within the biblical narrative repeatedly exhibits cycles of rebellion and impending judgment, interspersed with pleas for mercy and divine forgiveness. The story of the Israelites, from their bondage in Egypt to their repeated lapses in the wilderness, vividly illustrates how resistance to divine guidance often yields communal consequences. The deliverance orchestrated by Moses is both an act of judgment against oppression and an expression of mercy that rescues the chosen people. Yet as the Israelites frequently stray into idolatry and disobedience, God's judgments through plagues and discipline seek to correct and call them back. The prophetic literature, rich with vivid imagery and heartfelt appeals, reflects this same tension: prophets deliver dire warnings of judgment to awaken a wayward people but simultaneously offer visions of restoration and hope. The divine character expressed through these narratives is one of relentless pursuit, a God unwilling to abandon the covenant relationship despite persistent human failure.

Embedded deeply within these stories is the recognition of human autonomy and moral accountability. The biblical writers do not portray humanity as mere victims of divine caprice; rather, they emphasize the consequences that naturally follow from moral choices. This focus on free will and responsibility situates judgment as a rightful and necessary response to rebellion, maintaining cosmic and moral order. Yet this order is never rigid or fatalistic; the door to mercy remains open. Throughout Scripture, the tension between judgment and mercy also reflects an ongoing dialogue about the nature of justice itself. Divine judgment does not seek vindictiveness but aims at restoration, it is a loving correction designed to heal fractured relationships rather than perpetuate brokenness. In this light, judgment transcends mere penalty, functioning as a catalyst for introspection and transformation.

The prophetic voices in the Hebrew Scriptures emphasize that divine judgment is not indiscriminate wrath but a moral imperative against injustice and unfaithfulness. Prophets like Isaiah, Jeremiah, and Ezekiel portray God as both a righteous judge and a merciful parent. Their words lament societal corruption and idolatry yet echo promises of restoration and renewal that follow the acknowledgment of sin and sincere repentance. This dual emphasis suggests that judgment serves an educative and redemptive purpose, confronting evil to protect the vulnerable and uphold covenantal integrity while also offering pathways back into divine favor. The prophetic tradition underscores the patience of God, who repeatedly invites a stubborn people to change course, revealing a divine heart attuned to both justice and forgiveness.

In considering the broader biblical witness, the Psalms provide another rich layer of reflection on judgment and mercy. The psalmists express profound awareness of human sinfulness and the consequences thereof, yet their prayers often circle back to pleas for divine mercy, forgiveness, and restoration. These poetic meditations capture the emotional and spiritual reality of living under divine judgment, where fear and hope coexist. They reveal the seeker's trust that God is both just and compassionate, capable of remembering human frailty and extending grace beyond deserved punishment. This intimate spirituality complements the more external historical accounts, illustrating how individuals wrestled personally with divine judgment and reconciliatory mercy.

The interplay between judgment and mercy reaches a pivotal moment in the biblical narrative with the advent of the New Testament and the embodiment of divine mercy in Jesus Christ. The incarnation, life, death, and resurrection of Jesus reveal the fullness of God's patience and love in confronting human sin. Jesus' ministry consistently reflects the tension between acknowledging the reality and consequences of sin while extending forgiveness and new life. His parables and teachings underscore that judgment is inseparable from mercy, offering both a warning of impending consequences for unrepentant rebellion and an invitation to repentance and transformation. The crucifixion serves as the ultimate expression of this dynamic, where judgment, the penalty of sin, is borne by the Messiah, enabling mercy to flow freely to humanity. This profound act redefines judgment, shifting from external punishment to internal renewal, opening the way for restoration not only of individuals but of all creation.

This movement toward redemption through mercy does not negate the reality or seriousness of sin; rather, it intensifies the call to ethical responsibility and spiritual awakening. Early Christian writings interpret the echoes of Old Testament judgment within this new framework of grace, emphasizing that divine patience invites ongoing repentance and moral renewal. The New Testament's portrayal of judgment incorporates the hope of final restoration, where justice and mercy are ultimately reconciled in the eschatological vision. This vision stresses that perseverance in faith and transformation of the heart align humans with the divine will, thereby resolving the tension between justice and mercy forever.

Beyond theology, the realities of human psychology and social dynamics are deeply implicated in the patterns of judgment and mercy found throughout the Bible. Human resistance to moral order often arises from pride, fear, or misunderstanding, provoking consequences that extend beyond individuals to communities and nations. The divine responses recorded in Scripture thereby model a profound understanding of human brokenness, recognizing that judgment is essential to realign behavior and restore harmony, but mercy is indispensable to heal wounds and foster reconciliation. The sustained divine patience reflected in biblical narratives encourages readers to consider the profound mercy required for genuine transformation, reminding us that justice cannot be truly realized without compassion.

Moreover, the biblical theme of judgment and mercy invites readers into an active engagement with their own moral choices. It challenges contemporary believers and seekers alike to reflect upon how rebellion manifests in their lives, and how divine mercy operates even within contexts of failure and weakness. This reflection fosters spiritual humility and hope, acknowledging the painful consequences of sin while affirming the possibility of redemption. The biblical witness affirms that while judgment records the serious cost of disobedience, mercy embodies the eternal invitation toward restoration and renewal. This dual reality encourages lived faith marked by accountability coupled with grace.

Throughout these ancient narratives, judgment and mercy emerge not as conflicting forces but as complementary aspects of a divine plan aimed at restoring a fractured world. Judgment asserts the reality that sin disrupts harmony and demands consequence, maintaining moral order and justice. Mercy insists that human ruin is never final, reflecting an abiding divine love that seeks to heal, forgive, and renew. Both are necessary for the fullness of life promised in the covenant relationship, together shaping a powerful drama of human fallibility and divine compassion that continues to resonate deeply. The echoes of this dynamic are felt not only in biblical times but in the spiritual and ethical struggles of all who wrestle with the consequences of their choices and the hope of restoration.

As the narrative of judgment and mercy unfolds in biblical history, it invites a profound contemplation of the divine-human relationship, one marked by tension yet overflowing with compassion. It reveals a God who is just and holy, responding rightly to rebellion and sin, yet whose patience and love persist against all odds. This enduring divine forbearance compels us to imagine a world where justice is not separated from mercy but fused in the heart of God's action, a world where consequences both remind and redeem, where hope arises from judgment's shadow. Through this lens, readers are encouraged to see their own moral journeys as part of a grand, ongoing dialogue, a dialogue between fallibility and grace, between sin's echo and the promise of redemption. This dialogue ultimately beckons toward spiritual awakening, ethical transformation, and renewed commitment to align with the merciful justice that has shaped the biblical story from the beginning of human history.

Conquest and the Cycle of Sin

Entering the Promised Land

The moment Israel stepped into the Promised Land was charged with the weight of destiny, hope, and a daunting divine promise that had been spoken generations earlier through Abraham. For centuries, this land had symbolized more than just physical territory; it was the embodiment of God's covenantal faithfulness and the aspiration for security, prosperity, and spiritual identity. Yet, the conquest was not simply a grand march into victory, nor was it the seamless realization of an idyllic homeland. Rather, it was a complex tapestry of military struggle, moral testing, and theological tension that would characterize much of Israel's early settlement and set the tone for a turbulent era that followed, the epoch of the Judges. This period, often viewed through the lenses of chaos and fragmentation, is equally a profound narrative of divine discipline, human frailty, and the recurring cycles of rebellion and redemption that echo throughout biblical history.

The initial conquest of Canaan, under the leadership of Joshua, bore the marks of divine orchestration couched within human endeavor. The narratives describe sweeping campaigns against formidable city-states and entrenched peoples whose cultures and religious practices stood in stark opposition to the God who had delivered Israel from Egyptian bondage. To modern readers, the stark imagery of warfare and destruction can be jarring, but within the ancient context, these acts were framed as necessary judgments against entrenched idolatry and moral corruption, a purging required to establish a new, sanctified community under God's laws. Joshua's leadership was marked by an unwavering commitment to obedience, as the people crossed the Jordan by miraculous means and encircled the walled city of Jericho, bringing down its walls through faith-fueled strategy. Victory was not merely a product of military might but a testament to Israel's reliance on the divine promise.

However, the conquest was not uniform nor absolute. While some cities fell swiftly, others resisted, and Israel's dominion remained patchy and incomplete. The command to utterly dispossess the inhabitants and avoid assimilation was a continual challenge. The land itself, fertile but fiercely contested, became the stage for ongoing conflict between the Israelites and the remnants of Canaanite populations who maintained practices that provoked divine wrath, such as idolatry and child sacrifice. This incomplete conquest introduced an ambiguity into Israel's relationship with the land and God's instructions, sowing seeds of future downfall. Israel's disobedience, whether through tolerating pagan customs or failing to fully drive out hostile peoples, brought consequences that unfolded over generations.

As the torch passed from Joshua to the generation beyond him, the unity and fervor that had propelled the initial conquest began to dissipate. The book of Judges captures this era vividly, presenting a cyclical pattern where Israel drifts into sin and idolatry, suffers oppression at the hands of neighboring peoples, cries out to God, and is delivered by a series of charismatic leaders, judges, raised by God for specific purposes. These judges, such as Deborah, Gideon, and Samson, were complex figures whose leadership was marked by both remarkable heroism and significant personal failings, embodying the ambiguous tension between divine blessing and human weakness. Their stories reveal a society struggling to maintain covenantal fidelity amidst the pressures of tribalism, cultural assimilation, and moral compromise.

One cannot understand this period without appreciating the concept of divine discipline so vividly portrayed by the biblical narrator. The recurring distress inflicted by oppressors, whether Philistines, Moabites, or Midianites, is interpreted as a form of corrective judgment, a painful yet redemptive chastisement intended to bring Israel back to wholehearted dependence on God. The cycle of sin and deliverance is itself a striking testament to the merciful nature of divine justice: God's unwillingness to abandon a wayward people despite their repeated failures. This theological motif challenges simplistic notions of punishment, instead presenting a dynamic relationship where human freedom to choose coexists with divine sovereignty and grace.

The Judges era, while chaotic, produced notable moments of spiritual renewal and tribal cohesion, even as the decentralized system planted the seeds for eventual demands for monarchy. The absence of a strong, unified government highlighted inherent weaknesses in Israel's social structure at the time. Tribal loyalties occasionally overshadowed national identity, and the refrain repeated in Judges, "In those days there was no king in Israel; everyone did what was right in his own eyes," signals a profound crisis of leadership and morality. This fragmentation exacerbated social injustices and led to the marginalization of vulnerable groups, further complicating Israel's covenantal obligations.

Embedded in these narratives is the enduring tension between human initiative and divine mandate, between the need for order and the reality of brokenness. The stories of individual judges emerge not simply as episodes of political or military success but as spiritual dramas, where the hero's faithfulness, or lack thereof, profoundly impacts the fate of the entire community. Consider Gideon, who with a small band of warriors overcame overwhelming odds through reliance on God's guidance, yet later faltered in idolatry, reflecting the fragile nature of faith amid prosperity and political power. Or Samson, whose immense strength derived from his Nazirite vow and God's empowering spirit, but whose personal weaknesses precipitated ruin and unrest, symbolizing how intimate betrayals can parallel national crises.

The land itself during this period was both a gift and a battleground. Agricultural patterns shifted as tribes settled regions, relationships with indigenous peoples fluctuated between war and uneasy coexistence, and the spiritual landscape was marred by syncretism. The persistence of pagan worship, Baal and Asherahic cults, fertility rites, and occult practices was a constant challenge that undercut Israel's exclusive covenant. Prophetic voices began to emerge, calling for repentance and social justice, sowing early seeds of theological reflection that would blossom in later prophetic literature. These calls were not mere religious rhetoric but urgent appeals to restore the people's foundational relationship with their God, emphasizing ethical conduct as intrinsic to covenantal identity.

The interplay of sin, judgment, and redemption during the Judges period also had profound social ramifications. Tribal leaders exercised varying degrees of justice and mercy, disputes erupted between clans, and vulnerable groups, widows, orphans, and foreigners often suffered. The biblical text, especially through the Song of Deborah and narratives like that of Jephthah, highlights how justice was both administered and subverted, revealing tensions that would inform Israel's later legal and societal developments. These stories underscore a theme central to the book's broader message: the consequences of human choices extend beyond individual morality to shape societies' spiritual health and stability.

Amidst this fractured epoch, the persistence of hope and the promise of restoration remained steadfast. The cyclical narratives of Judges affirm that despite the repeated failures and the heavy toll of discipline, Israel was never abandoned. Each deliverance foreshadowed a greater hope, a longing for a king who would embody perfect justice, wisdom, and covenantal fidelity. This eschatological anticipation would ultimately find its fulfillment in the monarchy, particularly in the idealized reign of David, and later in the messianic promises that permeate the biblical canon.

The transition from Judges to monarchy itself was marked by profound awareness of the limits of human governance and the need for divine guidance. The experiences of conquest and settlement, fraught with moral ambiguity and political instability, revealed the complexity of inhabiting God's promises in a flawed world. The Promised Land was as much a spiritual reality as a geographical one, requiring ongoing commitment to God's covenant and ethical demands. Sin was never just a private matter; it reverberated through the social fabric, calling Israel to continuous self-examination and repentance.

Reflecting on this formative period invites us to consider how deeply intertwined land, identity, and moral agency are within the biblical worldview. The story challenges modern readers to recognize that the promises we seek, be they spiritual, moral, or communal, are inseparable from the responsibilities and disciplines they entail. The echoes of sin evident in the Judges' era remind us that human choices wield power not only to destroy but to restore, that divine justice balances judgment with mercy, and that true redemption emerges in the tension between human fallibility and steadfast divine love.

In contemplating the conquest and settlement era, we also encounter enduring questions: How do communities navigate the challenges of incomplete obedience amid complex social realities? What does it mean to be faithful to a transcendent ethical call in the midst of imperfect leadership and social fragmentation? The chaotic dynamics of the Judges teach us that spiritual fidelity is a continuous journey, marked by setbacks and resurgence, failures and renewed hope. This cyclical rhythm resonates beyond the ancient past, inviting readers today to recognize the patterns of sin's echo in their own lives and societies, and to embrace the processes of repentance and grace as vital to moral growth.

Ultimately, the saga of entering the Promised Land exposes the persistent tension between divine promises and human responsibility, a tension that remains central to the biblical understanding of sin and redemption. It challenges us to see beyond simplistic narratives of conquest to the profound spiritual and communal struggles that define our existence. The Judges' era, with all its messiness and moral complexity, becomes a mirror reflecting the perennial human condition and God's unwavering commitment to restoration, beckoning us to walk with wisdom and courage into our own promised places, ever aware of the echoes from the past shaping our steps forward.

Cycles of Apostasy

The era of the Judges, a period often described as a turbulent and tumultuous chapter in the history of Israel, unfolds as a vivid, cyclical narrative of human frailty, divine patience, and relentless grace. This epoch, sandwiched between the conquest of Canaan and the establishment of monarchy, reveals patterns of apostasy that repeat with almost hypnotic regularity, echoing the spiritual struggles of a nascent nation wrestling with its covenant identity. To understand these cycles, these recurrent lapses into sin followed by episodes of repentance and deliverance, is to peer deeply into the essence of human nature itself, marked by a restless oscillation between turning away from God and returning in desperate need. Each turning away was not merely a private or isolated sin but a communal rupture, a fracture in the fabric that bound Israel to her divine covenant, and each return was a collective act of humility and recognition of God's sovereign mercy.

The cycle begins invariably with the Israelites turning their backs on Yahweh, abandoning the worship and commandments that defined their unique relationship with the divine. This turning away was often manifested through the adoption of pagan practices, idol worship, and alliances with neighboring peoples that contravened God's law. It was a rejection not only of faith but of identity, a failure to live out the distinctiveness that God had called them to embody. What stands out vividly in these narratives is how this apostasy was rarely a single act but a gradual sliding into moral and spiritual decay. It was as if the people, seduced by the familiarity of the surrounding cultures or frustrated by their hardships, slowly drifted from the foundational truths that once buoyed their communal spirit. The abandonment of covenantal fidelity often led to social chaos, moral confusion, and the erosion of communal values, creating fertile ground for oppression and suffering.

This turning away invited divine discipline, a key theme in the cycle, expressed most dramatically in the form of foreign domination. As the Israelites descended into sin, God permitted external enemies to rise against them, Philistines, Moabites, Midianites, and others, inflicting suffering that was both punishment and a catalyst for repentance. The razor-edge justice of divine discipline was unrelenting, but embedded within it was a profound hope: these periods of oppression were not the end but a redemptive instrument designed to awaken the people's conscience. The suffering was tailored to expose the consequences of disobedience, confronting Israel with the stark reality that their distress was not random but causally linked to their spiritual rebellion. Far from being mere historical footnotes, these episodes echo perennial human experience: the painful but necessary reckoning when choices estrange us from sources of life and blessing. The divine hand, stern yet loving, sought to bring the people to their senses, a call to introspection and transformation.

The next phase in the cycle, the cry for help, unfolded as a bleak reality set in across the land. Under the yoke of foreign oppression, the Israelites found themselves weakened, vulnerable, and desperate. This desperation was not simply physical but existential, a deep awareness that their plight was a consequence of their broken relationship with God. It is here that the narrative reveals a remarkable psychological and spiritual dimension: sin's consequences often precipitate a profound acknowledgment of human limitation and need. The crying out was a collective confession, an anguished recognition of past failures, and a heartfelt plea for divine intervention. What is striking is the consistency of this cry throughout the Judges' stories, an unspoken acknowledgment that God remained the ultimate source of salvation despite the people's unfaithfulness. This moment reveals the enduring human capacity for repentance, even after prolonged periods of wanderings in spiritual wilderness.

Responding to these cries, God would raise up judges, charismatic, divinely appointed leaders who served as instruments of deliverance. These judges were more than military champions; they were prophetic figures who restored the social and religious order, reestablishing the covenantal norms that the people had abandoned. Their rise was a manifestation of divine mercy and grace, embodying God's desire not to abandon His chosen people but to redeem them from their plight. The judges were often flawed themselves, deeply human and complex, yet their leadership was pivotal in bringing temporary peace and spiritual realignment. Whether it was Deborah, the warrior prophetess; Gideon, the hesitant hero; or Samson, the tragic figure of strength and weakness, each judge embodied the possibility of restoration. Their stories stand as powerful testimonies to the resilience of faith and the potential for renewal, even amidst widespread apostasy.

However, the deliverance brought by the judges was typically temporary, marking not a final reconciliation but a cyclical reset. Once peace was secured and threats subdued, the people's hearts would invariably drift back into complacency and sin, restarting the pattern of turning away. This pattern underscores a profound reality about human nature and collective memory: the ease with which lessons learned are forgotten, and how quickly gratitude can be replaced by entitlement or forgetfulness of divine provision. The cyclical aspect of the Judges' narrative reads almost like a moral parable, illustrating the fragility of covenantal faithfulness and the persistent allure of disobedience. Each cycle of apostasy and restoration serves as a mirror, reflecting both the stubbornness of human sinfulness and the persistence of divine mercy.

Throughout these cycles, a tension unfolds between divine justice and mercy that is central to understanding the spiritual dynamics at play. God's justice is enacted in allowing the consequences of sin to flow naturally, punishments that result from turning away rather than arbitrary wrath. At the same time, God's mercy shines in the repeated opportunities for repentance and forgiveness, in the raising of deliverers, and in the restoration offered to a wayward people willing to return. This divine interplay resists simplistic interpretations; God is neither distant nor capricious but deeply invested in the moral restoration of His people. The Judges' era invites reflection on the delicate balance between allowing freedom to choose (with all its attendant consequences) and the ongoing offer of grace that encourages realignment with divine intention. It reveals a God who disciplines not to destroy but to preserve, who punishes not to abandon but to redeem.

Another layer of complexity emerges when considering the social and cultural ramifications of this cyclical apostasy. The oscillation between faithfulness and sin had profound effects on Israel's social cohesion and identity. The recurring lapses into idolatry and disobedience weakened the communal bonds, fractured trust, and often led to internal strife as well as vulnerability to outside aggression. The anguish of oppression under foreign rulers exposed not only political weakness but also spiritual decline. Yet, within this chaos, the stories of the Judges offer glimpses of hope and divine faithfulness, reminding readers that even fractured communities are not beyond redemption. This dynamic also invites contemporary readers to consider how cycles of neglect, repentance, and restoration operate in their own spiritual and communal lives, highlighting the ongoing relevance of these ancient patterns.

Beyond the immediate historical context, the cycles of apostasy during the Judges period resonate as a universal theme in human existential experience. They speak to the repeated human tendency to stray from ideals and truths, to succumb to temptation and forgetfulness, yet also to the equally persistent capacity for repentance and renewal. The Judges' stories, with all their rawness and complexity, offer a mirror not only to ancient Israel but to each reader's moral and spiritual journey. They challenge one to confront personal and communal failures without despair, to recognize the inevitability of stumbling but also to embrace the possibility of restoration. Through these narratives, sin is not an ultimate destiny but a condition shadowed by the hope of grace, inviting ongoing reflection and transformation.

The protracted nature of these cycles, their repetition over generations, also reveals a theological truth about the nature of covenant relationship itself. It is not a static contract but a dynamic engagement, marked by phases of intimacy and estrangement, fidelity and rebellion. God's covenant with Israel, tested repeatedly through the era of the Judges, underscores the profound patience and commitment of the divine partner. Each cycle of apostasy and return serves as a new writing of the covenant story, a renewal of the relationship in the face of human weakness. This dynamic tension echoes throughout biblical history, setting the stage for the prophetic calls to repentance and ultimately pointing toward the hope found in the New Testament's message of ultimate redemption.

Reflecting on the era of the Judges and the cycles of apostasy invites readers into a deeper understanding of sin not merely as individual failure but as a communal and historical force with far-reaching consequences. It challenges modern readers to see how turning away and returning to foundational truths continue to shape communities and individuals alike. These ancient patterns illuminate the complexity of moral decision-making, the costs of disobedience, and the enduring hope that forgiveness and renewal remain possible despite repeated failures.

In the end, the cycles of apostasy in the Judges' period serve as a profound meditation on the nature of human choice and divine response. They reveal a God who is simultaneously just and merciful, who disciplines but also delivers, who allows the painful consequences of turning away but never ceases to call His people back into relationship. This dynamic interplay invites readers to embrace a spiritual journey marked not by perfection but by the persistent movement toward grace, a journey that continues to echo through the corridors of history into every individual life and age. The ancient patterns of the Judges thus remain alive and vital, teaching timeless lessons about sin, repentance, and the boundless reach of divine mercy.

Judges as Deliverers

The era of the Judges stands as a tumultuous and stirring chapter in the tapestry of Israel's history, an embodiment of the divine interplay between human frailty and steadfast grace. Against a backdrop of social and spiritual chaos, the Judges emerged not merely as military champions but as God's chosen deliverers, heralds of divine discipline and mercy. This period, sprawling across centuries, unfurled a recurring cycle of sin, punishment, repentance, and redemption, a rhythm that shaped not only the fate of Israel but also etched profound lessons about leadership, obedience, and divine sovereignty into the consciousness of the people.

In the absence of a centralized monarchy, the land of Israel was a mosaic of tribal territories, fragmented and vulnerable to external pressures and internal discord. As the tribes grappled with idolatry, lawlessness, and moral decay, their collective disobedience invoked God's chastisement through the oppression of surrounding nations. These oppressions, often cruel and relentless, were not mere historical footnotes; they were divine instruments meant not to annihilate but to awaken. The bondage was both physical and spiritual, pressing the Israelites into the crucible of suffering that would eventually ignite their heartfelt cries to God, the pleas that beckoned the emergence of the Judges.

Each Judge was a unique figure, imbued with divine calling and human imperfection, raised up from within the people to confront immediate peril and to restore a delicate equilibrium between the sacred and the profane. Their stories are more than chronicles of battlefield valor; they are complex narratives woven with moments of doubt, fervent faith, flawed humanity, and remarkable courage. They reveal an intimate picture of a God who chooses unlikely agents, works through imperfection, and persistently invites a returning people to repentance.

Take, for instance, the story of Deborah, a prophetess and judge whose singular leadership radiated wisdom and strength in a male-dominated society. Her call to battle against the Canaanite oppressor Sisera was more than a military campaign; it was a revitalization of faith and covenantal loyalty. In Deborah's voice, we hear the stirring summons for Israel to rise from complacency and reclaim their God-given identity. Her story highlights the intricate relationship between divine empowerment and human agency, showing how leadership was not only about strategic skill but also about spiritual attunement and justice. Through her, the narrative transcends mere deliverance; it becomes a testament to the synergy of prophecy, courage, and communal redemption.

Similarly compelling is the account of Gideon, whose initial hesitation and self-doubt reveal the often fraught human response to divine commissioning. Called to lead a vastly outnumbered Israelite force against the Midianites, Gideon exemplifies how God's power is magnified through human weakness. His refining journey from fearful farmer to victorious commander and judge underscores an essential truth: deliverance is not reliant upon human might but upon God's sovereign intervention. Yet, Gideon's story also carries a cautionary thread, warning of the dangers that accompany earthly glory. His creation of an ephod, a religious artifact that inadvertently became a snare for Israel's future idolatry, reveals the complexities and unintended consequences woven into leadership.

The judge Samson presents another vivid portrait of divine deliverance entangled with personal weakness. His life story pulses with dramatic contrasts, superhuman strength bestowed by God to combat the Philistines, juxtaposed with moments of impulsiveness, moral lapses, and tragic downfall. Samson's saga illuminates how God's redemptive purpose often navigates and redeems human folly. His final act of destruction against the Philistine temple, while a devastating climax, simultaneously marks the fulfillment of divine justice and the complex intersection of sacrifice, vengeance, and liberation. Samson's tale beckons reflection on the paradox of divine power manifesting through human brokenness and the persistent hope embedded within the cycle of sin and redemption.

Beneath these individual narratives stretches the broader canvas of the Judges' era, one punctuated by recurring patterns that speak volumes about Israel's spiritual condition and God's patient justice. This cyclical narrative forms a theological heartbeat: Israel's apostasy leads to oppression; in anguish, they cry out to the Lord; God raises a Judge to deliver and restore; a period of peace ensues, only for the cycle to begin anew. This pattern reveals both the stubbornness of the human heart and the endless compassion of the divine. It is a history that does not shy from the messy realities of rebellion and restoration, highlighting the consequences of choice while simultaneously extending a hand of grace.

One must also consider the social and cultural milieus in which these Judges operated, times marked not only by external threats but by internal fragmentation and identity crises. Tribal loyalties often clashed, leading to disputes and alliances that complicated efforts at unified resistance. The absence of strong centralized leadership prior to the monarchy meant that the Judges' authority was often localized, temporary, and sometimes contested. Their deliverance was as much about restoring order and justice within Israel as it was about defending against foreign domination. These leaders stood at the crossroads of law and grace, judgment and mercy, weaving a fragile social fabric amidst the persistent tug of chaos. Their legacy underscores the divine commitment to uphold covenantal justice even amid human volatility.

Divine discipline during this era served both as correction and catalyst. The oppressions that befell Israel were not punitive ends in themselves, but signals pointing back to the covenant and calling the people to genuine repentance. The suffering placed upon Israel compelled a reckoning, a collective recognition that the land and the people were not autonomous but intricately bound to the holiness and commands of Yahweh. This theological underpinning framed the Judges' deliverance not as random acts of salvation but as deeply rooted responses to covenantal breaches, reflecting Yahweh's dual commitment to justice and mercy.

In reflecting on the Judges as deliverers, one cannot overlook the narrative's implicit invitation to contemporary readers to engage with the complex dynamics of leadership and moral responsibility. These leaders were not perfect; they embodied the tensions inherent in any human endeavor to align with divine will amidst fractured societies. Their stories offer a rich wellspring for understanding how spiritual authority is often exercised within constraints, uncertainties, and failures, yet remains potent through God's enabling presence. The Judges' rise and fall embody a lived theology of redemption, not a once-and-for-all event but an ongoing process of returning, restoration, and renewal.

Moreover, the Judges' era challenges modern notions of heroism and power by reframing human strength as ultimately dependent on divine empowerment, and human leadership as a sacred trust fraught with the risk of moral compromise. Their narratives resist simplistic idealization and instead confront the shadows that trail any human attempt to mediate divine will. They reveal a God who works within history's imperfections, who calls flawed individuals to confront formidable enemies, both external and internal, and who redeems failure into new opportunities for deliverance and hope.

As the chapters of Israel's history progressed beyond the Judges, into the united monarchy and prophetic voices, the echoes of this era remained, a reminder that deliverance is never merely political or military triumph but a deeply spiritual journey demanding repentance, faithfulness, and communal alignment with divine purpose. The Judges' stories serve as both prologue and prism, refracting light onto the ongoing interplay between sin, justice, mercy, and leadership, a dance that continues to resonate through the corridors of faith and history.

In sum, the Judges stand as living testaments to the extraordinary ways God chooses to act through history's upheavals: imperfect leaders raised in times of crisis, embodying God's dual roles as righteous judge and merciful savior. Their era teaches us that divine deliverance often emerges not from human perfection but from the willingness to heed God's call amidst turmoil and uncertainty. It invites us to see the brokenness not as final but as a stage within a larger redemptive narrative, where sin's consequences are met by the softness of divine grace, and where hope can flicker anew in the hands of those brave enough to lead, repent, and believe. Through the Judges, we glimpse the enduring truth that God's faithfulness outlasts human failure, and that deliverance, though fraught and fragile, is ever possible in the midst of life's most daunting challenges.

The Monarchy and Moral Decline

Saul's Rise and Fall

The story of Saul's rise and fall is a compelling narrative woven into the very fabric of Israel's early monarchy, a profound exploration of human frailty, divine expectation, and the dramatic consequences that arise when personal ambition and insecurity collide with national destiny. In many ways, Saul stands as a tragic figure, not merely a flawed king, but a man whose inward turmoil and external pressures resonate with the universal human experience. His trajectory from humble beginnings to the throne, followed by a gradual unraveling, serves as a poignant illustration of the complex interplay between personal character, leadership responsibilities, and the weight of divine mandate.

Saul's ascent to kingship emerges against a backdrop of profound uncertainty and transformation within Israelite society. For centuries, the Israelites had lived under the decentralized rule of judges, charismatic leaders raised intermittently to meet specific crises. This patchwork leadership, while effective in moments, failed to provide enduring stability or unity. The people's clamor for a king, a political figure who could wield consolidated authority, reflected both practical needs and a deeper longing to be like the neighboring nations. This demand presented a delicate dilemma: while God's ideal for Israel was a theocratic community led by divine law, the people's insistence on monarchy introduced a level of complexity and potential deviation. Into this fraught atmosphere stepped Saul, anointed by the prophet Samuel as the Lord's chosen sovereign.

Saul's physical description in the biblical text conveys both his royal suitability and his underlying contradictions. Tall, handsome, and commanding in presence, he embodied the ideal visage of a king, a man who could inspire confidence and awe. Yet, beneath this striking exterior, Saul struggled with profound insecurities and a restless spirit. His initial reluctance to embrace the role of king suggests a man caught between humility and destiny, uncertain whether he was qualified and burdened by the enormity of the responsibility thrust upon him. This tension foreshadows the tragedies that would later define his reign.

Early in his kingship, Saul achieved tangible successes that solidified his legitimacy among the Israelites. He demonstrated military prowess, rallying and leading disparate tribes against external foes such as the Ammonites. His victories offered a moment of hope for a united and strong Israel, capable of defending itself and asserting its place in a turbulent regional landscape. These achievements were essential in fostering initial public support and establishing his authority. However, even at this promising stage, subtle signs of Saul's flawed character began to emerge, his impatience, a propensity for impulsive decisions, and a yearning for immediate acclaim rather than patient obedience.

The spiritual dimension of Saul's kingship is crucial to understanding the unfolding drama. God, through Samuel, had imposed clear conditions for Saul's rule, outlining that obedience to divine commands was paramount. This divine expectation set a standard against which Saul's actions would be measured. Unfortunately, Saul's reign became marked by a pattern of disobedience and compromise, often justified by pragmatic concerns or fear of losing favor. One notable episode illustrating this struggle is Saul's premature offering of a sacrifice to God before battle, a role reserved for the prophet. This act reveals Saul's anxiety and desire to control outcomes, even at the expense of established religious protocols. It also signals the beginning of a fracturing relationship with Samuel and, symbolically, with God.

Saul's most significant failure unfolded during the prolonged conflict with the Amalekites, an ancient enemy that God had commanded him to utterly destroy. Instead of following through with this divine decree, Saul allowed his army to spare King Agag and seize the best livestock. This partial obedience was a critical turning point, it demonstrated Saul's hesitancy and presumptuousness in handling sacred commands, substituting his judgment for God's will. Samuel's rebuke was stark and unequivocal, marking a rupture in Saul's favor with the Lord. The prophet's words, "Because you have rejected the word of the Lord, he has rejected you as king," resonate as a tragic indictment, setting the stage for Saul's downfall.

The personal ramifications for Saul were profound. The rejection by God, as communicated through Samuel, stoked an inner turmoil that fueled jealousy, paranoia, and despair. Saul, once buoyed by the promise of divine favor, now found himself haunted by the knowledge that he had lost God's blessing. This spiritual crisis manifested outwardly in erratic and often destructive behavior, which further eroded his standing among the people and his own family. His growing obsession with the young David, who emerged as a courageous warrior and a man after God's own heart, epitomized the tragic spiral of Saul's decline. Instead of recognizing and nurturing David's gifts, Saul perceived him as a rival and a threat, unleashing a relentless and violent pursuit that drove David into exile.

Saul's deteriorating mental state reflected how the burdens of leadership, compounded by a fractured relationship with God, can distort a person's judgment and lead to catastrophic decisions. His swings between bouts of hope and despair, moments of repentance and renewed defiance, created a volatile environment within the nascent kingdom. While his reign began with promise, it devolved into a chaotic struggle characterized by mistrust and fear. The once unifying figure became increasingly isolated, a cautionary emblem of what happens when leaders prioritize power over principle and human ambition overrides divine guidance.

Moreover, Saul's personal failings had profound national consequences. The instability of his reign weakened Israel's political cohesion and moral unity, sowing seeds of division that would reverberate through subsequent generations. His inability to fully embrace God's will created openings for factions and undermined the vision of a God-centered monarchy. The deepening hostilities with David's loyalists not only distracted from external threats but also fractured the social fabric, destabilizing the hopes for a united Israel. In this way, Saul's story underscores the intertwined nature of personal sin and communal suffering; leaders' choices invariably echo beyond their own lives, shaping the destinies of entire peoples.

Despite Saul's tragic flaws, the biblical narrative offers a nuanced portrayal that resists one-dimensional condemnation. Throughout his struggles, moments of genuine remorse and spiritual seeking emerge, revealing a man caught in the tension between fallibility and grace. Saul's lamentations and prayers indicate an awareness of his shortcomings and a desire for restoration, even if inadequate to reverse his course. These glimpses of vulnerability invite readers to see him not simply as a failed king but as a deeply human figure wrestling with profound existential and moral challenges.

In contemplating Saul's rise and fall, one is invited to reflect on the timeless complexities of leadership and the moral responsibilities it entails. Saul's narrative probes essential questions about ambition, obedience, the use of power, and the tragic cost of disobedience. It challenges the reader to consider how personal weaknesses, when left unchecked, can escalate into patterns of failure with far-reaching implications. At the same time, it opens space for mercy and redemption, highlighting that even flawed individuals remain within the purview of divine concern, their stories serving as cautionary tales and sources of wisdom.

Ultimately, the legacy of Saul's reign serves as a mirror reflecting the perennial tension between human imperfection and the call to holiness. His life, marked by both promise and failure, invites a compassionate understanding of the struggles inherent in the pursuit of moral and spiritual integrity. As readers journey through his story, they encounter echoes of their own battles with fear, pride, and the desire for acceptance, reminders that leadership, whether in ecclesial, social, or personal realms, demands humility, faithfulness, and an ongoing commitment to align one's will with a higher calling. Saul's narrative endures not merely as a historical account but as a living dialogue on the enduring dynamics of sin, choice, and the hope for restoration within the human heart.

David's Triumphs and Sins

David's narrative unfolds like a grand tapestry woven with threads of profound triumph and devastating failure, a rich complexity that resists simple categorization. His reign as king of Israel is a study in contrasts, illustrating the staggering heights of human potential alongside the depths of personal weakness. From his improbable ascension as a shepherd boy to the throne, David's life is marked by inspired leadership and pious devotion, yet equally by moments of grave sin and moral compromise, each decision rippling through the fabric of his nation's destiny. This duality makes David one of the most compelling figures within the biblical canon, a king whose story invites us to reflect on the intricate interplay between individual character and the fate of a people under God's sovereign gaze.

David's early years in leadership were adorned with remarkable successes that galvanized the fledgling nation of Israel. His defeat of Goliath is emblematic not only of personal courage but also of divine endorsement, the victory igniting hope and uniting a fractured people around a new monarch who seemed anointed by God for greatness. This initial triumph set high expectations; David was not just a military leader but a shepherd of his people spiritually and politically. His establishment of Jerusalem as Israel's capital was a masterstroke of nation-building, blending religious significance with strategic governance. By bringing the Ark of the Covenant into the city, David symbolically anchored the divine presence at the heart of the kingdom; this act was both a political and spiritual affirmation that intertwined the welfare of the nation with its faithfulness to God.

Yet, even as David crafted a legacy of unification and grandeur, the shadow of his personal failings began to grow. His sins, most notably the episode with Bathsheba and the orchestrated death of her husband Uriah, expose a king vulnerable to the allure of power and desire, capable of grievous ethical lapses. This incident is more than a personal moral failure; it reverberates with national consequences, eroding the king's integrity and fracturing the trust placed in him by the people and by God. The narrative does not shy away from the harsh realities of this transgression, portraying the domestic turmoil and social unrest that followed. The prophet Nathan's rebuke punctuates this moment with divine condemnation, reminding readers that leadership grounded in sin yields destructive outcomes, not only for the leader but for the broader community he governs.

David's internal struggle after his sin reveals a man torn between guilt and repentance, pride and humility. His psalms, many attributed to him, offer a transparent window into this spiritual wrestling, blending raw honesty with a deep yearning for divine mercy. Through these poetic expressions, David does not present himself as a flawless hero but as a flawed human seeking redemption, embodying the broader biblical theme of sin as a pervasive moral force from which no one is exempt. In this way, his life story adapts from a mere historical account into a profound theological reflection on the nature of grace and accountability. His contrition and God's subsequent forgiveness underscore a pivotal tension: while divine mercy can restore, the consequences of sin continue to unfold in the temporal realm, affecting relationships, leadership efficacy, and communal stability.

The repercussions of David's sins are manifest in the fracturing of his own household, as familial strife escalates into violence and rebellion. The tragic fate of his son Absalom, whose revolt against David's rule ultimately ends in death, symbolizes the high cost of compromised morality even within intimate spheres. This familial disintegration mirrors national fragmentation, as Israel's unity wavers in the face of internal discord. David's reign, once a symbol of national strength, now grapples with upheavals that threaten to unravel its political and spiritual fabric. The tension between the king's public role and private failings invites readers to consider the complex relationship between personal ethics and public leadership, illustrating how deeply intertwined they are in shaping a nation's trajectory.

Despite these challenges, David's legacy is not confined to his failures. His enduring commitment to God's covenant and his vision for Israel's future inject a hopeful dimension into an otherwise turbulent narrative. His efforts to bring the Ark to Jerusalem, his plans for the temple (later realized by his son Solomon), and his role as a prophetic figure foreshadowing the Messiah affirm that redemption and hope persist amid human frailty. Through David, the text reveals a dynamic interplay between judgment and mercy, sin and grace, despair and restoration, encapsulating the broader biblical motif of a God who engages deeply with human brokenness to bring about ultimate renewal.

In examining David's reign, one cannot overlook the political savvy and strategic acumen that complemented his spiritual passion. His alliances, military campaigns, and administrative reforms laid vital foundations for Israel's ascendancy as a regional power. Yet, the complexity of his character emerges vividly when we see how his personal ambitions sometimes blur with divine purpose, creating tensions between human will and divine guidance. This nuanced portrayal eschews simplistic heroism; instead, it invites us to meditate on the challenging realities of leadership where strength and weakness coexist. David's ability to navigate this precarious balance has ensured his story remains a touchstone for understanding the intricate dynamics of sin's influence on governance and society.

Moreover, David's story is deeply embedded in the broader theological context of the biblical narrative, framing sin as an active, dynamic force that disrupts harmony and relationships but also as a condition into which God continually intervenes with justice and mercy. David personifies this tension: his sins precipitate judgment, yet his repentance draws forth forgiveness and hope. This interplay heightens the dramatic intensity of his reign and provides a fertile ground for reflection on the enduring human dilemma of moral failure and the quest for restoration. The biblical text allows no easy resolution but instead portrays the ongoing struggle to reconcile human frailty with divine expectation, making David's life both a cautionary tale and a source of inspiration.

The echoes of David's sins transcend his historical moment, resonating through subsequent biblical narratives and theological interpretations. His lineage, traced to Jesus Christ in the New Testament, positions him as a pivotal figure in spiritual history, connecting his experiences with the ultimate act of redemption embodied in Christ's life and sacrifice. This continuity invites readers to see David's story not as an isolated episode but as part of a grand tapestry in which sin's reverberations shape the unfolding drama of salvation history. The complexities of his reign, therefore, serve as a microcosm of the larger human condition, a profound narrative of victory, failure, judgment, and grace that continues to inform contemporary understandings of morality and divine-human relations.

As we reflect on David's triumphs and sins, we are confronted with the sobering reality that those who wield power are not immune to the pitfalls of temptation and moral failure. Yet, his story also offers a radical vision of hope grounded in repentance and divine mercy, encouraging personal introspection and spiritual growth. David's life challenges us to recognize our own imperfections and the far-reaching consequences of our choices, while also reminding us that no failure is beyond the possibility of redemption. This rich complexity, captured through vivid storytelling and theological insight, makes David's reign a timeless study in the profound mysteries of sin and grace, leadership and humility, judgment and forgiveness, a narrative still reverberating within the human soul today.

Legacy of Leadership

The legacy of leadership in ancient Israel is a complex tapestry woven with triumphs and tragedies, where the personal failings of its rulers bore profound consequences for the nation's destiny. This intricate interplay between human weakness and divine mandate reveals that leaders were not merely figures of power but pivotal actors in a larger spiritual and cultural drama. The lives and choices of Israel's kings, from Saul's volatile reign to David's nuanced kingship, mirror the enduring tension between divine expectation and human frailty, a dynamic that shaped the collective identity and fate of a people striving to fulfill a sacred covenant. It is within this tension that the legacy of leadership emerges, offering an enduring lens through which to comprehend how personal shortcomings ripple outward, influencing social structures, religious life, and the very survival of a nation.

The story begins with Saul, anointed as the first king of Israel, whose reign was marked by a precarious balance between divine favor and his own insecurities. Saul's ascent to power was emblematic of Israel's transition from tribal confederation to monarchy, a transformation both political and symbolic, intended to unite the people under a single banner amidst swirling regional threats. Yet, Saul's failings were emblematic of the human struggle to live up to divine expectations. His repeated disobedience, whether in prematurely offering sacrifices reserved for the priesthood or his failure to fully execute divine commands against the Amalekites, exemplified a fractured obedience that led not only to his personal downfall but also to national instability. The loss of divine favor from Samuel, the prophet, was more than just a personal rebuke; it signified a fracture in the leadership ethos of Israel, signaling that kingship was not merely about wielding power but about embodying faithfulness to Yahweh's statutes. Saul's tormented reign culminated in his tragic demise, setting a precedent that leadership tainted by spiritual dissonance invites chaos, both for the ruler and the realm.

In stark contrast, the reign of David, Saul's successor, offers a nuanced study in leadership marked by both extraordinary faithfulness and profound complexity. David, the shepherd boy turned king, is often remembered for his heart after God, his poetic Psalms expressing intimate devotion and repentance, and his role in uniting the tribes into a cohesive kingdom. His legacy, however, is far from unblemished. David's personal failings, including his transgression with Bathsheba and the subsequent murder of Uriah, reveal the vulnerability of even the most anointed leaders to sin's corrosive power. This episode, vividly chronicled in the biblical narrative, is not merely a tale of moral failing but a study in how private sins can have public consequences. The murder incited familial strife, ignited internal rebellion through the revolt of his son Absalom, and sowed seeds of division that would haunt the monarchy for generations. David's experience underscores that leadership in Israel was deeply interwoven with accountability, not only to divine law but to the people whose welfare was inseparably linked to the king's character.

This duality of David's legacy, a man of both great blessing and deep brokenness, imprinted itself on Israel's future, laying the foundation for theological reflections on kingship, repentance, and divine mercy. His heartfelt contrition, articulated in his penitential psalms, modeled a posture of humility that allowed for restoration despite grave sin. This concept of repentant leadership became a benchmark for subsequent rulers and prophets alike, illustrating that sin, while devastating, was not irrevocable if met with genuine remorse and a return to covenantal fidelity. Yet, the persistent familial and political turmoil that followed David's reign revealed that redemption is a process, often fraught with ongoing consequences that outlast individual repentance. Indeed, his dynasty, the House of David, would be both a source of hope, as the lineage from which the messianic figure was anticipated, and a battleground for the competing claims of power, morality, and legitimacy.

The reverberations of personal sin extended far beyond the palace gates, affecting the social and spiritual fabric of Israel. The monarchy was not a closed system but a reflection of the collective soul of the nation. Kings embodied the nation's hopes and fears, their deeds a barometer of Israel's covenantal health. When leaders failed morally or politically, the social order frayed, sowing discord among tribes, exacerbating inequalities, and inviting external threats. The biblical accounts consistently link the prosperity and security of Israel to the righteousness of its leaders, revealing a societal notion that justice and fidelity at the top determine communal flourishing. This concept reached a critical point under Solomon, whose wisdom and wealth brought unprecedented splendor but whose later idolatry and political extravagance planted the seeds of division that ultimately fractured the united kingdom. Solomon's reign illustrated how the corruption of leadership, when indulgence replaces devotion, leads to a weakened polity vulnerable to external conquest and internal collapse.

The prophets, seers, and moral watchdogs of Israelite society were keenly aware of this dynamic. Their vociferous critiques of kings and nobles highlight the intimate link between personal sin and national consequence. Prophets such as Nathan, Samuel, Elijah, Isaiah, and Jeremiah served as divine mouthpieces, castigating leaders whose actions endangered Israel's covenantal relationship with God and, by extension, its survival. These prophetic voices reaffirmed that leadership was not a privilege for self-aggrandizement but a solemn stewardship requiring justice, mercy, and faithfulness. When leaders compromised these values, prophets warned, judgment would follow, not only on individuals but on the entire nation. This prophetic tradition entrenched the idea that sin within leadership was not merely a private failing but a public emergency affecting the spiritual and social order of the people.

The consequences of leadership failures extended into exile and diaspora, periods when the direct royal line was tested by foreign domination and cultural disruption. The exile was interpreted theologically as a consequence of Israel's collective sin, including the sin of its leaders. The narratives of this era emphasize that the downfall of the monarchy was not simply political misfortune, but divine discipline, underscoring the profound link between leadership morality and national fate. Yet amidst this judgment, even in exile, hope remained, a legacy of leadership reflected in the promises of restoration and return, built on the foundations of repentance and renewed covenant. These hopes were kept alive by prophetic messages envisioning a future king, the Messiah, who would embody perfect obedience and justice, restoring Israel and ushering in a new era of righteousness.

It is here that the legacy of Israel's ancient leaders intersects with the New Testament narrative, wherein Jesus Christ emerges as the fulfillment of this enduring hope. Jesus' life and ministry are portrayed not as a mere continuation but as a transformative reinterpretation of kingship, providing an answer to the failures of past rulers. Unlike the earthly monarchs marked by sin and human frailty, Christ's leadership encapsulates perfect obedience, sacrificial love, and the ultimate act of redemption through his death and resurrection. In this way, the legacy of leadership in Israel culminates not in the perpetuation of sinful patterns but in the promise of grace that overcomes sin's destructive echoes.

The impact of Israel's flawed leadership on its future thus operates on several intertwined levels. First is the historical and political, where personal sins precipitated social upheaval, division, and foreign domination, shaping the nation's trajectory through cycles of prosperity and exile. Second is the theological, where the narratives of kings' failures deepen understanding of sin as a pervasive moral force with communal consequences, inviting reflections on divine justice and mercy. Thirdly, there is an enduring ethical dimension, with ancient stories serving as cautionary tales urging leaders, ancient and modern alike, to embrace humility, accountability, and faithfulness. The story of Israel's monarchy challenges readers to grapple with the reality that leadership is never insulated from moral responsibility and that the consequences of sin extend far beyond the individual, influencing societies and futures.

Finally, this legacy calls contemporary readers to examine how past echoes of leadership sin resonate in modern contexts, where personal failings within positions of authority continue to have profound societal effects. The biblical narratives invite an ethical introspection that transcends time, encouraging an ongoing dialogue between history, faith, and personal growth. Understanding that every act of leadership carries weight not only invites greater empathy for the struggles of those who lead but also imposes a solemn responsibility on leaders to steward their charge with wisdom and grace.

In reflecting on Israel's legacy of leadership, one is struck by the paradox at its core: great leaders were deeply flawed human beings whose failures precipitated national consequences, but within these very failings lies an invitation to repentance, restoration, and transformation. The echoes of their sins reverberate through history, shaping not only the fate of Israel but also offering a profound mirror for all who bear the mantle of leadership today. It is a legacy that underscores how intimately human choices, fraught with weakness and hope, can shape the spiritual and social destiny of a people, and how divine mercy continually reaches beyond failure to offer a path toward redemption. In this light, the story of Israel's kings is not merely a record of sin and judgment but a vital testament to the enduring power of grace amidst human imperfection.

Prophetic Voices Against Sin

Prophets as Conscience

The prophets of ancient Israel stand as some of the most compelling and paradoxical figures in biblical history, embodying the fraught position of divine messengers in a world marred by social injustice, moral decay, and spiritual waywardness. They emerge amidst the clamor of human sinfulness not merely as oracles delivering cryptic predictions but as outspoken voices of conscience, challenging kings and commoners alike to confront their ethical failures and to heed the higher summons of covenantal faithfulness. Their role is intricately bound to the divine imperative to call the nation back to righteousness, to warn of impending judgment, and to foster hope for restoration. Yet, this mission is steeped in profound tension and hardship, as prophets grapple not only with the weight of their messages but also with resistance, hostility, and loneliness in a culture often unwilling to hear uncomfortable truths.

To appreciate the prophetic vocation fully is to understand it as a divine summons that transcends mere foretelling. The prophets function as moral agents who pierce the veil of societal complacency, exposing the oppression, exploitation, and corruption festering beneath the surface of national prosperity or religious ritualism. These men and women, from Amos to Isaiah, Jeremiah to Ezekiel, and the lesser-known prophets scattered through the biblical record, inhabit a liminal space. They stand between the divine and human realms, channeling divine indignation against injustice and calling forth repentance as a catalyst for transformation. Their pronouncements often articulate a fierce critique of the disparity between outward religiosity and inner ethical bankruptcy; they indict leaders who oppress the poor, priests who profane the holy, and communities that neglect their covenantal obligations. Social justice is not a peripheral concern but a central axis of their message, reflecting a God who demands justice and righteousness as the foundation of true worship.

Their prophecies are steeped in vivid imagery and striking metaphors, crafted not merely to warn but to awaken. When Amos denounces the crimes of Israel's elite, it is a searing indictment of how wealth and privilege are preserved through crushing the weak, twisting justice, and perverting the scales. The prophets do not shy away from naming systemic sin, identifying it as the root from which personal transgressions and social decay flow. These messages resonate with timeless urgency, reflecting God's righteous anger not as capricious punishment but as a necessary response to violation of divine order and human dignity. The prophetic voice becomes a thunderous echo across the ages, reminding us that sin is communal, structural, and embedded in the very fabric of social relations, demanding accountability not only of individuals but of entire societies.

Yet, the prophetic office is marked by immense challenges. The prophets walk a solitary path, often met with scorn, rejection, or active persecution by those they are sent to admonish. Jeremiah, branded the "weeping prophet," exemplifies this struggle, enduring imprisonment, despair, and even threats to his life for proclaiming God's warnings unapologetically. Hosea's life itself becomes a living allegory of divine love and judgment, as he marries a woman who betrays him, symbolizing Israel's spiritual unfaithfulness. This personal dimension underscores how the prophetic message is not abstract but embodied, costly, and transformative. Prophets are frequently caught in the crosscurrents of political power, religious tradition, and public opinion, needing to navigate these treacherous currents without compromising the integrity of their calling. To speak truth to power invites alienation and suffering, yet the prophets persevere, driven by an unyielding commitment to divine truth and the hope of redemption beyond judgment.

Their warnings are not merely punitive but deeply pastoral in intent. Prophetic literature blends oracles of doom with assurances of divine mercy, envisioning a future where the covenant relationship is renewed and justice flows like a mighty river. This delicate balance between justice and mercy reveals the heart of God's engagement with humanity, a God who disciplines but also redeems, who devastates but ultimately restores. The prophets remind their audiences that consequences are real and often severe, but they also offer visions of hope that transcend present despair. Isaiah's vision of a suffering servant, Micah's call to "do justice, love mercy, and walk humbly," and Zechariah's promise of a coming kingdom of peace encapsulate this tension. The prophetic message thus refuses simplistic dualities; it neither sugarcoats human failure nor resigns to hopelessness, but calls for repentance as a door to renewal and grace.

Furthermore, the prophetic role indicates a profound theological anthropology, emphasizing human responsibility and freedom within a covenantal relationship. Prophets highlight that sin is a choice with consequences, not an inevitable condition beyond control. Their words insist on moral agency and the possibility of reform, even while acknowledging human stubbornness and sinfulness. The recurring theme of divine patience alongside judgment reveals a God who earnestly desires repentance and community restoration. This dialectical tension reinforces the complexity of divine justice and mercy as coexisting forces shaping the course of history. The prophetic call is ultimately an invitation to participate consciously in the divine narrative, to choose life and covenant fidelity over destruction and exile.

In the wider historical and cultural setting of ancient Israel, prophets often arose during times of crisis, political upheaval, military threat, and social inequality that exposed deeper spiritual malaise. Their appearances coincide with moments when the social fabric unravels and the legitimacy of political and religious institutions is questioned. This context amplifies the urgency of their call; they function not only as spiritual guides but as social critics pointing to the underlying causes of communal distress. The prophets' emphasis on ethical leadership serves as an implicit and explicit rebuke to kings and rulers who exploit power for personal gain or nationalistic expansion at the expense of justice and righteousness. Samuel's anointing of Saul, Nathan's confrontation with David, and Elijah's showdown with Ahab illustrate the dynamic interplay between prophetic authority and royal power. This tension frames a recurring biblical motif: the contest between worldly might and divine justice mediated by prophetic voices.

The prophetic message also reveals the tension between continuity and change within Israel's religious life. While deeply rooted in the covenantal traditions and legal frameworks of the Torah, prophets often push beyond ritualistic observance to demand a transformed heart and ethical integrity. They challenge superficial religiosity that ignores the plight of the marginalized and exalts empty sacrifices while neglecting justice. This theme is poignantly expressed in the prophetic declaration that God desires "mercy, not sacrifice," "to do justice, and to love kindness, and to walk humbly." The prophets thus recast true worship as inseparable from social ethics, emphasizing that God's presence is not confined to the temple but is manifest through just living and faithful community relations. This reorientation situates social justice at the heart of true covenantal faithfulness.

Moreover, prophetic literature often employs poetic and symbolic language, drawing readers into a dynamic interplay of hope, judgment, and renewal. The vision of the valley of dry bones coming to life, the imagery of lion and lamb resting together, or the depiction of a new heaven and earth enrich the thematic complexity of sin and redemption. These evocative images not only capture theological truths but also invoke emotional and spiritual responses that deepen the reader's engagement with the prophetic call. This artistry demonstrates that prophetic words are not just information but embodied truths, inviting transformation at the level of both intellect and heart.

The prophets also serve as bridges between the Old Testament world and later theological developments, particularly in the New Testament. Their portrayals of sin, judgment, and hope find new dimensions in the life and teachings of Jesus Christ, who fulfills and transcends old patterns by embodying divine mercy and bringing the possibility of ultimate reconciliation. The prophetic tradition thus forms a crucial background for understanding Christian conceptions of sin and redemption. By tracing how prophets wrestled with the moral crises of their times, contemporary readers gain insight into their struggles with faithfulness, justice, and grace, a legacy that continues to challenge and inspire.

In summary, the prophets as conscience represent an indispensable voice within the biblical narrative, one that relentlessly confronts sin's corrosive effects on individuals and societies while holding fast to the hope of divine restoration. Their calling to champion social justice and proclaim divine warnings is marked by courage, perseverance, and profound spiritual depth. Though often marginalized and misunderstood, they embody the tension between judgment and mercy that defines much of biblical theology. Their legacy endures as a clarion call to listen intently to the moral demands of the divine, to recognize the systemic and personal dimensions of sin, and to embrace the transformative power of repentance. The prophetic voice echoes through history, standing as a beacon for all who seek to align human conduct with divine justice, underscoring that true faithfulness is inseparable from a passionate commitment to making justice roll down like waters and righteousness like an ever-flowing stream.

Messages of Judgment

Throughout the tapestry of biblical history, the voices that cry out with urgency and conviction are those of the prophets, uncompromising heralds of divine truth whose purpose was to deliver messages of judgment. These warnings were not mere admonitions delivered in a vacuum; they were fervent calls against the persistent backdrop of human sinfulness, a sin that threatened the very fabric of society and the sacred alliance between God and His people. In the unfolding drama of biblical times, the prophets assumed the perilous role of standing at the intersection of heaven and earth, channeling divine displeasure against social injustice, idolatry, and moral decay. Their messages resonated far beyond the immediate context, touching on themes so timeless they continue to reverberate through the corridors of our moral consciousness today.

At the heart of these prophetic oracles lies a profound awareness that sin is not merely a list of infractions but a corrosive force that gnaws at the relationships binding individuals to one another and to God. The most common refrain in their speeches is an impassioned indictment against social injustice, a lament over the exploitation of the vulnerable, widows, orphans, strangers, and the poor, and a call to return to the covenantal ethics that demanded righteousness and mercy. These messages of judgment vividly illustrate that divine justice transcends ritualistic observance and instead demands a lived morality rooted in equitable treatment and genuine compassion. The prophets lamented, often with piercing clarity, the hollow religiosity that masked the corruption of societal elites, condemning empty sacrifices while systemic oppression flourished unchecked. Such duality made the warnings all the more biting: outward piety without inward transformation would not shield Israel from the consequences of collective sin.

The prophetic writings articulate a consistent theme: the consequences of sin are not confined to individual misfortune but manifest in national calamity and divine retribution. Whether through military defeat, exile, famine, or other disasters, the text ensures that the punishment is portrayed not as arbitrary torment but as a sober outcome of violated covenantal terms. For example, Isaiah's scathing critiques reveal how the rulers and people neglect justice and righteousness, relying instead on alliances with foreign powers and self-serving policies, which ultimately lead to their downfall. His warnings bear an unsettling duality of hope and doom, hope hinging on repentance and restoration, doom looming in obstinacy and unrepentance. This prophetic dialectic shapes much of the literature from Jeremiah, Ezekiel, Amos, and Hosea, who tirelessly invoke the theme that judgment is both just and necessary, an inevitable consequence of persistent sin threatening to unravel the chosen people's relationship with God.

These messages of judgment frequently raise the issue of communal responsibility, emphasizing that sin is not merely the sum of individual acts but can become a collective contagion that infects the entire body politic. Prophets expose how leaders who stray from divine principles jeopardize not only themselves but their subjects as well. Nor is the blame limited to kings and priests; the communal nature of sin implicates everyone in the social order. Amos, in particular, scorns those who live in luxury while the poor suffer destitution, warning that the gods of wealth and self-indulgence are deceptive idols leading to destruction. In this way, corruption and callousness are not abstract offenses but concrete sins with devastating implications. These indictments resonate deeply because they touch on everyday realities where power unscrupulously marginalizes the weak, turning human dignity into a casualty of greed and oppression. The prophets insist that such societal sin inevitably provokes divine justice, a reminder woven into the biblical narrative that social ethics are inseparable from spiritual fidelity.

Moreover, the prophets challenge their contemporaries, and us, to consider the long-term consequences of their choices. Judgment is portrayed as both a present reality and a future certainty. This temporal tension is crucial; it underscores the belief that divine patience is real but finite. Idolatry and injustice may thrive for a season, but consequences loom inevitably, often catching people unprepared. It is within this tension that many prophetic warnings take on a dramatic urgency, imploring a rapid course correction lest the people face irrevocable ruin. Ezekiel's vivid visions of destruction function as unsettling mirrors reflecting society's present sins while depicting a world on the brink of collapse. Yet, even in the shadows of judgment, the prophets hold out a vision for repentance and renewal, affirming that divine discipline is ultimately restorative and redemptive, not purely punitive.

The interplay between divine judgment and mercy emerges with exquisite complexity in these messages. The prophets do not simply declare doom but invite the possibility of reprieve through genuine repentance. Hosea's poignant portrayal of Israel's unfaithfulness conveys a heartbroken God yearning for reconciliation despite persistent waywardness. The drama of judgment thus becomes a powerful theological expression of divine love's paradox: justice is necessary, but mercy remains available for those who turn away from sin. This balance is part of what makes prophetic literature particularly rich and nuanced. Their messages compel listeners to face uncomfortable truths about sin while simultaneously holding space for hope and forgiveness. This dynamic invites a deep psychological and spiritual engagement; one cannot simply shrink from judgment without risking greater harm, nor can one despair entirely because grace abides even amid judgment.

In the narratives underpinning these warnings, the role of temptation takes center stage as a force that entices and misleads, pulling individuals and nations into sin's destructive orbit. Prophets reveal temptation's subtlety, often wrapped in political alliances, economic expediency, or cultural assimilation, that gradually erodes commitment to divine statutes. Jeroboam's golden calves represent not only the physical idols but also the temptation to short-circuit true worship with visible, convenient substitutes. Such images resonate deeply because they depict sin not as sudden rebellion but as incremental compromise that blinds a people to their deeper covenantal responsibilities. The warnings against temptation thus serve as both diagnosis and cure, cautioning against the normalized small betrayals that accumulate into insurmountable spiritual breaches.

These messages also boldly confront idolatry, a sin that prophetically symbolizes broader spiritual infidelity. The prophets utilize powerful imagery to expose idols as lifeless, impotent substitutes that cannot deliver safety or justice. Isaiah's vision of smashed and discarded idols embodies the futility of trusting in human-made objects or foreign powers rather than the living God. Idolatry, therefore, is not just a religious offense but a social and political betrayal. To follow foreign gods or human rulers rather than God's ethical covenant is to choose destruction. The dire warnings associated with idolatry emphasize that sin's worst consequence is alienation from God, from community, and ultimately from self. This alienation is portrayed as the root of many other forms of social injustice and moral crisis, making idolatry a central concern in prophetic judgment.

The execution of judgment often includes vivid metaphors and symbolic acts intended to awaken an often complacent or resistant audience. Prophets frequently employ striking imagery, ranging from droughts and famines to sieges and exile, to dramatize the consequences of sin. These symbolic acts serve as tangible manifestations of divine disapproval, emphasizing the seriousness of the warnings given. They disrupt ordinary life and ordinary thinking, forcing a reckoning with the underlying social and spiritual evils. Such methods underscore the prophets' deep conviction that words alone are insufficient; lived experience and historical events bear the unmistakable marks of divine judgment. This vivid storytelling invites readers to imagine the profound impact these warnings must have had in their original context, heightening the emotional and ethical stakes.

The historical context of these judgments cannot be overlooked if one seeks to appreciate their full significance. The prophetic warnings often came at crucial moments, before exile, in the midst of oppressive empires, or during periods of national flourishing that bred complacency. For instance, Jeremiah delivers his message in the shadow of an impending Babylonian invasion, adding a palpable tension to his attempts at urging repentance. His lamentations reveal a prophet painfully aware of the cost of ignored warnings, as the people spiral deeper into sin and face catastrophic consequences. Thus, these messages are not abstract moralizing; they are urgent, grounded in the lived realities of communities on the brink of disaster. The intertwining of historical crisis and theological reflection enriches the texture of judgment, underscoring that sin's consequences are both personal and communal, immediate and enduring.

Yet, amid the sobering tone of judgment, the prophetic messages consistently envision a future restoration that hinges on a transformed heart and a re-oriented society. Judgment is never portrayed as the ultimate end but as a necessary phase toward healing and renewal. Isaiah's vision of a new heavens and a new earth stands as a powerful testament to this hope, an eschatological promise that divine justice is ultimately restorative. The path to this renewal requires embracing divine standards of justice, righteousness, and mercy, thus reversing the patterns of sin that led to judgment. Prophets remind their hearers that divine judgment serves not only as punishment but as a refining fire that purifies and reclaims. Through this lens, the messages of judgment become invitations to participate in a shared journey of repentance, healing, and hope.

One of the most compelling aspects of these warnings is the way they call for ethical self-examination on both individual and societal levels. The prophets do not allow their audiences to evade responsibility by attributing blame solely to external enemies or circumstances. Instead, they hold up a mirror reflecting internal moral failures and demand accountability. This inward focus deepens the psychological import of judgment, as it exposes the insidious nature of sin that corrupts both heart and society. It reinforces that genuine repentance must involve a process of transformation rather than mere ritual confession. This ethical imperative resonates with contemporary readers who grapple with similar questions about personal and systemic sin and the consequences of failing to address injustice.

Moreover, the prophetic messages of judgment critique the often automatic association of prosperity with divine favor. They challenge the prevailing notion that material success is proof of righteousness, revealing instead the complexity of divine providence that does not exempt the wicked from correction. Prophets use irony and paradox to jar their audiences, for example, King David's descendants enjoy political power yet fail to uphold covenantal justice, leading inevitably to judgment. This critique deconstructs simplistic understandings of blessing and curse, inviting a deeper engagement with the reality that sin's consequences are multifaceted and that divine judgment prioritizes moral integrity over material prosperity. Such insights enrich the theological reflection surrounding judgment, reminding readers that spirituality is inseparable from ethical conduct.

In reflecting on these rich and complex messages, it becomes clear that the warnings against sin and their consequences serve not only as historical records but as enduring moral and spiritual touchstones. They invite us into a dialogue across millennia, challenging contemporary societies to assess their own complicity in injustice and to heed the sobering lessons embedded in biblical tradition. The echoes of judgment resonate with clarity: persistent sin breeds decay, alienation, and disaster, but repentance opens the door to restoration and grace. In a world still grappling with issues of poverty, oppression, violence, and broken relationships, the prophetic call remains urgent and relevant.

This ancient strain of divine warning encourages readers to engage with sin not as a distant, abstract concept but as a living reality that demands an ethical response. It pushes beyond individual guilt to consider the structural sins that sustain injustice and harm communities. The profound social consciousness embedded in these messages teaches that judgment is integrally connected to social transformation and reconciliation. As the prophets contended with the realities of their age, so contemporary readers are challenged to confront the echoes of sin in their world and to participate in the ongoing work of justice, mercy, and healing.

Ultimately, these prophetic messages of judgment represent a crucial facet of biblical theology's rich dialogue between divine justice and human responsibility. They portray sin as a serious breach with far-reaching consequences but simultaneously reveal a God who remains deeply invested in restoration. This tension between judgment and mercy forms a theological heartbeat, pulsing through scripture and theology alike, summoning readers into a journey of honest self-examination, moral courage, and hopeful renewal. The compelling narrative arc from warning to judgment to redemption invites all who encounter it to consider their place in this unfolding story and to respond with wisdom and grace, mindful of the lasting effects of their choices both for themselves and for the community of faith.

Hope for Restoration

Amidst the tapestry of human failing and divine reproof that colors the biblical narrative, a persistent thread of hope for restoration gleams with resolute brightness. This hope is not merely an abstract notion or a passive wish but a profound promise woven into the fabric of Scripture, a promise that despite the depth of sin and the severity of consequences, there remains a pathway to reconciliation, renewal, and justice. The biblical texts portray this hope both as a divine initiative and a human summons, intimately tied to ideas of social justice and the imperative to heed divine warning. To explore these promises is to delve into the soul of biblical spirituality, where the brokenness of humanity is met not with final abandonment, but with steadfast mercy and an uncompromising call to restoration.

From the earliest echoes in the prophetic literature, the divine voice is both stern and reassuring, wielding warning not as a threat of arbitrary punishment but as an invitation to relent and recover the covenantal relationship fractured by sin. This dialectic of warning and hope is palpable. Take, for instance, the voice of the prophet Isaiah, whose words frequently lament the injustice, idolatry, and violence that have ravaged the community yet invariably pivot towards anticipation, anticipation of a new day when righteousness will flourish and the desolation of sin will be lifted. Isaiah's vision of restoration is striking in its vivid symbolism: deserts blooming into lush gardens, the deaf hearing, the blind seeing, and the wolf dwelling with the lamb without harm. Such imagery transcends mere physical renewal to capture a holistic transformation of society, where broken relationships are healed and justice is actualized. Social justice here is not an optional virtue but the very axis upon which divine restoration turns, emphasizing that hope is inextricably bound to ethical living and communal integrity.

The promises of future redemption thus emerge as an ethical imperative and a theological assurance intertwined. They offer a paradoxical comfort that redemption will come, though it demands genuine repentance and systemic change. The prophetic calls for justice highlight the reality that sin's reach is not confined to private transgressions but extends to societal structures that perpetuate inequality, oppression, and violence. The cries of the widows, orphans, and strangers, those vulnerable members of society, resonate throughout the biblical witness as a measure of faithfulness. The divine warnings are stark reminders that ignoring such cries invites judgment, not out of vindictiveness, but as a consequence of violated covenantal values. Yet, within these warnings, the promise gleams clear: when justice reigns, when mercy triumphs over vengeance, the community is restored to its intended harmony under divine rule.

Consider also the shape of restoration in the exilic and post-exilic contexts, which offer poignant paradigms of hope amid catastrophe. The exile was a crushing judgment, a result of persistent disobedience and injustice; however, the exilic prophets reveal the depth of divine compassion through assurances that the community will be gathered once more from the farthest lands, the temple will be rebuilt, and the covenant renewed with renewed zeal for righteousness. Jeremiah's "new covenant" prophecy is especially profound, it envisions a transformation that goes beyond external compliance with the law to the internalization of divine will, written not on tablets of stone but on human hearts. This intimate restoration suggests that redemption is not simply a return to a former state but a movement toward a higher spiritual and ethical condition.

Central to this idea of restoration is the challenge and opportunity presented in the tension between divine justice and mercy. Justice insists on accountability, the rectification of wrongs, and the restoration of order disrupted by sin. Mercy, however, softens the harsh edges of judgment, extending grace and mercy to repentant hearts. The biblical narrative often presents these qualities not as contradictory but as complementary facets of God's character. Divine warnings serve as the mechanism by which justice calls humanity to account, while the promises of hope underscore the merciful willingness of God to forgive and restore. This theology finds its most profound expression in the New Testament, where the life, death, and resurrection of Jesus Christ embody and fulfill the ultimate hope for restoration, a hope that encompasses not only personal salvation but the full reconciliation of creation itself.

In examining the social justice dimension of these promises, it becomes clear that the restoration hoped for is communal as much as it is individual. Sin fractures not only personal souls but the social fabric; hence, restoration must heal both. The prophets, in particular, articulate this communal focus with unrelenting clarity. They decry exploitation, corruption, and selfishness that place the powerful above the vulnerable and call for a just society modeled on divine righteousness. The promises of restoration thus become a vision of a world where peace and equity prevail, a world where every person has dignity and where the social order respects the sacredness of human life. This is no utopian fantasy but a deeply rooted conviction that the divine purpose for humanity includes flourishing relationships marked by justice and love.

The hope for restoration articulated in the biblical texts also functions as a spiritual lifeline amid human despair and brokenness. In moments when the consequences of sin appear overwhelming, when exile and alienation seem permanent, the prophetic promises breathe life into despairing hearts. This hope insists that no human situation is beyond the reach of divine redemption and that the cycle of sin and consequence, though painful and rigorous, is not endless. The biblical voice here becomes a beacon that invites self-examination and repentance, yet it also extends an open hand toward renewed life. It is a hope that challenges complacency and despair alike, asserting that true renewal flows from an openness to divine grace and a commitment to ethical transformation.

Moreover, the promises of future redemption carry an eschatological dimension, linking hope for restoration with the ultimate fulfillment of God's kingdom. This future-oriented hope reconfigures present struggles as part of the larger divine narrative. Prophets like Ezekiel, Jeremiah, and Isaiah offer glimpses of a glorious future where God's presence dwells fully with the people, where war and suffering cease, and where a new heaven and earth emerge. The eschatological vision reframes the tension between justice and mercy as the climax of God's plan, a hope that transcends temporal trials and resonates through history into eternal restoration. This vision nurtures perseverance, inspiring communities to embody justice now while trusting in the ultimate triumph of divine reconciliation.

Integral to the biblical hope for restoration is the transformative power of repentance. This dynamic process is not simply an apology or regret but a profound turning away from sin and turning toward God and neighbor. Through repentance, individuals and communities acknowledge their failings and embrace the possibility of change, thus participating in the very renewal promised by God. The biblical texts underscore this process by portraying repentance as both a human responsibility and a response enabled by divine grace. The intertwining of divine promise and human response multiplicatively enriches the discourse on restoration, emphasizing that hope is not passive but active, demanding engagement, humility, and perseverance.

In exploring these promises, it becomes evident that they are not uniform or simplistic but layered and multifaceted, reflecting the complexity of human existence and divine purpose. The hope for restoration, while future-oriented, continuously interacts with present realities, challenging individuals and societies to reflect divine values in tangible ways. This interplay underlines a crucial insight of biblical theology: restoration is both a gift and a task, a future assured by divine fidelity but requiring human cooperation. The ethical implications are profound, calling readers to examine their own lives and contexts in light of divine expectations and promises.

The theme of restoration also bridges the Old and New Testaments, connecting the ancient hopes expressed through the prophets with the fulfillment revealed in Christ. Jesus's ministry is characterized by acts of healing, liberation, and proclamation of the kingdom of God, demonstrations of restoration breaking into human history. The cross and resurrection embody the paradox of judgment and mercy, a decisive victory over sin's consequences, transforming the hope long yearned for into a living reality. This New Testament revelation recasts prior promises, now centered on grace, forgiveness, and the indwelling presence of the Spirit as agents of ongoing restoration.

In contemplation of these expansive promises, readers are invited into a deep reflection on the nature of sin, justice, and mercy, and the transformative hope that God offers. The biblical narrative does not downplay the reality of sin or diminish its consequences; rather, it illuminates a divine trajectory that moves decisively toward healing, justice, and grace. This journey invites a continual return to covenant faithfulness, an embrace of repentance, and a participation in the divine mission of restoration. It is a hope that resonates through time, echoing in the lives of individuals and communities striving to live out faith in the face of brokenness and longing for renewal.

Ultimately, the promises of future redemption in the biblical tradition reclaim the possibility that the deepest wounds inflicted by sin can be healed, that justice can indeed prevail, and that mercy extends beyond human fault. They assure that the moral and spiritual bankruptcy of humanity is not the final word; there is always an invitation to rise again, to repair what has been broken, and to embody a renewed vision of community and relationship under God's unfailing grace. This hope does not erase suffering nor bypass accountability, it confronts darkness with light, brokenness with wholeness, and despair with enduring expectation. It is, in essence, the echo of a divine promise that continues to call humanity forward, urging all who hear to journey toward restoration with courage, faith, and love.

Exile and Reflection

Fall of Jerusalem

The fall of Jerusalem stands as one of the most heartrending and pivotal moments in biblical history, a catastrophe that shook the identity of an entire nation and echoed through the ages, shaping not only theological reflections but social and spiritual consciousness for generations to come. This tragic event did not merely signify the physical destruction of a city; it embodied an intense, multifaceted upheaval that conveyed profound lessons about divine justice, human frailty, the consequences of collective choices, and the complex interplay of judgment and mercy. The protracted siege, eventual breach, and violent devastation of Jerusalem by Babylonian forces in 586 BCE marked the rupture of the covenantal relationship in an utterly tangible way, a rupture witnessed, lamented, and ultimately mourned by a people whose very sense of self was intertwined with the sacred city and the Temple, the dwelling place of God among them. This chapter of suffering and exile challenges readers to contemplate identity in the face of loss, the role of repentance amid calamity, and the seeds of hope that sprouted from the ashes of devastation.

The story begins against a backdrop of political instability and spiritual decay. Jerusalem, once a beacon of covenantal fidelity under the united monarchy of David and Solomon, had devolved into a complex matrix of alliances, betrayals, and moral compromise. The divided kingdoms of Israel and Judah experienced recurring cycles of rebellion against the laws God had ordained, and while prophets like Jeremiah and Ezekiel fiercely pleaded for a return to righteousness, their voices were often drowned out by the clamor of political expediency and idolatry. To the inhabitants of

Jerusalem, the city was not just a physical stronghold or a political capital; it was the heart of their religious and communal identity, the visible symbol of God's presence and promises. Yet, with every ignored warning and forsaken covenant, the city edged closer to catastrophe. As Babylonian armies encircled Jerusalem, the sense of impending doom grew palpable, a dark shadow looming over every household, every whispered prayer.

The siege itself was brutal and relentless. For months, the city's walls enclosed thousands trapped within, their hopes dwindling in the face of starvation, disease, and despair. The very air must have thickened with the cries of anguish, the sound of desperation carried through narrow, dust-choked streets where families clung to one another amid the ruin. Beneath the threat of war, internal divisions surfaced between those who advocated surrender in the hope of mercy and those who insisted on fighting to the bitter end, believing in divine deliverance no matter the cost. This internal conflict reflects a profound theme that resonates far beyond its historical moment: the tension between human agency and divine sovereignty, a tension still wrestled with in the moral and spiritual struggles of individuals and nations alike. The siege laid bare the fragility of earthly power and the consequences of collective disobedience, as well as the complex emotions stirred by desperation and hope intertwined.

When the walls finally fell and the Babylonians breached the city, the destruction was merciless and total. The Temple, the very epicenter of Israel's worship and symbol of God's dwelling, was razed to rubble. Palaces were sacked, homes reduced to ash, and countless lives were torn apart in an instant. This devastation was more than military strategy; it was a poignant and deliberate act of divine judgment, expressed through the hands of foreigners but interpreted by the captives as the fulfillment of God's warnings through prophets long ignored. For the exiled leaders, priests, and common people who were taken to Babylon, the so-called Babylonian Captivity, it was a wrenching uprooting from everything familiar, an identity crisis on a colossal scale. The land, the Temple, and their city were inseparable from who they were as God's chosen people. Without these, the question overwhelmed them: Who are we now? Was the covenant severed forever? Was God abandoned?

This crisis of identity led to some of the most profound theological reflections in the entire biblical canon. In exile, the people wrestled with the silence of God and the confusion of divine purpose. Yet, in that space marked by loss and displacement, new forms of faithfulness emerged. The destruction of the Temple forced a reconceptualization of worship and relationship with God, shifting from place-bound ritual to a faith centered on Torah, prayer, and communal memory. The prophets, both during and after the fall, proclaimed that this calamity was not the end but part of a redemptive process, an invitation to repentance and renewal. The lamentations, with their raw grief and honest questioning, did not merely express hopelessness but voiced a yearning for restoration, a steady, fragile hope that God's mercy was not spent. The exile became a paradoxical space where punishment and promise coexisted, where judgment was harsh but filled with the possibility for transformation.

This nuanced understanding brought burgeoning questions about the nature of sin and repentance to the forefront. The people came to see that sin was not limited to individual misdeeds but was embedded in the collective life, the social structures, the religious leadership, and the complacency that allowed injustice to flourish. The fall of Jerusalem was a mirror reflecting the consequences of turning away from God's path. Yet repentance was more than regret; it was a radical turning toward God, a reorientation of the heart and community life. In these moments of profound loss, the seeds for national and spiritual restoration were planted, nurtured by prophetic promises that God would make a new covenant, write the law on hearts rather than tablets of stone, and gather the scattered people once again. These promises offered nourishment for a people adrift, sustaining faith and identity even in exile.

The experience of exile deeply shaped the future trajectory of Judaism and, by extension, Christian theological thought. It was a time when identity was reimagined through the prism of suffering and hope. The stories of exile remind us that faith is not immune to suffering but rather often forged within it. This redefinition of identity, born of rupture and displacement, offers a powerful lesson for any reader confronting the fissures in their own lives or communities. The narrative of Jerusalem's fall prompts reflection on how trauma and loss can become spaces where new understandings and deeper commitments arise. It shows that faith is dynamic, responsive to history, and capable of transformation even when the foundations seem irrevocably shattered.

In this way, the fall of Jerusalem resonates far beyond its ancient moment, inviting contemporary readers to ponder their own experiences of brokenness, repentance, and the longing for renewal. The echoes of sin that brought about the city's destruction still reverberate today in collective and individual struggles with moral failure, injustice, and the consequences that unfold over time. Yet, intertwined with those echoes is the call to hope, the invitation to lean into the possibility of mercy and restoration. The story underscores that destruction does not preclude redemption, and exile can be a passage, not merely a punishment, but a crucible for a new life of faithfulness.

Moreover, the fall of Jerusalem challenges readers to reflect on the communal nature of sin and repentance. It was not merely the failing of kings or priests but the entire society that bore responsibility. This communal aspect extends to the modern moment, reminding us that moral and spiritual failures often intertwine with systems and shared choices. Therefore, the path to restoration also requires collective reflection, justice, and transformation. Jerusalem's destruction and exile remain a sobering testimony to the stakes of disobedience, but they also bear witness to the enduring power of divine mercy, which transcends destruction to offer a horizon of hope and renewal.

In the end, as the narrative unfolds beyond the fall, the story of Jerusalem's destruction is not simply one of despair but becomes a beacon of spiritual resilience. The biblical texts emerging from exile, the prophecies of restoration, the psalms of lament, and the reforms of returnees chart a course for a community learning to live in the tension of memory and hope. This tension invites readers into a deeper understanding of faith, reminding us that while sin fractures, grace can rebuild. The echoes of Jerusalem's fall thus continue to reverberate through time, prompting ongoing reflection on identity, sin, repentance, and the transformative power of God's redeeming love, which calls a fractured people toward wholeness and peace.

Life in Captivity

Life in captivity unfolds as an intricate tapestry woven from threads of despair and resilience, of loss and fervent hope. The very notion of captivity, a physical and spiritual confinement, reverberates deeply throughout biblical history, casting long shadows that stretch into the hearts of those ensnared in foreign lands, alien customs, and enforced servitude. To live in captivity is to grapple not only with the external chains that bind the body but also with the inner turmoil that threatens the soul's freedom. It is a crucible wherein identity is tested, faith is strained, and the profound questions of repentance and hope come to the forefront. Within this suffocating context, the captives face the challenge of preserving their heritage and maintaining their covenantal connection to God, even as they bear witness to the devastation wrought by disobedience and sin, both personal and communal, that led to their downfall.

At the heart of captivity lies a profound sense of dislocation, both geographic and spiritual. The captives find themselves uprooted from their homeland, severed from the familiar rhythms of temple worship, and thrust into an environment that often derides or seeks to erase their very identity. In these foreign surroundings, the struggle to preserve faith becomes synonymous with the struggle to preserve selfhood. When exiled from Zion, the pilgrimage site of sacred promises and divine presence, the descendants of Israel confront an existential crisis: how to remain God's people when stripped of the land, the temple, and the political sovereignty hitherto understood as integral to their covenantal status. This crisis is not merely a historical fact but a spiritual odyssey, an inward journey through which captives confront the echoes of sin reverberating across their history, the collective failures of their ancestors' hearts and nations' leaders that precipitated this fall.

The biblical narrative vividly captures this tension in the lamentations and prayers of those in exile, voices imbued with raw emotion yet tinged with a remarkable tenacity. The psalms and prophetic proclamations during this period reveal faith in extremis: a faith that does not deny pain or anger but acknowledges it as part of the journey towards deeper understanding and restoration. Repentance becomes a pivotal theme here, not an abstract theological concept but a living, breathing response to the harsh reality of captivity. The people are invited to look inward, to examine their roles in the collective sin that brought ruin upon them, to wrestle honestly with guilt and responsibility. This repentance is not merely about obedience in the moment but about rekindling a relationship with God, whose justice has been made manifest in their suffering yet whose mercy holds the promise of redemption.

But repentance in captivity is fraught with complexity. It is shaped by the tension between hope and desolation, between a yearning for return and the harshness of present circumstances. The exiles are forced to confront uncomfortable questions: What does it mean to be God's people when the temple stands desolate? Can God's promises remain valid when the nation lies in ruins? This existential wrestling is echoed in the writings of the prophets who speak within this era, voices that blend stern calls to ethical renewal with visions of future restoration. Their messages carry the weight of divine judgment but also the glimmer of unshakable hope. Through their words, the captives find that while the consequences of sin are severe, they are not irrevocable; the boundaries of captivity do not confine God's capacity for grace.

As the days stretch into years and generations in exile, the challenge of preserving faith becomes a matter of daily survival and spiritual choice. The community's identity, once tethered strongly to land and temple rituals, must adapt and find new means of expression. Religious leaders emerge who emphasize the study of the Torah, communal prayer, and moral rectitude as anchors for sustaining a people bereft of traditional symbols of sanctity. In these adaptations, the seeds of transformation are sown, redefining the contours of faith from an external, place-bound practice into a more internalized, covenantal commitment. The practice of remembering, through recited prayers, songs, and ritual observances, becomes a lifeline that connects the dispersed communities back to their sacred history and collective destiny. This reimagining of faith in captivity exemplifies the dynamic and resilient spirit of a people who refuse to allow their suffering to erase their identity or sever their bond with the divine.

Moreover, the captivity experience serves as a mirror reflecting the consequences of earlier disobedience, a theological lens through which sin's reach is revealed not merely as an individual failing but as a collective force with far-reaching repercussions. The exile is a narrative marker, a historical and spiritual moment demanding introspection at the communal level. It is a sobering reminder that sin's echoes resonate beyond immediate acts, shaping entire nations and defining epochs. The captives' plight is thus interwoven with broader themes of justice, divine justice that disciplines desires, restoration yet. It invites readers to see how human frailty and divine sovereignty interact dynamically, underscoring the inescapable link between moral choices and their consequences. Yet, even amid this somber recognition, the story brims with invitations to trust in hope, no matter how faint it may seem, grounded in the steadfastness of God's promise to reconcile and renew.

Within this tension between judgment and hope, the promise of return begins to kindle a renewed vision, a future illuminated by the prophetic assurances of restoration and grace. This promise does not dissolve the pain of exile nor erase the memories of failure; rather, it offers a vision that transcends immediate suffering, a horizon where the land will be regained, the temple rebuilt, and the covenant reestablished in deeper, more profound ways. The prophets convey that redemption is not a simple reversal of fortune but a transformative process that involves purification, renewed commitment, and a moral realignment with God's will. The captives come to understand that hope is not passive waiting but an active striving toward holiness and righteousness, even in the midst of desolation.

The psychological and spiritual dynamics of captivity expose the intensity of the human condition when removed from familiar anchors and confronted with the stark consequences of sin. The trauma of forced displacement combines with the existential questioning that plagues individuals and communities alike. This dual struggle pushes the captives to wrestle with the very understanding of God's character. Is God's justice purely punitive, or is there scope for mercy and forgiveness amid judgment? Do divine promises endure beyond the collapse of institutions and political power? These inquiries resonate not only within historical captivity but also within the personal spiritual journeys of believers today, who may face seasons of desertion, doubt, or loss. Thus, the captivity experience, while rooted in ancient history, offers a timeless paradigm for understanding the interplay between sin, consequence, repentance, and hope.

The endurance of faith in captivity is not merely an act of nostalgia for a lost past but a radical expression of trust in divine faithfulness. This faith assumes an active posture, cultivating spiritual disciplines that guard the heart against despair and nurture communal bonds. The community's steadfastness is exemplified by figures who lead prayer, teach the laws, and remind their people of God's enduring presence despite physical displacement. Such leaders embody the hope that sustains the people, guiding them toward holistic renewal. Their role highlights the critical importance of memory and narrative in constructing a resilient identity, a reminder that who we are is inseparable from the stories we tell about ourselves and our relationship with God.

This complex interplay between identity, repentance, and hope in captivity has profound implications for understanding sin and grace in biblical theology. Sin is revealed as a disruptor of relationships between human beings and God, among communities, and with creation itself, but also not as an unbreakable chain. The experience of captivity vividly dramatizes sin's consequences, making tangible the cost of broken covenant and moral failure. Yet, interlaced within this somber reality is an enduring thread of grace, manifest in the persistent possibility of repentance and the promise of restoration. This dual recognition invites humility, urging readers to consider the weight of their choices while also embracing the hope that transcends human frailty.

In contemplating life in captivity through this multifaceted lens, a profound lesson emerges about the nature of spiritual resilience. Captivity does not represent a final defeat but a stage in a larger divine narrative, one that encompasses fallenness and redemption in intricate balance. The captives' story models an essential truth about faith: that it can survive and even flourish in the most desolate landscapes when nurtured by repentance and sustained by hope. This truth offers a deep wellspring for personal reflection, encouraging readers to confront their own seasons of captivity, whether literal or metaphorical, and to seek liberation not only from external circumstances but from internal bonds of despair and alienation.

Ultimately, life in captivity becomes a witness to the enduring power of divine mercy and human repentance intertwined. It is a testament to the fact that even in the depths of exile, the human spirit, anchored in covenant faithfulness, can look beyond immediate ruin and sight toward the dawn of redemption. The echoes of sin that once brought devastation resonate still, yet they are met by the louder, resounding call of grace that beckons a new chapter, one where identity is reclaimed, broken relationships are healed, and hope is born anew amid the ruins. This narrative invites every reader to consider how the lessons embedded in captivity can illuminate their own journeys, offering pathways through darkness toward spiritual renewal and restoration.

Calls for Renewal

In the vast tapestry of biblical history, there emerges a recurrent, compelling voice, one that calls not merely for change but for a profound renewal, a turning back to the essence of identity and purpose in the divine relationship. This prophetic call for renewal resonates deeply within the human heart's longing for restoration and hope amid the realities of failure, exile, and the pervasive shadow of sin. It is a summons that transcends mere repentance as an act of regret; it beckons toward a holistic transformation that touches every facet of human life, community, and spiritual orientation. The prophets, those enigmatic and passionate messengers, stand as both witnesses to the brokenness of their times and heralds of a future replete with mercy, justice, and the re-establishment of a covenantal bond centered on grace rather than mere lawfulness. Their words, far from being distant echoes from antiquity, pulse with vital urgency, inviting a dialogue between our ancestral past and the moral complexities of present existence.

To grasp the meaning embedded in these calls for renewal is to begin with an intimate understanding of identity, for the prophets consistently challenge Israel, and through this narrative, all humanity, to reconsider who they are in relation to God. This identity is not static but dynamic, grounded in the acknowledgment that to be chosen is to be called to righteousness, justice, and compassion. In their stark admonitions, prophets like Isaiah, Jeremiah, and Hosea unveil a fundamental dissonance between Israel's self-understanding and its reality; they have strayed from the true essence of their vocation. Yet, amid this confrontation, there is no abandonment, no final verdict of despair. Instead, the prophetic vision harbors an expansive hope, one that sees beyond current judgment to the possibility of restoration. This restoration is not merely external or superficial but a total recalibration of heart and community. It is about recovering the original intention of harmony between the divine and human, between neighbour and neighbour, dissolving the barriers erected by sin and alienation.

Repentance, in this prophetic framework, extends far beyond the individual acts of confession or sorrow. It is portrayed as a communal and existential turning, teshuvah, that requires a return to God's ways in sincerity and action. The prophets underscore the insufficiency of ritual sacrifices or ceremonial piety if they are divorced from justice and mercy. The call is for an authentic inner conversion that naturally flows outward in ethical living. Jeremiah's lamentations, for example, reveal a desire for a heart transformed, a "new heart" and a "new spirit" to replace the hardened soul that has resisted correction. This transformation embodies both the pain of acknowledging failure and the liberating hope in divine forgiveness. Such repentance is not a fleeting moment of regret but a lifelong orientation toward God's redemptive purposes. It demands courage, humility, and a willingness to confront uncomfortable truths about oneself and society. The prophets advocate not only for the turning away from sin but for a turning toward the divine justice that uplifts the downtrodden, protects the vulnerable, and restores broken relationships.

Within these calls for renewal lies an inexhaustible reservoir of hope, anchored in the anticipation of a future where the consequences of sin will be overturned and new life will flourish. This hope is vividly imagined as a time when the desolation wrought by human failure will be replaced by flourishing gardens, peaceful cities, and nations singing in unity. It is a hope that holds on to God's promises as a sure foundation, despite the evident signs of judgment and exile. The prophetic literature often portrays this hope with breathtaking imagery, prophesying the coming of a Messiah or an anointed leader who will mediate justice and peace, reassert divine sovereignty, and inaugurate an era of righteousness. In texts like Isaiah's visionary chapters, the lion shall lie down with the lamb, and swords shall be beaten into plowshares, images that evoke an ultimate reconciliation not only between God and humanity but within creation itself. This future is not a distant abstraction but a tangible horizon drawing nearer through faithfulness and obedience.

The prophetic calls for renewal are also deeply communal. They do not isolate the individual but address the entire people, recognizing that sin's ripple effect shapes societies, economies, and political structures. The prophets call Israel to a renewal that includes justice for the widow, the orphan, the stranger, and the poor. Their scathing critiques of corruption and exploitation reveal a vision of society reconfigured according to divine standards. This renewal requires collective responsibility and the willingness to rebuild not only personal morality but social institutions. The prophetic voice pierces through the noise of superficial religiosity to demand a society where the marginalized find justice and where peace is more than the absence of conflict but the flourishing of right relationships. It is a call not merely to individual piety but to systemic change anchored in covenantal fidelity. Thus, the prophetic hope is also a blueprint for societal transformation, an invitation to live into the fullness of divine justice on earth.

Embedded in these calls is a recognition of the tension between judgment and mercy, a theme woven tightly into the fabric of renewal. The prophets do not shy away from the harsh realities of divine justice, acknowledging that sin has real consequences and that accountability is essential. Yet, this justice is always tempered by mercy, portraying a God who longs to forgive and restore rather than to condemn outright. This precarious balance invites readers to wrestle with the profound nature of divine character, where holiness requires righteousness but love yearns for restoration. The notion of covenant renewal encapsulates this paradox; even when the covenant is broken, God's promise persists, offering a pathway back through repentance and grace. The tension between the inevitability of judgment and the possibility of mercy creates a dynamic space where hope can thrive amid despair and where transformation is possible despite the weight of past failures.

Moreover, the prophetic voice extends beyond Israel's borders to encompass a vision of universal renewal. Some prophets articulate an inclusive hope that transcends national boundaries, envisioning a day when all nations will come to know the one true God and live in peace and justice. This broader perspective underscores the idea that sin, while rooted in human history, is not confined to specific peoples but affects all creation. Consequently, the renewal called for is comprehensive and cosmic, promising a restoration that includes all peoples and the entire created order. The prophetic imagination thus opens a horizon far beyond immediate circumstances to encompass the destiny of humanity within God's sovereign plan. This universality invites contemporary readers to reflect on the global implications of moral renewal and justice, reminding us that the prophetic hope remains unfinished work, necessitating ongoing engagement.

In exploring the nuances of prophetic encouragement, one cannot overlook the deeply personal dimension these calls contain. The prophets speak to individuals not only as members of a collective but as agents of change who bear responsibility for the course of history. Their words stir the conscience, urging self-examination and encouraging a courage that embraces both vulnerability and action. The path of renewal is often portrayed as arduous, fraught with resistance and painful sacrifice, yet illuminated by the assurance of divine presence and support. This dynamic invites a spiritual encounter where personal faith is tested, refined, and deepened through the challenges of repentance and commitment. In this way, the prophetic call is not a distant mandate but an intimate invitation to participate in the unfolding drama of redemption, experiencing firsthand the power of grace to overcome sin's entrenched hold.

The richness of prophetic literature also lies in its ability to speak across temporal boundaries, engaging readers from ancient times to the modern era with its timeless relevance. Contemporary individuals and communities find in these ancient voices a mirror reflecting their own struggles and aspirations. The calls for renewal resonate with enduring human experiences, the search for meaning, the wrestling with guilt and forgiveness, the desire for justice, and the hope for a world where peace and righteousness prevail. The prophetic insistence on an inner and outer transformation challenges complacency and invites active engagement with both personal faith and social responsibility. This dual focus offers a holistic approach to renewal that integrates spiritual renewal with ethical living, fostering a coherence that sustains hope amid complexity and contradiction.

Furthermore, the prophetic calls underscore the importance of memory and narrative in renewal. By recalling Israel's formative experiences, the Exodus, the Sinai covenant, and the teachings of the law, the prophets anchor their call in a rich historical consciousness that validates identity and galvanizes commitment. This collective memory functions as a source of strength and inspiration, reminding the people of their origins and of God's steadfast faithfulness despite recurring failures. Through this lens, renewal becomes a re-encounter with foundational stories, a reclaiming of heritage that empowers present and future generations to live authentically in accordance with divine intention. The past, then, is not a burden but a beacon, illuminating the path forward and infusing the present with purpose.

In addition to recollecting history, the prophetic calls for renewal often employ poetic and symbolic language that evokes the imagination and stirs the soul. This rhetorical brilliance serves to communicate complex theological truths with emotional power and artistic beauty, making the message memorable and transformative. The symbolic imagery, whether of dry bones coming to life, blossoming deserts, or a new covenant inscribed on hearts, creates a vivid experience that transcends mere intellectual assent. It invites readers into a participatory encounter where the abstract concepts of repentance, justice, and hope become tangible realities. This aesthetic dimension enriches the prophetic appeal and enhances its capacity to inspire deep reflection and lasting change.

The prophetic message of renewal also embraces the themes of endurance and perseverance, recognizing that the journey out of sin's shadow is neither quick nor easy. The prophets acknowledge resistance, opposition, and the persistence of hardship, yet they consistently affirm that steadfastness in faith and obedience will ultimately yield fruit. This encouragement fortifies the weary and emboldens the hesitant, offering a vision of victory that is both present and eschatological. The promise of renewal is not simply a distant hope but a living reality that begins now and culminates in the fullness of God's kingdom. This tension between present struggle and future fulfillment creates a rhythm of hope that sustains individuals and communities through trials, inviting them to embody the prophetic vision in tangible ways today.

Moreover, the intertwining of judgment and hope in prophetic calls functions as a corrective to any simplistic or sentimental notions of forgiveness. They confront the complexity of moral failure honestly, rejecting denial or trivialization of sin's harm, yet simultaneously affirming the power of divine grace to heal and restore. This nuanced understanding encourages a balanced perspective that neither dismisses accountability nor loses sight of compassion. It frames renewal as an ongoing process rather than a one-time event, fostering humility and openness to continual growth. This dialectic invites individuals and communities to embrace transformation as a lifelong undertaking that requires vigilance, repentance, and the constant renewal of hope.

The prophetic calls for renewal also reveal an invitation to participate in a divine-human partnership, where human agency and divine initiative intertwine. While God's mercy and justice set the framework for restoration, human response is integral to the unfolding of the renewal narrative. This cooperative dynamic emphasizes responsibility and empowerment, asserting that change is possible not only because of God's grace but also through human commitment to embody divine values in daily life. The prophets' insistence on ethical living and social justice underscores this active role, urging people to be co-workers in the healing of the world. This understanding offers a hopeful vision that neither fatalism nor self-reliance alone can supply, but one grounded in faithful collaboration that transforms history.

Finally, the prophetic calls for renewal open a conversation about the enduring impact of sin and the perpetual need for renewal in every generation. They remind readers that sin is not a static event but a pervasive force that continually challenges human integrity and community cohesion. The need to return, to be renewed, to reorient one's life toward God's will recurs throughout biblical history and remains relevant in contemporary contexts. This cyclical pattern calls for vigilance and humility, recognizing that no generation is immune to the temptation or consequences of sin, but all are invited into the redemptive process. In this light, the prophetic call becomes a timeless invitation, a lifelong journey marked by repentance, hope, and the persistent pursuit of justice and mercy. It is an invitation that beckons each reader into their own story of renewal, encouraging an embrace of grace that transforms not only individuals but the entire community of faith and the world beyond.

Through the evocative and determined voices of the prophets, the call for renewal emerges not as a mere echo from ancient times but as a living, breathing summons to repentance, justice, and hope. It challenges us to reflect deeply on identity and vocation, compelling an authentic turning toward the heart of God's purposes. This renewal, filled with both sobering judgment and radiant mercy, offers a pathway from sin's shadow to the dawn of grace, inviting a future where brokenness is healed, justice prevails, and the enduring relationship between divine and human is restored. In embracing these prophetic calls, contemporary readers step into a transformative dialogue that bridges time and culture, illuminating the path to personal and communal wholeness, and inspiring an ever-deepening journey of faith enlivened by hope.

Return and Rebuilding: Sin's Aftermath

Return from Exile

The return from exile marked one of the most pivotal moments in the saga of Israel's storied relationship with God, a profound transition from despair to hope, from captivity to renewal, and from desolation to a tentative rebuilding of identity. The journey home was not simply a geographical relocation; it signified the rekindling of a covenantal bond fractured by sin, disobedience, and the weighty consequences of rebellion. As the sun cast its first light over the ruins of Jerusalem and the silent stones of the once-mighty Temple, the returning exiles faced not just the physical task of reconstruction but the daunting spiritual challenge of rebuilding a community whose faith and social fabric had been eroded by years of displacement, foreign domination, and cultural fragmentation. It was within this delicate moment that two towering figures arose with remarkably distinct yet complementary calls to leadership: Ezra, the scribe and teacher dedicated to spiritual restoration through the law, and Nehemiah, the pragmatic and resolute governor whose vision encompassed not only walls and city gates but the restoration of order and justice among the people.

The journey home itself was arduous, bristling with uncertainties and dangers, both natural and political. The exiles, many of whom had become deeply assimilated into Babylonian and Persian cultures over decades, carried within them the dual burdens of nostalgia and fear. Their memories of a distant homeland were shaded by the grief of loss, the shame of exile, and the wounds of a people scattered across foreign lands. For some, the promise of return was fraught with skepticism, did their God still watch over this land? Would their neighbors receive them as rightful inhabitants or as vulnerable remnants of a defeated nation? The physical journey wove through landscapes scarred by neglect, where villages lay abandoned and fields had gone fallow, striking a sharp contrast to the vibrant hope blossoming in the hearts of those who dared to dream of rebuilding. Yet the emotional and spiritual journey proved far more complex. The collective psyche wrestled with the legacy of sin, the idolatry, the neglect of the law, and social injustices that had provoked divine judgment. A profound sense of accountability lingered, coloring the return with humility and a resolve that the mistakes of the past would not be repeated.

Ezra's arrival in Jerusalem introduced a transformative spiritual dynamic aimed at re-centering the community's identity around the Torah. His leadership was distinguished by a profound conviction that the law of God must serve as the foundation for societal renewal and personal repentance. Unpacking the sacred scrolls before the people, Ezra's voice carried both gravity and promise, urging a people long removed from their covenantal roots to listen, understand, and embrace the statutes that defined their special relationship with Yahweh. His public reading of the law was not a mere ritual but a radical act of reclamation, a call to remember who they were as a people chosen to embody holiness and justice in a world beset by moral decay. This moment rekindled a collective consciousness steeped in reverence but also challenge. How could a fractured community, marked by intermarriage and diluted traditions, reclaim its sanctity? Ezra's response was uncompromising: renewal required repentance, reformation, and a rigorous commitment to the law's demands. The social and religious implications were immense. The people had to confront sins that were both communal and personal, including the painful issue of intermarriage with surrounding nations deemed incompatible with the covenant. This crisis underscored the tension between the desire for unity and identity preservation and the realities of diasporic blending.

Meanwhile, Nehemiah's practical and resolute leadership focused on the tangible restoration of Jerusalem's defenses and infrastructure, recognizing that the physical security of the city was inseparable from its spiritual vitality. When Nehemiah arrived as the appointed governor under Persian authority, the city was vulnerable, its gates broken down, walls shattered, leaving the inhabitants exposed to threats from hostile neighbors and internal disorder. Nehemiah's plan was bold and urgent; he rallied the people to labor side by side, defending their families while rebuilding the city's walls in the face of mockery, threats, and sabotage. His leadership was marked by a rare combination of administrative acumen, unyielding faith, and strategic diplomacy, as he engaged both the Persian court and local adversaries to secure the city's viability. The reconstructive effort was symbolic on multiple levels: the walls represented not only security but the re-establishment of communal boundaries and a necessary barrier against the corruption and lawlessness that had plagued the nation previously. The rebuilding of physical boundaries thus paralleled a spiritual boundary-setting, inviting the people to rededicate themselves to purity, justice, and covenantal obedience.

However, the challenges Nehemiah and Ezra faced extended well beyond the stones and scrolls. Returning from exile meant navigating complicated social dynamics, including reopening wounds of past betrayals and dealing with economic exploitation that had intensified during their absence. Many of the returning exiles found themselves impoverished, while a class of wealthy elites, often those who had remained or prospered under foreign rule, controlled the land and resources. Nehemiah's confrontation with these injustices reflected a broader biblical theme linking sin to social inequality and the neglect of the vulnerable. He called for debt relief, the return of lands, and an end to the oppression of widows and orphans, challenging the community to live out the ethical demands of the Torah. This required courage because it involved confronting entrenched interests as well as collective complicity in systemic sin. The narrative of return thus transcended physical restoration to encompass moral and economic reformation, emphasizing that sin was not merely individual but embedded in structures and relationships.

The community's struggles included confronting internal dissent and skepticism. Not all inhabitants embraced the radical vision of covenantal renewal. Some resisted the imposition of strict legal codes, while others remained indifferent to the spiritual revival that Ezra championed. This tension highlighted the complexity of communal restoration, the necessary interplay between law and grace, justice and mercy, discipline and forgiveness. Ezra's public confessions of sin and collective mourning sessions modeled a penitential posture designed to heal divisions and awaken spiritual sensitivity. These moments of liturgical repentance functioned as communal catharses, reminding the people of their collective accountability and the grace available through genuine contrition and divine forgiveness.

Moreover, the return raised profound questions about identity in a world progressively shaped by imperial powers and cultural crosscurrents. The returning exiles did not re-enter a blank slate; Jerusalem and its territory were inhabited by individuals and groups who had settled in their absence, including Samaritans and other peoples with competing religious and political claims. Nehemiah's stern refusal to allow foreigners to participate fully in the rebuilding project reflected a protective stance toward preserving the purity of Israelite worship and identity. Yet these exclusivist measures also echoed the ongoing biblical tension between holiness and hospitality, separation and integration. The narrative of return thus embodied a paradox: the longing to re-establish a distinct covenant community within the complexities of an ever-changing world order that demanded adaptability without losing foundational faith commitments.

In the spiritual dimension, the return from exile was a profound exercise in hope mingled with mourning. The people were acutely aware that their restored city and temple could never fully compensate for the grandeur lost during the exile or the innocence forfeited in Eden. Yet the journey home also revealed the persistence of God's covenantal promises amidst human frailty and failure. The prophets who had preceded and punctuated the exile, such as Jeremiah and Ezekiel, had spoken of a new covenant and a hope that transcended the calamities of the past. The return was the beginning of that prophetic fulfillment, not as a final destination but as a step in an ongoing journey of restoration and redemption. It was a testament to the divine balance of justice and mercy, a recognition that while sin had caused exile, divine mercy facilitated return, and divine grace sustained the reluctant yet hopeful people through the arduous task of rebuilding.

The emotional texture of this time was woven with longing for a restored past and a cautious trust in a hopeful future. The returned community had to wrestle daily with memories of exile's pain, challenges of poverty, and the persistent shadows of guilt. Yet this fragility was met with moments of spiritual renewal, festivals celebrated with renewed fervor, public readings of the law that reanimated communal identity, and the rekindling of religious practices that formed the core of Israelite life. It was a time of fragile beginnings, marked by tentative steps toward a horizon illuminated by divine promise but shadowed by human sinfulness.

Ezra and Nehemiah's combined leadership modeled the intricate balance needed in such a period: a commitment to spiritual purity and covenantal fidelity paired with pragmatic governance and social justice. Their stories remind us that returning home, whether from exile or from any form of dislocation, entails confronting both the visible ruins and the invisible fissures within the self and community. It requires courage to face not only external enemies but internal divisions, not only structural rebuilding but heart renewal. Their legacies urge modern readers to consider how restoration always invites not only physical rebuilding but moral and spiritual awakening, and how the echoes of ancient sin continue to whisper in the challenges of community, identity, and faith.

The return from exile was thus a complex and tumultuous journey, a pilgrimage of accountability and hope, destruction and rebuilding, judgment and mercy. It pressed the people of Israel to reevaluate what it truly meant to be a chosen people in covenant with their holy God, a task as demanding then as it remains relevant today. In embracing the law with renewed passion and reconstructing the walls with steadfast resolve, the returning exiles took their first collective steps toward a future shaped by redemption but always shadowed by the echoes of their shared sin. Their story invites us into a reflective dialogue on how communities recover from brokenness, how leadership must balance firmness with compassion, and how the interplay of history and theology shapes our understanding of justice, mercy, and grace across time.

Rebuilding the Temple

In the aftermath of exile, when the people of Israel found themselves scattered and their homeland a shadowed memory, the task of rebuilding both a physical edifice and a fractured identity became paramount. The destruction of the Temple in Jerusalem was not merely the loss of a building; it was a profound rupture in the spiritual heart of the nation. The Temple was more than stone and timber; it was the focal point of worship, the tangible symbol of God's presence among His people, and the center around which social cohesion revolved. With the return from Babylonian captivity, the challenge was not only to restore the Temple's walls and altar but also to rekindle a community that had been splintered by displacement, despair, and disillusionment. This monumental endeavor of spiritual and communal restoration found its most resolute champions in Ezra and Nehemiah, who emerge from the biblical narrative as visionary leaders, deftly navigating the complex terrain of rebuilding a nation's faith and social fabric amidst daunting opposition.

Ezra, the scribe and priest, returned to Jerusalem charged with a sacred mandate to renew the covenantal relationship between God and His people. Arriving several decades after the initial return, his mission was not merely architectural but theological, to restore the law of Moses as the cornerstone of Israelite identity and to revive worship practices that had grown lax or were compromised by prolonged exile. His leadership was marked by a profound understanding that the physical reconstruction of the Temple was incomplete without the reformation of the people's hearts and the reinstatement of a holy lifestyle. The Temple had to be a living reality rather than a hollow relic, so Ezra undertook the daunting task of reading the Law publicly to an assembled crowd, many of whom had grown distant from their heritage. The public reading on the first day of the seventh month, marked by the Feast of Trumpets, resonated deeply as a profound moment of awakening. The people wept as they heard words that spoke of covenantal obligations, divine commands, and the blessings and curses tied to loyalty or rebellion. Yet, Ezra's purpose was not to condemn but to invite repentance and renewal. His passionate exhortations called for a recommitment to God's statutes, and though initially met with sorrow for past failures, the community gradually embraced a renewed vision of holiness and obedience.

Simultaneously, the communal restoration demanded attention, for years of exile had eroded social bonds and blurred tribal and familial identities. Marriages had been intermingled with foreign peoples, economic disparities had widened, and the land itself lay untended in many places. Ezra confronted these issues head-on, addressing the intermarriage between Israelites and surrounding peoples, which he perceived as a threat to the purity of the covenant and the distinctiveness of Israel's identity. His stance, while controversial and difficult, reflected a deep concern that without clear boundaries and a return to the covenant's demands, the fragile restoration would unravel. This meant not just military or political power but spiritual fidelity was essential for the survival and flourishing of the community. Ezra's leadership was grounded in the belief that obedience to the Law constituted the core of Israel's identity and destiny, a responsibility given by God to His chosen people. Through his instruction and reforms, the people were reminded that their fate was intertwined with their faithfulness, spurring a movement of collective repentance and recommitment.

In this milieu, Nehemiah's leadership complementarily addressed the more tangible, social, and political dimensions of restoration. While Ezra focused on spiritual renewal, Nehemiah took on the formidable task of rebuilding the city's physical defenses. Arriving in Jerusalem as a cupbearer to the Persian king Artaxerxes, Nehemiah's heart burned with concern for the broken walls and exposed vulnerability of the city. His marriage of diplomatic savvy, organizational acumen, and prayerful dependence on God was the catalyst that galvanized the community into action. The broken walls were not merely a security risk; they symbolized the community's shattered dignity and exposed weakness. Nehemiah understood that without these walls, the people of Jerusalem could hardly thrive, vulnerable to both external attacks and internal chaos.

What Nehemiah achieved was nothing short of remarkable. He mobilized the diverse inhabitants of the city, priests, nobles, goldsmiths, merchants, to labor side by side. This collective effort, punctuated by the constant threat of opposition from hostile neighbors and internal discouragement, was a powerful statement of communal solidarity and shared destiny. The physical rebuilding of the walls was undertaken not just with bricks and mortar but with a renewed sense of identity and purpose. The threat of sabotage from surrounding peoples, who derided and threatened the workers, served to strengthen rather than break the resolve of the Israelite community. Nehemiah's leadership also involved instituting social reforms, as he confronted abuses such as the exploitation of the poor by wealthy elites who demanded exorbitant interest on loans, leading to widespread poverty and bondage. His call for economic justice, including the cancellation of debts and restoration of property, was deeply tied to the Torah's concern for equity and compassion within the community. This integrated vision, where physical security, social justice, and religious devotion were inseparable, fundamentally shaped the trajectory of the restored Jerusalem.

More than simply rebuilding structures, the efforts of Ezra and Nehemiah represent a profound model of holistic restoration. Their work elucidates how spiritual revival and practical governance are intertwined in the process of reconstituting a broken people. The Temple, as reconstructed, stood as a beacon of hope and a tangible reaffirmation of God's enduring presence. It was no longer a distant memory but a renovated heart of worship, inviting the community into a renewed covenantal relationship. The restoration efforts extended beyond stone and rituals; they touched on the deep human need for belonging, identity, and meaning. The community had to reclaim their story, their laws, and their God in order to flourish in a world that was no longer the same as before exile.

The narratives recorded in the biblical accounts of Ezra and Nehemiah also reveal the complexity of restoration. This was not a seamless process but one fraught with opposition, setbacks, and prayers of supplication. The enemies of Jerusalem sought to disrupt and discourage the work, reflecting the ongoing spiritual warfare that borders on the mundane reality of leadership. Yet, through steadfast faith and pragmatic action, the leaders and their communities persisted. They constantly turned to God in prayer, asking for protection, wisdom, and favor, demonstrating that restoration is as much a matter of divine grace as human endeavor.

This restorative period also reinvigorated the importance of the Law, not merely as a static code but as a living framework for relational and communal life. The recitation and understanding of the Law cultivated a collective consciousness centered on God's justice, mercy, and holiness. Ezra, as a teacher and interpreter of the Law, empowered the people to see their history and identity through a theological lens, connecting their past to a hopeful future. In this way, the Law became a lens for ethical behavior, social responsibility, and communal cohesion that would sustain the people in the years ahead.

As the Temple was rededicated and the city walls rebuilt, the community celebrated not only physical achievements but spiritual victories. Their renewed worship included offerings, festivals, and public readings of the scriptures that reinforced their commitment to God and to one another. This was more than ritual; it was an act of public identity that proclaimed a collective hope despite past trials. It was a testimony to the resilience of faith when embraced with sincerity and courage.

The work of Ezra and Nehemiah holds profound implications even today. Their story challenges contemporary readers to contemplate the depth and scope of restoration needed in personal and communal life. Just as Israel needed both spiritual repentance and tangible acts of rebuilding, modern communities face intertwined challenges of moral renewal and social reconstruction. The balance of faith and works, prayer and action, repentance and justice remains crucial. Furthermore, their legacy invites reflection on leadership that is both visionary and practical, one that listens for divine guidance while confronting harsh realities with determination and compassion.

In the end, the rebuilding of the Temple under Ezra and Nehemiah stands as a testament to the enduring power of restoration. It is a narrative steeped in courage, faith, and resilience, reflecting the ancient conviction that no matter how profound the ruin, the hand of God can restore and that human cooperation with divine purposes is essential in that process. Their combined efforts encapsulate a profound truth that echoes across time: that true restoration involves the transformation of hearts, communities, and environments alike, forging a renewed covenant that reaches beyond bricks and mortar to the very core of human existence. In this ancient story of rebuilding, we find a living blueprint for how fractured lives and societies can be renewed with patience, faith, and collective endeavor, guided by a God who remains present in the midst of brokenness and hope.

Renewed Covenant Commitment

The narrative of renewal and recommitment encapsulated in the books of Ezra and Nehemiah stands as a stirring testament to the enduring power of covenant, an emblem not only of divine promise but also of human resolve. After decades of exile and displacement, the return of the Jewish people to Jerusalem was nothing short of a seismic moment, suffused with the weight of history, hope, and a determined desire to restore what had been lost. Yet, this return was not merely geographical; it was a profound spiritual and communal reawakening, declaring unequivocally that the covenant between God and His people remained alive, though tested, fragile, and in dire need of affirmation. At the heart of this movement were Ezra and Nehemiah, two figures whose leadership, distinct yet complementary, coalesced around the urgent necessity of reaffirming God's law as the foundation of Israel's identity and future stability.

Ezra, a scribe and priest of profound learning and spiritual conviction, emerges as the central instrument in restoring not only the physical presence of God's people in their ancestral land but also the authority and sanctity of the Mosaic Law that defined their relationship with God. The law had been neglected, misunderstood, or outright ignored during the years of exile and oppression, allowing sin and disorder to infiltrate the social fabric of Israel. Ezra's mission was a clarion call to return to the original covenant, to the statutes and commandments handed down from Sinai, which were now the keystone in rebuilding the shattered community's moral and spiritual compass. His reading of the law before the gathered assembly by the Water Gate was nothing short of revolutionary, a public declaration that the covenant was not a relic of the past but a living document to which Israel was bound by divine mandate and collective memory. The event was charged with emotion, people wept openly as they confronted their failings and the vast chasm between their current state and the holiness prescribed by God. Yet, this was not an act of despair; rather, it was an opening of hearts, a communal confession that set the stage for true repentance and renewal.

Nehemiah's role complements Ezra's spiritual revival with pragmatic and visionary leadership aimed at physical and social restoration. Tasked with rebuilding the walls of Jerusalem, Nehemiah understood that material security was indispensable to the flourishing of God's law and the covenant community. The walls were not mere stone and mortar; they were a bulwark protecting the sanctity of the restored city, a symbol of regained identity, dignity, and divine protection. This monumental task was fraught with external opposition and internal strife, yet Nehemiah's steadfast commitment and unyielding faith galvanized the people to overcome these obstacles. Through his stewardship, the covenant was not only renewed in words but also in deeds, laws and ordinances were enforced, social injustices addressed, and the community instructed in a way that revitalized the ethical and legal standards set forth by their ancestors. The rebuilding of Jerusalem under Nehemiah's guidance embodies the inextricable link between divine law and societal order; the restoration of one necessitated the restoration of the other.

Together, Ezra and Nehemiah's leadership dramatizes a dynamic tension between renewal through divine revelation and renewal through human action. The reiteration of God's law, superimposed upon the collective memory and experience of the people, was a deliberate and strategic endeavor to re-anchor Israel's identity amid a fragile geopolitical and spiritual landscape. The law was no longer just a divine command; it was a social contract and a means by which the people could guard themselves against the syncretism, corruption, and moral erosion that exile had wrought. This reengagement with the law required profound repentance, which entailed acknowledging communal sins such as intermarriage with foreign peoples, neglect of Sabbath observance, and failure to uphold justice and mercy, the pillars of godly living. The renewal was marked by rigorous covenantal pledges in which the people committed themselves anew to live according to the requirements of the law, consciously aware that their fortunes depended on their fidelity to God's covenant.

What makes this period particularly compelling and nuanced is the recognition that reaffirming God's law was not a mere administrative or religious formality. It was a deeply transformative process that invited the people into a renewed relationship with God and with one another. It was about restoring trust, rediscovering purpose, and reimagining the possibilities of communal life under God's sovereign rule. The covenant was a covenant of both privilege and responsibility, an invitation to live in conformity with divine holiness and to be a light to the nations around them. Ezra's public reading of the law did more than instruct; it inspired a collective moral awakening, while Nehemiah's reconstruction of Jerusalem's defenses signaled a readiness to defend and preserve this sacred heritage against all odds. This dual approach mirrored the original covenantal framework in which law and land, spirit and society, justice and faithfulness were inseparably intertwined.

In delving deeper into the theological significance of this covenant renewal, one cannot ignore the interplay between divine mercy and human accountability that characterizes the actions and motivations of both leaders. God's faithfulness amidst Israel's repeated failings is a thread that runs conclusively throughout these texts, underscoring that while sin has consequences and demands repentance, God's mercy remains steadfast, offering restoration rather than condemnation. This echoes earlier biblical narratives where, despite humanity's transgressions, God continually extends grace and invites His people back into fellowship through covenant reaffirmation. Yet, the renewed covenant also emphasizes that this mercy is not permissive but conditional, obedience to the law and genuine repentance are necessary responses to God's enduring love. The process of renewal was therefore as much about awakening dormant faith as it was about implementing practical reforms to tighten the community's adherence to God's statutes, reinforcing an ethic that intertwined personal sanctity with communal well-being.

This covenantal reestablishment under Ezra and Nehemiah also functions as a critical hinge point in biblical history, bridging the post-exilic period with the unfolding narrative of Israel's religious identity. The primacy given to the written law during this era solidified its place as the authoritative guide for future generations. It framed Israel's understanding of itself not simply as a people restored to a physical city, but as a people called once again to live out their distinctiveness through holiness, justice, and obedience to divine ordinances. The renewed commitment to the law carried with it profound implications for the social, political, and religious structures of the community, influencing everything from judicial proceedings and temple worship to family life and economic practices. It beseeched Israel to resist complacency, urging vigilance in guarding against the erosion of covenantal fidelity that had once led to disaster and exile.

What reverberates through the story of Ezra and Nehemiah's leadership is the recognition that covenant renewal is a cyclical and ongoing necessity. The challenges that precipitated exile, disobedience, disregard for God's commandments, and fragmented communal life, did not vanish with the rebuilding of Jerusalem's walls or the public proclamation of the law. Rather, these efforts were the beginnings of what the biblical narrative invites believers into: a continual process of repentance, restoration, and recommitment. The journey of the returned exiles encourages modern readers to reflect on the ways their own communities and personal lives require such revisiting and reaffirming of commitments to moral and spiritual principles. The covenant is presented not as a static agreement but as a living relationship that demands attention, renewal, and sometimes costly alteration in response to shifting circumstances and persistent temptations.

Moreover, the intertwined leadership of Ezra and Nehemiah exemplifies a model of faithful stewardship that balances adherence to divine law with the necessary courage and practical wisdom to enact reform. Their example is instructive not only for their immediate context but also for contemporary faith communities confronting the tension between tradition and renewal, spiritual ideals and real-world complexities. By acknowledging their failings and undertaking the tangible work of rebuilding, these leaders affirm that faithfulness is both an inward devotion and an outward expression, requiring both contemplation and action. The comprehensive renewal they sought was as much about rebuilding hearts as it was about rebuilding walls, a holistic restoration that invites a fuller understanding of covenant as inclusive of law, grace, community, and individual responsibility.

The profound effect of this covenantal recommitment extended beyond the immediate generation. Its ripple effects can be traced in the subsequent prophetic voices and even in the New Testament's engagement with the themes of law, grace, and redemption. The renewed adherence to the Law re-centered Israel's spiritual life on its sacred texts and commandments, creating a foundation from which Christ's teachings and the early Christian movement would emerge, often positioning themselves in conversation with this reinvigorated tradition. In this light, Ezra and Nehemiah's work does not merely conclude a chapter of restoration but opens a horizon for further theological reflection and spiritual transformation, evidencing how the echoes of sin and redemption continue to resound through history, shaping the contours of faith and practice for generations to come.

Thus, the reaffirmation of God's law under Ezra and Nehemiah is a vivid illustration of how divine justice and mercy operate hand in hand, calling for accountability while offering restoration. It reveals a God who actively pursues His people despite their waywardness, inviting them back into covenantal intimacy through repentance and obedience. The narrative challenges individuals and communities alike to remember that the invitation to covenant fidelity is enduring and inexhaustible, requiring ongoing engagement and courage. In their leadership, Ezra and Nehemiah beckon readers to a deeper understanding of how covenant renewal can serve as a powerful catalyst for spiritual renewal, moral clarity, and communal resilience, a call to embrace the timeless challenge and grace of living lives rooted in God's law and mercy, ever mindful of the echoes of sin that demand vigilance, repentance, and hope.

Wisdom Literature: Sin and Human Choice

Proverbs on Wisdom and Sin

In the vast expanse of biblical literature, the Book of Proverbs stands as a timeless fountain of wisdom, its verses rippling through the ages with practical guidance and profound philosophical insight. It is within these ancient sayings that we find a distinctive approach to sin, not merely as a divine decree waiting to be broken but as a tangible reality woven into the fabric of human experience, a moral force that shapes lives in subtle and sweeping ways. The Proverbs invite us into a reflective dialogue, offering pearls of wisdom that transcend time, culture, and even theological boundaries, making it possible for all seekers of truth to engage meaningfully with the complexities of wrongdoing and virtue. They reveal a world where sin is not an abstract concept but an experiential truth to be recognized and navigated with deliberate care, underscoring the importance of wisdom as the compass that guides individuals through the thorny crossroads of moral decision-making.

At the heart of the Proverbs' discourse on sin lies a fundamental understanding of human nature, its frailty, tendencies, and capacity for both greatness and downfall. The writers of Proverbs paint sin not as a sudden, isolated act but as a progression, often beginning with a flawed thought or desire. The waywardness of the heart, the deceitfulness of intentions, and the allure of forbidden paths combine to set the stage for transgression. This portrayal brings an immediacy to sin; it is not merely the breaking of commandments or laws but the unfolding of character failures that manifest in choices, words, and deeds. The text cautions that sin often begins quietly, in the realm of thought and attitude, lurking unnoticed until it blooms into tangible harm, whether harm to oneself or others. This philosophical perspective invites a mindful vigilance, urging readers to cultivate self-awareness and moral clarity as the first line of defense against the entanglements of wrongdoing.

Wisdom, in this context, is not simply knowledge or intelligence but a lived, embodied understanding of how to align one's life with what is good and true. Proverbs frequently personifies wisdom as a noble woman calling out in the public squares, inviting all who pass by to embrace her counsel and thereby avoid the pitfalls of folly and sin. This vivid personification serves as a metaphor for an accessible, proactive choice to live with attentiveness and moral insight. Embracing wisdom means valuing prudence, discernment, and self-control, qualities that stand in direct opposition to the impulsiveness, arrogance, and deceit that often accompany sinful behaviors. The practical guidance here is both intimate and expansive; it recognizes that life unfolds in a web of relationships and choices, and that wisdom is the thread that holds this web together, tempting individuals toward grace rather than ruin.

One striking feature of Proverbs' philosophical reflections on sin is the emphasis on consequences, both immediate and far-reaching. Rather than minimization or relativism, the text presents a cause-and-effect dynamic with unwavering clarity. The seduction of sinners and the seductive words of the deceitful are depicted as nets or traps, ensnaring those who lack wisdom and leading them toward destruction. The parallel imagery of paths, one leading to life, the other to death, underscores the existential stakes of moral choices. This vivid framing grounds sin in real-world outcomes: broken families, shattered reputations, lost opportunities, and spiritual exile. This pragmatic approach avoids abstract condemnation and instead calls for careful stewardship of one's life, highlighting the gravity and seriousness with which sin should be regarded. It summons readers to consider that sin is not an isolated shame but a trajectory with tangible repercussions, rippling through personal existence and community wellbeing.

The social dimension of sin, especially within the Proverbs, further deepens our understanding of its pervasive effects. Sin is shown to corrode not only the individual but the fabric of human relationships and society at large. The dishonesty of a wicked man, the gossip of a slanderer, or the violence of a ruthless ruler, these actions are not confined to personal failings but actively undermine trust, justice, and peace. The Proverbs vividly articulate how systemic and interpersonal evils stem from moral failure, echoing the biblical theme that sin fractures the harmony that once existed in creation. Such insights challenge readers to look beyond personal guilt toward communal responsibility, to appreciate that ethical living demands more than avoiding personal sin; it requires active engagement in fostering righteousness within one's social environment. This communal emphasis resonates deeply with contemporary concerns, providing a robust foundation for ethics that transcends private spirituality and engages the public square.

Embedded within the practical advice of the Proverbs is a pervasive call to cultivate the "fear of the Lord," which anchors the entire discourse on wisdom and sin. Far from being a fear grounded in terror or dread, this reverence represents a profound respect and acknowledgement of divine authority and moral order. It is the wellspring from which wisdom flows and the framework within which human behavior is ordered. The fear of the Lord serves as a safeguard against hubris, introducing humility as an essential virtue to counteract the pride that often fuels sin. This theological grounding situates the moral struggle within an overarching spiritual narrative, linking human choice with divine expectation and cosmic justice. It elevates the discussion beyond mere human pragmatism, inviting readers into a transformative relationship with God that forms the foundation for genuine moral integrity.

Furthermore, Proverbs approaches the theme of sin with an acute awareness of human vulnerability and the allure of temptation. Sin is not depicted as an insurmountable obstacle but as a challenge to be confronted with wisdom and resolve. The seductions of wealth, pleasure, and power are portrayed as tests that require fortitude and reflection. This balances the severity of sin with the possibility of resistance and redemption, emphasizing personal agency amid human weakness. The practical guidance offered is not fatalistic but empowering; it charts a path where individuals can cultivate habits and character traits that fortify them against the enticements of sin. For instance, the warnings against the "adulterous woman" or the "scorner" are more than moralistic proscriptions, they are cautionary narratives about the dangers that ensnare those who fail to heed wisdom's call, highlighting the need for continual vigilance and self-discipline.

The Proverbs also provide profound insights into the nature of repentance and forgiveness within the moral order. While they extensively detail the outcomes of sinful behavior, they do not abandon hope for restoration. The recognition of sin is the first step on the path back to wholeness, and wisdom calls for humility to admit faults and seek correction. This dimension of the Proverbs is often subtle but nonetheless pivotal: it fosters a mindset open to transformation, learning, and growth. The tension between justice, the inevitable consequence of sin, and mercy, the possibility of renewal, is ever-present, reflecting a dynamic interplay rather than a static dichotomy. This nuanced approach encourages readers to engage honestly with their own failings while holding fast to the hope that change is always attainable through conscious effort and divine grace.

Engaging with Proverbs on wisdom and sin also invites reflection on the inner workings of the human heart and mind. The text recognizes that the battle against sin is not simply external but begins in the hidden chambers of impulse, motive, and desire. Wisdom calls for introspection, urging individuals to examine their own inclinations and to be wary of self-deception. The imagery of guarding one's heart is pervasive, emphasizing that the quality of life flows from the condition of one's innermost being. This psychological depth complements the ethical framework, highlighting that true moral living requires honesty and insight into oneself as much as compliance with external norms. Within this inward journey, wisdom serves as a guiding light, bringing clarity to complex inner terrain and pointing toward authentic transformation.

In addition to personal introspection, Proverbs underscores the importance of learned counsel and community support in overcoming sin. The admonition to seek advice, to listen to correction, and to remain teachable reflects a communal vision of moral growth. Wisdom thrives in dialogue and shared accountability, resisting isolation and arrogance. This social dimension illustrates that moral vigilance is a collective endeavor, where the wise are those who not only guard their own conduct but also contribute to the ethical health of their communities. Such insights resonate powerfully in contemporary contexts, where individualism often overshadows the significance of communal wisdom and mutual responsibility.

Moreover, Proverbs consistently highlights the contrast between wisdom and folly as a central axis upon which the discourse on sin revolves. Folly is characterized by impulsiveness, ignorance, and the rejection of moral order, traits that inexorably lead to downfall. The seductive allure of folly is not overlooked; rather, it is depicted as a choice made in blindness or rebellion against the voice of wisdom. This stark juxtaposition underscores the gravity of human freedom, each person stands at the crossroads of choosing wisdom or folly, life or death, wholeness or ruin. The clarity of this binary invites readers to recognize the moral clarity available even amid life's complexities and to appreciate that sin is ultimately aligned with folly, alienation, and destruction.

The practical orientation of Proverbs on sin also reflects a nuanced understanding of the moral landscape that includes subtle forms of wrongdoing. Not all sins are overt or catastrophic; many are embedded in everyday attitudes and behaviors, pride, envy, laziness, harsh speech, injustice. The cumulative effect of these "small" sins is acknowledged as corrosive, a slow erosion of moral character that ultimately leads to profound damage. This attention to the gradations of sin encourages vigilance toward the seemingly minor choices that often escape notice until they have hardened into patterns. The wisdom imparted is thus comprehensive and anticipatory, equipping individuals to recognize and address the early signs of moral slippage before they flare into full-blown transgression.

At the same time, Proverbs offers a refreshing perspective that treats humans not as doomed to perpetually fall but as capable of flourishing when wisdom is embraced. The celebration of righteousness, honesty, generosity, and humility reveals an alternative way of living marked by joy, security, and peace. These virtues are not abstract ideals but concrete expressions of a life in tune with divine order. Their benefits are tangible in social relations and personal well-being, providing a compelling incentive to pursue wisdom and resist sin. This positive vision elevates the discourse from mere rules to a holistic, life-affirming philosophy where moral living is synonymous with flourishing and fulfillment.

In the final analysis, the Proverbs on wisdom and sin constitute a rich philosophical and practical discourse that continues to resonate deeply in our contemporary moral and spiritual conversations. They challenge readers to acknowledge the pervasive presence of sin in human life without succumbing to despair, to embrace wisdom not as theoretical knowledge but as a vibrant way of living, and to appreciate the profound consequences of human choices. More than a collection of maxims, the Proverbs offer a framework for navigating the complexities of moral existence, highlighting the interplay of intellect, emotion, community, and spirituality. Their timeless call is to awaken to the possibilities of transformation, to live with intentionality and insight, and to pursue a path marked by reverence, integrity, and hope. In doing so, they invite each reader into a journey where the echoes of sin can be met not with resignation but with the courageous embrace of wisdom's enduring light.

Ecclesiastes: The Search for Meaning

The voice of Ecclesiastes resonates through the corridors of time with a haunting melancholy, a meditation on the ephemeral nature of human existence that pierces the heart of scripture's reflection on sin and meaning. This enigmatic book, often attributed to the figure of "the Preacher," known traditionally as Solomon, provides a profound philosophical lens through which we may examine the perplexing interplay between life's futility and the shadows cast by sin. Within its pages lies a relentless confrontation with the paradox of human endeavor, a ceaseless striving for significance in a world marked by impermanence and, often, unintelligible suffering. The fragile thread of purpose that holds together personal and communal identity is, according to Ecclesiastes, painfully thin and precarious, fluttering in the cold winds of vanity and shadow. This text dares to ask what meaning can persist when all human accomplishments, pleasures, and even wisdom itself seem to dissolve into the vapor of "hevel," a Hebrew term evoking breath, vapor, or mere fleetingness.

The persistent refrain, that all is "vanity of vanities" and "a chasing after wind", does not merely express despondency but a radical honesty about the human condition exposed to the ravages of sin and the inscrutable decrees of divine providence. Unlike other biblical narratives that emphasize clear pathways of righteousness and reward, Ecclesiastes plunges into the murkiness of existence where justice seems obscured and the consequences of choices remain unpredictably entangled with chance. The Preacher wrestles with the dissonance between the ideal and the real, between divine justice and human experience. Sin here is not presented solely as transgressions punctuating a moral ledger, but as an ingrained atmosphere, a pervasive condition that casts doubt on the ultimate efficacy of human seeking and the durability of all worldly things. The weight of death, the great equalizer, looms over every effort and ambition, reminding purposeful agents that mortality erases much of what they laboriously construct. This becomes a sobering backdrop to reflections on the vanity of both righteousness and wickedness, suggesting a cyclical and enigmatic order that refuses simplistic resolution.

Yet, the search for meaning, even amid such apparent futility, is not abandoned. Here, sin becomes a catalyst for deeper philosophical inquiry, an impetus to probe beyond superficial pleasures, achievements, and legalistic piety toward an existential assessment that demands humility before the inscrutable. The Preacher acknowledges that wisdom, whilst valuable, is also shadowed by sorrow, introducing a complexity that often escapes dogmatic readings. The accumulation of knowledge intensifies the awareness of life's fleeting nature and the inevitability of death, intensifying the paradox instead of resolving it. In this light, sin is not only personal wrongdoing but an element of cosmic tension, a condition that corrupts the natural order and distorts human understanding. The futility of vanity, pleasure, and toil is unmasked, revealing an existential vacuum that traditional metrics of success or righteousness fail to fill. The book thereby challenges readers to reconsider where true value lies in a world dominated by the brevity of life and the ubiquity of moral imperfection.

This sobering exploration reaches its theological crescendo in the recognition that despite the mysteries and ambiguities, there is a divinely ordained response appropriate for humanity. "Fear God and keep his commandments," the Preacher asserts, positioning this reverence and obedience as the anchor amidst life's ephemeral currents. This conclusion, far from a simplistic formula, resonates as a profound surrender, a mode of navigating the ambiguities imparted by sin and mortality. To "fear" God here is not mere terror but a reverent acknowledgment of divine sovereignty, a recognition of human limitation, and an acceptance of moral boundaries etched by the Creator. This provides a counterbalance to vanity, offering a grounding principle for living amidst uncertainty and moral ambiguity. It recognizes that the pursuit of meaning cannot be detached from a relationship to the divine, one that transcends human logic and temporal achievements. The reverential obedience suggested is thus an ethical and spiritual posture, a response born from grappling with sin's consequences and life's inherent paradoxes.

Intriguingly, the book's discourse on sin does not yield a neatly packaged theology of blame or punishment but rather an invitation to embrace paradox and live authentically within its tension. Sin's "echo," as it reverberates through Ecclesiastes, is less a series of didactic injunctions and more a profound awareness of limitation, frustration, and moral perplexity. The Preacher's narrative unfolds as a voice inviting listeners into a mature spirituality that acknowledges the limitations of human wisdom and control, calling forth patience, reflection, and a contemplative recognition of divine mystery. This philosophical stance is a rare voice in biblical literature, embracing ambiguity rather than always seeking resolution, inviting a humble embrace of the question marks that accompany human history and personal experience. In this way, the book contributes a vital dimension to the understanding of sin: that it is not only an outward act of disobedience but a condition that invites us into a deeper theological and existential reckoning.

The metaphorical "chasing after the wind" can be seen as both condemnation and an honest appraisal of life's struggles against the confines imposed by sin and the fractured human condition. Every human project, every quest for immortality through legacy or accomplishment, is susceptible to loss and decay. The text's somber realism guards against illusions that one's own efforts can fully transcend the frailty embedded in creation. This extends not simply to individual sin but to communal and social realities, where patterns of injustice and sorrow persist despite legal codes and moral aspirations. The Preacher's stark observations paint a picture of a world in which sin's manifestations destabilize the meaning-making frameworks of society, where even wisdom's light casts long shadows of despair. Such sobering reflections compel a humility about moral certainty, a recognition that sin disrupts neat moral dichotomies and reveals the complexity lurking beneath human choices.

Moreover, Ecclesiastes' reflections invite us to appreciate the tension between divine omnipotence and human agency, a dynamic fraught with complexity, especially when observing the prevalence of sin and suffering. The Preacher wrestles with the arbitrary distribution of fortunes and misfortunes, noting that the righteous may suffer and the wicked prosper, complicating simplified models of divine justice. This apparent disjunction urges a more nuanced theology, where sin's consequences are neither immediate nor always comprehensible. The book suggests that the divine ordering of the world operates on levels beyond human understanding. Such insight can both humble the self-righteous and comfort those battered by life's inequities, providing space for patience and trust amidst unanswered questions. It reframes sin not as a puzzle to be neatly solved but as a profound reality calling for faith that endures despite mystery.

In this light, the role of repentance and redemption is implied rather than elaborated in explicit terms but remains central to the book's ultimate message. The acknowledgment of life's vanity and the need to "fear God" gestures toward a path of alignment with divine will, even when clarity is absent. This posture fosters a spirituality that holds both the darkness of sin and the hope of grace in tension, calling for ongoing ethical vigilance and spiritual humility. The Preacher's reflections do not abandon the possibility of meaning but situate it within a framework that survives paradox and embraces the complexity of human existence. Such a stance enriches contemporary conversations around sin by emphasizing that meaning can emerge precisely through wrestling with ambiguity, repentance, and reverence, rather than through denial or oversimplification.

When viewed against the broader biblical narrative, Ecclesiastes stands as a profound counterweight to more triumphant or legalistic portrayals of sin and righteousness. It amplifies the voice of the "everyman," the seeker who struggles with doubts, disillusionment, and the oft-painful realities of life in a fallen world. Its embrace of existential questioning enables believers to wrestle with the shadows of sin not as passive subjects but as active participants in a moral and spiritual odyssey. This dynamic underscores that sin's consequences ripple not only through acts of wrongdoing but through the often-painful search for meaning in their wake. The Preacher invites readers to lean into this tension without retreating into despair or facile optimism, modeling a faith that is honest, reflective, and ultimately hopeful.

The philosophical richness of Ecclesiastes provides a crucial perspective for modern readers grappling with sin's manifestations in personal, social, and global spheres. It confronts the temptation to reduce life's difficulties to simplistic moral formulas or to gloss over the pain and ambiguity that sin engenders. Instead, it advocates for a mature engagement with the realities of human limitation and divine mystery. This engagement fosters resilience and openness, cultivating a spirituality that holds fast to reverence and ethical living even when the outcomes remain uncertain. The recognition that many efforts in life are transient invites a redirection of focus from transient things to eternal values, including the cultivation of wisdom, justice, and compassion, qualities that resist the corrosive effects of sin and contribute to the restoration of broken relationships.

Ecclesiastes also implicitly voices a critique of idolatry, the human tendency to invest ultimate hope in things that are inevitably insufficient. The "vanity" critiqued is not merely the absence of substance but the misplacement of value onto temporal and fallible sources of meaning. This fall into misplaced trust can itself be understood as a form of sin, leading to disillusionment and despair. Thus, the Preacher's reflections act as a spiritual corrective, beckoning readers back to a divinely centered view that acknowledges human frailty without capitulating to nihilism. Sin's echo in the form of misguided aspirations and illusions becomes a recurrent call to spiritual alignment, urging a recalibration of priorities toward the divine order.

In the end, the search for meaning articulated by Ecclesiastes is not simply an intellectual exercise but a deeply spiritual journey through the terrain of sin, mortality, and grace. The book's poetic melancholy coexists with a sober hope that invites transformation. It situates the human subject within a vast cosmic narrative, where sin's ripples provoke reflection, repentance, and an ultimate, if sometimes elusive, encounter with divine mercy. The humility and awe that conclude the book's reflections invite readers not only to contemplate the frailty of existence but also to embrace the mystery and wonder of a Creator who remains sovereign over life's perplexities. In this embrace lies the possibility of sincere faith, ethical maturity, and an enduring quest for meaning that transcends the shadows cast by sin.

Thus, as we reflect on Ecclesiastes, we are drawn into a dialogue that balances skepticism and faith, despair and hope, futility and reverence, a dialogue that continues to shape theological and moral understanding. The acceptance of life's paradoxes opens space for a nuanced encounter with sin and redemption that honors the complexity of real human experience. This aged voice, echoing through biblical history, challenges each generation to wrestle honestly with the nature of sin, the limits of wisdom, and the boundless grace that ultimately redeems. It teaches us that the search for meaning, though fraught with difficulty, is itself a sacred endeavor, one that perseveres beyond the fleeting chase of the wind toward a horizon illumined by divine presence and eternal truth.

Job's Suffering and Faith

In the vast panorama of biblical narratives grappling with the complexity of sin and its consequences, the story of Job occupies a uniquely profound place, delving deeply into the nature of suffering, divine justice, and human endurance. Unlike many accounts that straightforwardly associate sin with punishment, Job's ordeal presents a nuanced, almost perplexing challenge to the simplistic equation of wrongdoing leading inevitably to misery. His narrative is a cornerstone for theodicy, the philosophical endeavor to reconcile the existence of evil and suffering with the notion of a just and omnipotent God. And within this age-old dialogue, Job's unwavering faith amidst relentless turmoil glimmers as a beacon of steadfastness, embodying the human capacity to endure and seek meaning beyond immediate pain.

Job begins as a man of remarkable righteousness, described explicitly as blameless and upright, one who feared God and shunned evil. His life is ordered, prosperous, and blessed with family and wealth, making him an exemplar of divine favor. Yet, this very perfection sets the stage for a cosmic challenge, wherein Satan questions the sincerity of Job's fidelity, insinuating that his piety is dependent solely on his blessings. This celestial wager becomes the catalyst for Job's profound descent into suffering: first, his livestock is stolen or destroyed, his servants murdered, his children tragically killed, and finally, he is beset with a painful plague. Each blow strips away not only his material wealth but also his social standing, health, and psychological peace. It is here that the theodicy of Job's story invites us to confront the unsettling question: why do the innocent suffer?

The philosophical implication at the heart of Job's suffering confronts believers and thinkers alike with what seems an intractable dilemma. If God is both loving and omnipotent, why allow innocence to be ravaged by pain and grief? The book's architecture refuses to provide a facile answer, instead threading through Job's dialogues and monologues a series of intense theological debates and human reflections that expose the discomfort of this mystery. Job's friends, who arrive to console him, represent traditional understandings of justice, they insist that suffering must be deserved, a consequence of sin. Their arguments echo the retributive justice common in the ancient world, a worldview that made sense of misfortune by linking it tightly to moral failure. But Job vehemently contests this logic, maintaining his innocence and asserting that his suffering is unjust, thus shaking the very foundations of the simplistic moral calculus of his time.

This contestation between Job and his friends opens the door to a broader meditation on the nature of sin itself and the role it plays in divine judgment and human suffering. Sin, rather than being a set of clearly definable transgressions, emerges here as a complex force that interacts with myriad human experiences in unpredictable ways. Job's innocence challenges the stereotype of deserved suffering, suggesting that human beings live in a world where suffering can be random, and pain is not always a direct reflection of one's moral state. This sobering insight not only complicates the assessment of sin and consequence but also introduces a profound empathy for human suffering that transcends facile moral judgments. Job's plight reveals the tension between a theological ideal of divine justice and the often harsh realities of life, where misfortune may befall the just and the wicked alike.

Amidst this cacophony of voices, Job's personal response to his suffering becomes a study in the endurance of faith. Despite his anguish, bitter lamentations, and at times anger towards God, Job does not abandon his quest for understanding or his ultimate trust in the divine. His speeches are raw and unfiltered, reflecting a sincerity and intimacy with God that many narratives shy away from in their portrayal of the faithful. Even when he cries out, "Why did I not perish at birth, and die as I came from the womb?" and when he questions God's justice with poignant honesty, Job clings to hope. His endurance is not passive submission but an active engagement with his circumstances, an insistence that suffering be heard, acknowledged, and wrestled with, rather than ignored or simply accepted.

The climax of Job's encounter with the divine comes not in the form of a direct answer to his questions but in a majestic and humbling revelation of God's sovereignty and inscrutability. When God finally speaks out of the whirlwind, the focus shifts dramatically from human concerns about justice to the awe-inspiring complexity of creation itself. God's questions to Job about the foundations of the earth, the control over the seas, the mysteries of the dawn, and the behavior of wild animals emphasize humanity's limited understanding and the vastness of divine wisdom. This divine discourse does not negate Job's suffering nor does it provide a neat moral equation; instead, it invites Job, and by extension, the reader, to trust in the divine governance of the world despite its mysteries and apparent injustices.

Philosophically, this shift suggests that attempts to rationalize all suffering within human frameworks of justice may be inherently inadequate. The divine response highlights the limits of human perspective and knowledge, challenging the hubris of assuming complete comprehension of suffering's origins or purposes. This is not to say that suffering is meaningless but that its full context is wrapped within the grander design of creation, which transcends human categorization. For Job, this encounter rekindles a humble faith, an acknowledgment of his smallness and the necessity of trust even in the absence of clear answers. This posture of faith does not erase pain but enlivens a relationship with God characterized by reverence, patience, and perseverance.

Moreover, Job's eventual restoration, his fortunes returned double, his family renewed, his health restored, should not be read merely as recompense for suffering or as divine favor regained. Rather, it symbolizes a restorative hope anchored in the possibility of redemption and renewal even after profound despair. It is a testament not only to God's mercy but to the resilience of the human spirit when tethered to faith. Yet, this restoration comes after the posturing of suffering and questioning; it acknowledges that faith and redemption often travel a winding road marked by doubt, courage, and honest grappling with pain.

Job's story, therefore, serves as a powerful refutation against simplistic attributions of suffering to sinfulness and, simultaneously, as a profound model of how endurance grounded in faith can sustain a person through the darkest trials. It provides a theological framework that embraces complexity, affirming that human beings are caught in an intricate web where sin, suffering, divine justice, and mercy intersect in ways that defy easy answers. The narrative insists on recognizing the legitimacy of questioning and lament, validating these as vital components of genuine faith rather than signs of weakness or failure.

This rich exploration of Job's suffering also invites readers into a deeper empathy for those who endure inexplicable pain in the modern world. It challenges contemporary believers and seekers to refrain from hasty judgment regarding others' hardships, encouraging compassion grounded in humility. It suggests that endurance is not passive resignation but an active, courageous participation in the mystery of life, marked by persistent faith and a refusal to abandon hope.

In sum, Job's experience embodies the enduring tension between human frailty and divine inscrutability, urging ongoing reflection on the nature of sin, suffering, and justice. His story transcends its ancient setting to speak to the universal human condition, a condition fraught with ambiguity, struggle, and the profound need for grace. Through Job, theodicy emerges not as a neat intellectual exercise but as a deeply personal journey of faith, perseverance, and ultimately, a sublime encounter with the transcendent mystery of God. The echoes of his endurance reverberate across time, inviting each generation to confront suffering with honesty, wrestle with the complexities of sin and justice, and emerge, like Job, with a faith tempered by both questioning and trust.

The New Testament Fulfillment

Jesus' Teachings on Sin

In the landscape of biblical teachings, the figure of Jesus Christ stands as a transformative presence, uniquely redefining the understanding of sin, grace, forgiveness, and redemption. His teachings on sin transcend the prevailing notions of his time, offering a profound moral and spiritual framework that extends beyond mere rule-keeping into the realm of heart transformation and new beginnings. Jesus' approach to sin reveals a compassionate awareness of human frailty while simultaneously calling for a rigorous ethical standard motivated by love and sincere repentance. This dual emphasis on mercy and moral integrity reshaped the divine-human relationship, inviting followers into a deeper experience of God's grace that is both personal and communal.

To grasp the fullness of Jesus' message about sin, one must first appreciate the cultural and religious context into which he entered. The Jewish tradition of the first century was steeped in a legalistic interpretation of sin, characterized by a heavy emphasis on adherence to the Mosaic Law. Sin was often perceived as a violation of external commandments demanding ritual purity and compliance with strict codes. Offenders were frequently subject to public judgment, ostracism, or divine retribution. This paradigm, while affirming the holiness of God and the necessity of righteousness, risks reducing sin to a checklist of infractions, obscuring the deeper realities of the human heart and the need for genuine transformation. Jesus confronted this paradigm by redirecting attention from mere outward compliance to the intentions, attitudes, and desires that dwell within, thereby exposing sin not only as discrete acts but as pervasive conditions that corrupt the very core of human existence.

In his Sermon on the Mount, Jesus articulated a revolutionary vision that unmasked the inner roots of sin. He proclaimed that anger, lust, envy, and pride are not peripheral issues but, in fact, manifestations of sin that defile a person far more profoundly than external acts. By equating anger with murder and lustful intent with adultery, Jesus illuminated the spiritual dimensions behind visible behavior, compelling his listeners to reconsider self-righteousness and judgment. His teachings pierced through the superficial righteousness of religious leaders and called every individual to authentic purity of heart. This radical emphasis on inward transformation challenged societal and religious norms, highlighting the moral responsibility humans bear not only for what is done but for what is harbored internally. Sin, therefore, became understood as a condition that entangles the mind and spirit, necessitating holistic restoration rather than mere ritual compliance.

Yet, Jesus did not dwell solely on exposing sin's depth and consequences; he also unveiled the transformative power of grace and forgiveness as the ultimate answers to human brokenness. His interactions with societal outcasts, sinners, and those burdened by guilt embodied a mercy that both surprised and scandalized the religious establishment. Pregnant with compassionate longing, Jesus extended forgiveness freely, inviting the repentant into a restored relationship with God. Through parables such as that of the Prodigal Son, he depicted a God who pursues the lost with relentless love, eager to restore, redeem, and reconcile. This message redefined sin not as an insurmountable barrier but as an opportunity for renewal, emphasizing that divine grace is not merited by human perfection but offered unconditionally to all who turn toward God with a contrite heart.

The moral implications of this grace-centric teaching on sin are profound. Jesus did not minimize the seriousness of sin; rather, he heightened the awareness of its pervasive influence while simultaneously proclaiming the hope of liberation through forgiveness. This balance curbs despair on the one hand and complacency on the other, fostering a dynamic moral responsiveness characterized by humble acknowledgment of fault, sincere repentance, and a continual turning toward God's healing power. Such a framework empowers individuals to transcend cycles of guilt and condemnation, inviting them into a new life marked by ongoing surrender, ethical renewal, and spiritual growth. The consequences of Jesus' forgiveness reach beyond individual salvation, cultivating communities rooted in mercy, reconciliation, and collective holiness.

Central to Jesus' teachings on sin is the idea of new beginnings. Forgiveness is not merely the wiping away of past failure but the inauguration of a restored identity and life trajectory. In his ministry, Jesus frequently declared the advent of the Kingdom of God, a reign characterized not only by divine authority but also by renewed ethics and transformed relationships. The forgiveness he offered was integrally linked to participation in this Kingdom, a radical reordering of social, spiritual, and moral spheres. Those who embraced his message entered into a new covenantal existence where sin's power was broken, and they were empowered by the Holy Spirit to walk in righteousness. This transformative dimension of sin and forgiveness is evident in the narratives of individuals whose lives were irrevocably altered by encounters with Jesus, demonstrating that grace facilitates authentic change and hopeful futures rather than mere absolution without consequence.

Moreover, Jesus' teachings challenge the prevailing human tendencies toward judgment and exclusion. His repeated encounters with tax collectors, prostitutes, and sinners highlight a profound inclusivity that defies societal stigmatization. By forgiving the woman caught in adultery and reprimanding those quick to condemn, Jesus underscores the perils of self-righteous judgment and elevates compassion. His message advocates for a community where sin is acknowledged honestly, but where forgiveness creates space for restoration rather than alienation. This ethic dismantles barriers that divide, inviting even the most marginalized into communion with God and others. The spiritual implications of such inclusivity are vast, fostering empathy and humility while countering attitudes of superiority and exclusion that perpetuate division.

The interplay of grace and accountability is also striking in Jesus' approach. While he offers forgiveness abundantly, he also calls for genuine repentance and transformation as evidence of receiving that grace. Forgiveness is not a license to sin; instead, it inaugurates a process of sanctification, a turning away from sin's bondage toward holiness. The imperative to "go and sin no more" demonstrates that moral renewal is inseparable from forgiveness, framing sin as a condition to be overcome rather than a static identity. Jesus emphasizes personal responsibility and persistent effort in embracing this new life, thereby integrating mercy with ethical rigor. This balanced vision negates fatalistic resignation, encouraging believers to actively participate in their own moral and spiritual healing with the aid of divine grace.

Jesus' teachings also illuminate how sin fractures not only the individual's relationship with God but also the broader social fabric. Through parables and exhortations, he reveals that sin's consequences extend into communal injustice, brokenness, and alienation. The call to love one's neighbor, to forgive seventy times seven, and to bear one another's burdens highlights the interconnectedness of spiritual and social ethics. Sin fosters estrangement while grace nurtures reconciliation and harmony. This broad perspective expands the scope of moral living to include social responsibility and justice, demonstrating that true forgiveness encompasses reconciliation both vertically with God and horizontally with others. Jesus challenges his followers to embody mercy as a lived reality that transforms relationships and communities, signaling that the echoes of sin are overcome not only through personal change but through collective restoration.

Spiritually, Jesus reorients the human understanding of sin by emphasizing its defeat through his life, death, and resurrection. Sin is portrayed as a power undermined by the incarnation and sacrificial love of Christ, which breaks the chains of condemnation and restores access to God's presence. This theological dimension provides believers with hope that forgiveness is grounded in divine action, rendering sin not merely a human dilemma but a cosmic one addressed by divine intervention. The cross becomes the pivotal event where sin's penalty is absorbed, opening the way for reconciliation and eternal life. Thus, Jesus' teachings invite believers to participate in this victory, living in the freedom and power afforded by his redemptive work, a reality that transforms the spiritual experience of sin from despair into hope.

In addition to these profound theological themes, Jesus' teachings on sin are marked by their practical application in daily living. He calls his followers into a lifestyle marked by humility, sincerity, and love, confronting hypocrisy and legalism at every turn. The Beatitudes exemplify this ethic, blessing those who mourn, are meek, or hunger for righteousness, signaling that transformation of character must precede societal change or religious success. The emphasis on mercy, purity, and peacemaking as marks of the blessed reflects a spiritual economy where sin is dethroned not by power or religious strictness but through the cultivation of virtues that align with God's Kingdom. This practical dimension empowers believers to embody forgiveness and grace in tangible ways, shaping not only their inner lives but also their social interactions, offering a countercultural witness to the enduring power of God's redemptive love.

Furthermore, Jesus' approach to sin includes a recognition of the complexity of human experience and the pervasive nature of temptation. He acknowledges the reality of spiritual struggle, the presence of evil, and the human propensity to fall short. Yet, his teachings provide a pathway to transcend these limitations. By encouraging prayer, reliance on divine strength, and a vigilant heart, Jesus fosters resilience and perseverance in the moral life. The Lord's Prayer, for instance, not only petitions forgiveness but also protection from temptation, encapsulating a holistic understanding of sin's multifaceted challenges. This anticipates the ongoing nature of moral growth and sanctification, inviting believers into a lifelong journey marked by dependence on God's mercy and grace.

The revolutionary nature of Jesus' teachings on sin also challenges social structures and religious authorities that had institutionalized exclusion and judgment. By proclaiming that tax collectors, Gentiles, and sinners were welcomed into the Kingdom, Jesus shattered established boundaries, reaffirming the universality of God's mercy. This inclusive vision upends hierarchical systems predicated on purity and exclusion, opening a spiritual democratization where sin no longer segregates but calls forth grace toward all. Such a stance carries radical social implications, emphasizing that no one is beyond redemption and that communities must embody forgiveness as a norm rather than an exception. This challenges contemporary believers to mirror this radical hospitality and grace within their own contexts.

In conclusion, Jesus' teachings on sin encapsulate a dynamic interplay of moral awareness, spiritual depth, and divine grace that redefine human existence. Sin, in his view, is not simply wrongdoing but a profound condition affecting the heart, mind, and community, necessitating holistic transformation. Jesus exposes the root causes of sin, reveals its seriousness, and simultaneously announces the possibility of forgiveness and new life through God's mercy. His message balances accountability with compassion, justice with grace, and individual repentance with communal reconciliation. Through his life, death, and resurrection, Jesus embodies the ultimate defeat of sin, inviting all into a restored relationship marked by hope, renewal, and continuous growth. As such, his teachings resonate across time, offering enduring wisdom for moral living and spiritual vitality, encouraging readers to embrace forgiveness as a path to freedom and to pursue holiness with courage and love. This transformative message remains a beacon illuminating the shadows of human fallibility with the light of divine mercy, inviting an ever-deepening journey into grace and ethical authenticity.

Crucifixion and Atonement

In the shadowed moments of history's greatest sacrifice, we find ourselves standing at the intersection of divine justice and overwhelming mercy, where human sinfulness meets the boundless compassion of God. The crucifixion and atonement of Jesus Christ constitute the ultimate fulfillment of a story that began long ago in the Garden of Eden, a poignant narrative arc that stretches from the brokenness of humanity's first disobedience to the redeeming hope etched out on a wooden cross. This event does not merely stand as a grand historical incident; rather, it embodies the profound depths of grace and forgiveness that permeate the biblical testament, offering new beginnings that resonate through time and into our own personal spiritual journeys. As we consider the gravity of the crucifixion, we confront the raw reality of sin's devastating power alongside the radical offer of restoration made possible through what appears as defeat but is in truth victory, a paradox that demands careful reflection and invites transformative contemplation.

The crucifixion itself is a tableau of injustice, pain, and sacrifice. Jesus, often depicted as the innocent lamb, is subjected to a cruel death that simultaneously reveals humanity's capacity for brutality and God's majestic plan for redemption. It is a spectacle that draws together the threads of prophecy, law, and mercy into one tragic yet hopeful tapestry. The brutality of Roman execution, nails driven through flesh, the weight of a crossbeam crushing weakened shoulders, the suffocating agony of hanging between heaven and earth, casts a somber veil over the scene. Yet beneath this physical suffering lies a theological significance that transcends human comprehension. The crucifixion is not simply an execution; it is a redemptive act imbued with deeper meaning, whereby the innocent voluntarily embraces the punishment deserved by sinners, effectively bearing the weight and consequence of humankind's transgressions. This mysterious exchange is central to understanding the atonement.

Atonement, in its biblical sense, is more than just payment for sin; it is the restoration of a broken relationship. In the ancient Hebrew tradition, rituals of sacrifice functioned to symbolize this restoration, an offering that bridged the gap between a holy God and a sinful people. The blood of animals, shed in ritual cleansings, was never sufficient to fully remove sin's stain, but these sacrifices pointed forward to a perfect act of reconciliation, a once-for-all sacrifice that could cleanse and heal not only externally but inwardly, spiritually. Jesus' death on the cross is that perfect sacrifice, an atoning gift that fulfills and surpasses the old covenant's limitations, making a profound and eternal provision for humanity's sins. His crucifixion represents the fullness of divine love manifested in incredible vulnerability and hope.

The theological richness of the atonement unfolds through the lens of grace, a grace that is both unearned and transformative. The crucifixion reveals God's willingness to forgive despite human rebellion, offering mercy where judgment was deserved. Herein lies an overwhelming tension: the just judgment of a holy God demands sin's penalty, while the love of God provides a means to escape that penalty through sacrifice. This divine paradox is the heart of the gospel message: justice is satisfied, and mercy triumphs. The crucifixion, therefore, becomes the focal point where grace flows abundantly, inviting believers to experience freedom from guilt, shame, and the entrapments of sin. It is an invitation to a new way of living defined not by condemnation but by renewed identity in Christ.

The imagery of grace extended through the crucifixion is deeply evocative. It calls to mind a bridge stretched over an abyss, connecting estranged humanity to God's presence. Those who accept this grace embark upon a journey of restoration, not merely through declaration but through transformation. The power of forgiveness is a cornerstone of this process; it dismantles walls built by sin and opens doors previously locked by despair. Forgiveness offered and received in the context of atonement is a radical act that frees hearts and communities from cycles of hurt and retaliation. It echoes loudly through the pages of the New Testament, where the early church grappled with what it meant to live in light of a cross that marked the end of the old order and the birth of a new covenant grounded in unconditional love.

New beginnings pulse at the center of the cross's shadow. The crucifixion is not the terminus but the genesis of hope and renewal. It echoes God's promise that sin and death, though fierce and destructive, will not have the final word. Through resurrection, the power of sin is decisively broken, and believers are invited into a resurrected life, a life steeped in the hope of restoration and eternal significance. This hope is not merely theoretical but meant to be lived out in the present, influencing daily actions, relationships, and ethical choices. The participants in this grace-filled narrative are called to embody the forgiveness received, extending mercy to others as a reflection of the divine mercy bestowed upon them. This shaping of character and community highlights the ongoing implications of the crucifixion and atonement for human existence.

The crucifixion also challenges simplistic notions of justice and punishment by introducing a profoundly relational view of redemption. It reveals sin as relational rupture, not only an offense against a divine code but a break in relationship with God, self, and others. The cross becomes a meeting place where these fractures begin to be healed. Here, justice is not merely retributive but restorative, aiming to bring wholeness to what was shattered. This perspective reframes the human predicament and God's response, suggesting that sin's ultimate defeat is realized not through condemnation but through the embrace of grace that renews rather than obliterates.

Furthermore, the cultural and historical dimensions surrounding the crucifixion enrich its significance. In an era dominated by imperial power, executions like crucifixion were symbols of shame and ultimate defeat aimed at maintaining control through terror. Yet God's act subverts this dynamic, transforming a symbol of humiliation into one of hope and salvation. This inversion communicates a powerful theological statement to both contemporaries and modern readers: God's kingdom operates under a logic distinct from worldly power, one of sacrificial love and self-giving rather than domination. The cross thus serves as a radical critique of human systems rooted in sin and a beacon of divine justice that transcends those systems.

The psychological and emotional resonance of the crucifixion is equally profound. Though Jesus endured unimaginable isolation, betrayal, and physical torment, his words from the cross echo a message of forgiveness and compassion. "Father, forgive them, for they know not what they do," he prays, embodying the depth of mercy that defines the crucifixion experience. This utterance encapsulates the invitation extended through atonement, not only for forgiveness but for understanding the human condition marked by ignorance and brokenness. It is a model of grace that challenges readers to reconsider their own responses in moments of suffering and injustice.

Examining the crucifixion through the lens of contemporary relevance reveals its continued power to inspire ethical reflection and personal growth. The narrative challenges individuals to confront the realities of sin in their own lives and to recognize the availability of forgiveness and transformation. The notion that one can be freed from the consequences of past wrongs resonates deeply in a world grappling with guilt, shame, and fractured relationships. Moreover, the crucifixion models a path for responding to wrongdoing, not through vengeance but through sacrificial love and active reconciliation. This radical ethic calls for courage and humility, inviting believers into a pattern of living marked by grace-filled resilience.

The ultimate sacrifice for sin, as shown in the crucifixion, opens pathways for dialogue across religious, cultural, and philosophical traditions. Its themes of suffering, sacrifice, justice, and mercy transcend specific doctrinal contexts, offering a universal meditation on human nature and divine compassion. This universality enriches its appeal and challenges communities to embody the principles exemplified. It also invites ongoing theological exploration, pushing believers to delve deeper into the mystery of God's redemptive work and the practical applications for contemporary moral life.

The grandeur of the cross's message unfolds through the resurrection, underscoring the inseparability of sacrifice and new life. Without resurrection, the crucifixion risks being misinterpreted as a tragic defeat. Instead, the resurrection illuminates the atonement's completeness, it demonstrates God's power to bring life from death, good from evil, hope from despair. This triumphant dimension expands the implications of the crucifixion beyond immediate forgiveness to eternal renewal. It reassures believers that sin's consequences, though real and serious, are ultimately temporary in the face of divine restoration.

As the narrative of crucifixion and atonement passes into the lived experience of believers, it becomes a transformative lens through which all other biblical stories and personal experiences are interpreted. It deepens understanding of earlier episodes of sin and judgment, framing them within a larger redemptive context. The lives of figures like Adam and Eve, Cain and Abel, and the Flood bear the marks of sin's tragic consequences. Yet the cross offers a horizon of hope beyond judgment, a promise that even the darkest stories can find light in God's mercy. This perspective fosters empathy for human frailty and conviction for spiritual growth.

In conclusion, the crucifixion and atonement represent the pinnacle of God's engagement with human sin, an encounter marked by pain, sacrifice, and incredible love. It is a divine act that simultaneously demands justice and invites mercy, exposing the devastating cost of sin while illuminating the boundless potential for forgiveness and restoration. Through this ultimate sacrifice, grace flows freely, inviting new beginnings for all who accept its gift. The echoes of the cross resonate endlessly, calling humanity into a lifelong journey of healing and hope, shaping moral vision and spiritual identity in ways both eternal and immediate. This event stands as a profound testament to the transformative power of love, proving that even amidst the shadows of sin, light and life prevail, forever changing the narrative of human existence.

Resurrection and Redemption

The story of resurrection and redemption stands as the culminating chapter in the vast narrative of sin's unfolding throughout biblical history, a vivid testimony to the profound power of grace, forgiveness, and new beginnings. It is a narrative that transcends mere historical recounting to embody the very heart of divine mercy and the renewal of existence itself. Forged in the crucible of suffering and betrayal, yet blossoming in the radiant dawn of hope and transformation, the resurrection story echoes across time as the ultimate triumph over sin and death's crushing dominion. To grasp the full magnitude of this event, one must immerse oneself deeply not only in its theological contours but also in the emotional and spiritual landscape it reveals, an invitation for all humanity to partake in a resurrection of spirit and life.

At its core, the resurrection is a profound act of divine intervention, a radical reversal of what seemed irrevocably lost. The narrative of Jesus Christ rising from the dead shatters the finality that sin and death appeared to impose on the human condition. This victory is not merely a physical event but the manifestation of a cosmic restoration, where the chains of human frailty and the shadow of eternal separation are broken. Throughout the Gospels, the resurrection stands as the pivotal moment where darkness yields to light, despair gives way to hope, and death's cold grip dissolves into life-giving breath. It propels the story of humanity from the despair of a tomb sealed in silence to the jubilation of an empty grave marked by the promise of new beginnings. The resurrection's significance lies not simply in what it conquered, sin and death, but also in what it reveals about the nature of God's love: unwavering, self-sacrificial, and boundless in its grace.

This grace, so vividly displayed through the resurrection, defies human expectations. The sin that once alienated humanity from God, creating a chasm of guilt and fear, encounters forgiveness that restores rather than condemns. The power of forgiveness, unmatched in its reach and depth, redefines the human encounter with sin. Instead of an endless cycle of judgment and punishment, forgiveness extends an olive branch toward reconciliation and healing. This divine forgiveness exemplifies a radical inclusivity: no sin too great, no failing beyond repair. The resurrection illustrates that God's mercy permeates even the darkest corners of human transgression, illuminating the possibility of renewal no matter the depth of fallibility. It is through this lens that the resurrection becomes more than an event; it transforms into a living invitation that waves to all humanity, beckoning each individual into the tender embrace of grace.

The narrative tension here is palpable because forgiveness in the face of sin is not passive. It demands a response, a turning of the heart, a repentance that aligns with the possibility of redemption. But this redemption is unlike the conditional bargains or transactional exchanges often seen in human relationships. It is a gift freely bestowed, a divine offering that calls forth a transformation of the self. Redemption, as revealed in the resurrection, is the sweeping away of the old identities forged in guilt and shame, replaced by a renewed existence characterized by freedom, dignity, and purpose. This renewal is not shallow; it is profound and all-encompassing, touching every facet of human life. It breathes vitality into the spiritual breathlessness wrought by sin and beckons toward a wholeness that transcends mere human attainment.

Alongside forgiveness and grace, the resurrection powerfully symbolizes new beginnings, both the literal rebirth of Christ and the metaphorical rebirth offered to all who embrace its truth. Its presence within the biblical canon climaxes not in a static victory but in an ongoing dynamic of life renewed and transformed. This new beginning ruptures the cycle of sin's ripple effects documented so thoroughly throughout scripture. Where ancient transgressions once founded fear, distrust, and fragmentation in human relationships, the resurrection offers a bridge toward unity, reconciliation, and hope. It posits a future that is open, unbounded by the weight of past errors. From the barren soil of failure and brokenness, it plants seeds of resurrection life that flourish into the fruits of love, peace, and joy. Each new day emerging from the resurrection is a call to embrace this gift, not as a mere concept but as an embodied reality, a way of life suffused with the resurrected presence.

The historical and cultural context surrounding the resurrection further underscores its revolutionary nature. In a world that often equated death with defeat and moral downfall, the resurrection stood starkly at odds with prevalent ideologies and expectations. It challenged the finality attributed to death by earthly powers and religious authorities while revivifying ancient hopes long cherished yet often dimmed by despair. The resurrection's triumph communicated a profound theological message: death, often seen as the final punishment for sin, is not the terminus of human existence. Instead, it reveals the mystery of life's endurance through divine power and the prospect of eternal communion with God. For the early followers of Jesus, grappling with oppression and uncertainty, this message ignited a transformative hope that would fuel faith communities and shape the very fabric of emerging Christian identity.

Understanding the resurrection's deep implications also requires reflection on how grace and redemption impact individuals and communities beyond the original biblical event. The narrative invites believers throughout the ages to identify with the themes of death and rising, of surrender and renewal. Every personal story marked by failure or despair can find resonance within the resurrection's rhythm. It promises that no human condition is exempt from the possibility of change, that sin's grip is never absolute when met with grace. This understanding fosters spiritual resilience and an enduring hope that sustains believers even amid life's darkest moments. The resurrection is thus continuously relevant; it creates a space where personal brokenness and communal sinfulness are not end points but openings for divine intervention and restoration.

Moreover, the resurrection's implications resonate profoundly in the moral and ethical spheres of life. Sin's persistent presence in human choices and social systems often seems insurmountable. Yet the resurrection embodies a higher principle that transcends despair: the potential for transformation and justice rooted in divine love. It challenges humanity to envision a world where forgiveness triumphs over vengeance, reconciliation over division, and renewal over decay. This vision compels individuals and communities toward active participation in the healing of broken relationships and systems. The resurrection is not simply a message of private salvation but a clarion call for social redemption, a stirring of the conscience toward creating justice and mercy in tangible ways.

To truly appreciate the resurrection's place in this grand narrative is to perceive how it harmonizes the themes of divine justice and mercy in a way that neither abolishes the reality of sin nor succumbs to its despair. It holds a divine tension, a balance where sin is acknowledged and confronted, yet met with compassion that seeks restoration rather than destruction. In this tension lies the transformative power of the resurrection: acknowledging the gravity of human failure while simultaneously opening the door to unmerited grace and life renewed. The resurrection does not erase the past but recontextualizes it, offering a future that is not dictated by sin's residue but by the hope infused by grace. It is an enduring symbol and reality of the new creation God envisages: a world where death and sin no longer have the ultimate word.

Finally, the resurrection points forward to a consummation of history still awaited, where the fullness of redemption will be realized. It anticipates an eschatological hope deeply rooted in biblical tradition but newly revealed in the person of Christ. This hope assures believers that the victory over sin and death witnessed in the resurrection is no isolated event but the harbinger of a restored cosmos. It beckons all toward a horizon where suffering, injustice, and spiritual alienation will be vanquished. The resurrection thus remains a living, breathing force within faith, transforming how the past is viewed, how the present is lived, and how the future is hoped for. It is the ultimate echo of sin's story, a resounding decree of victory that promises grace abounding, forgiveness unending, and beginnings anew.

In sum, the resurrection and redemption narrative is an inexhaustible wellspring of hope that shatters the finality of sin and death, illuminating the profound depths of divine love and mercy. It invites continual reflection on how grace can rewrite even the darkest chapters of human experience, guiding individuals toward spiritual renewal and communities toward justice and peace. It confronts humanity with the possibility of transformation that transcends sin's ripple effects and ushers in a new reality, marked not by condemnation but by restoration, not by despair but by steadfast hope. Through this victory, the timeless dialogue between human imperfection and divine mercy finds its most eloquent expression, inspiring countless generations to embrace the power of resurrection in their own lives and in the world around them.

Echoes into Modern Life

Sin and Society Today

The echoes of sin are not confined to the dusty scrolls of ancient texts or the distant epochs of biblical history; they are insistent whispers threading through the very fabric of our modern existence. To understand sin as a dynamic force that shaped civilizations and spiritual trajectories in biblical times compels us to confront its persistent presence and manifestations in contemporary society. Sin, in its essence, is a disruption, an aberration that fractures harmony, distorts relationships, and invokes consequences that ripple far beyond a single act or moment. Today, as in ages past, sin operates both invisibly and overtly, woven into the collective psyche, social structures, and individual choices that define the moral landscape of modern life. Yet, faced with the complexities of our world, it becomes crucial to recognize how ancient lessons on sin profoundly inform and challenge us now, urging reflection on the subtle ways transgression permeates contemporary culture and personal existence.

Sin's enduring influence in society today manifests through its insidious capacity to infiltrate systems and mindsets, shaping inequities and moral failures on both micro and macro scales. In the labyrinth of modern social dynamics, marked by rapid technological advancement, political turmoil, economic disparity, and cultural pluralism, the age-old tensions between selfishness and altruism, truth and deceit, justice and injustice remain agonizingly familiar. Consider, for instance, the ways systemic sin appears through structures that perpetuate inequality, exploitation, and injustice. Like the biblical narratives where communal sin led to disintegration and divine judgment, societal sins today reverberate in oppression, corruption, and environmental degradation. These are not isolated lapses but symptoms of a collective turning away from ethical stewardship and compassionate justice, reflecting the ancient warnings of prophets who decried social sins such as arrogance, greed, and neglect of the vulnerable. The persistent marginalization of communities, the widening chasm between wealth and poverty, and the exploitation of natural resources all echo calls from ages long past to reevaluate our priorities and values.

Moreover, the digital age has ushered in new arenas where sin's subtleties thrive and proliferate. The virtual landscape, with its anonymity and immediacy, exposes profound human vulnerabilities and temptations, often exacerbating selfish behaviors, envy, deception, and disconnection. Social media platforms, while enabling unprecedented global connectivity, simultaneously harbor spaces for slander, judgment, and the distortion of truth, modern manifestations of what biblical texts depict as the corrosive effects of sinful speech and deceit. The compulsion to curate idealized identities fosters pride and hypocrisy, while cyberbullying and misinformation sow division and harm on large scales. In this context, ancient admonitions against bearing false witness or harboring envy resonate anew, challenging us to cultivate integrity and empathy amid pervasive digital noise. The temptation to substitute authentic relationships with virtual façades invites us to reflect on the biblical injunctions toward genuine community and accountability.

Individual sin, too, remains palpably present in the struggles that define human experience today. Despite great strides in knowledge, communication, and ethical discourse, the personal battles with temptation, pride, selfishness, and moral blindness endure, emblematic of the enduring conflict between human frailty and divine expectations. These personal failings, though often hidden beneath layers of social veneer, contribute cumulatively to societal malaise; the ripple effect of an individual's choices invariably touches broader communal realities. Addiction, dishonesty, betrayal, and apathy all highlight how sin, when unacknowledged or unrepentant, corrodes not only selfhood but relationships and the social fabric. In this light, the ancient stories from Eden's fall to David's repentance underscore the timelessness of human moral struggle, offering both cautionary exemplars and redemptive hope. The biblical models teach that acknowledging sin is the first step toward restoration, a lesson increasingly vital in an era that sometimes glorifies denial or relativism over accountability.

At a deeper level, the existential dimension of sin challenges modern society's often secular frameworks that prioritize individual autonomy detached from transcendent moral anchors. The loss or marginalization of a shared ethical foundation rooted in divine revelation leaves many grappling with subjective moralities that may inadvertently harbor forms of spiritual rebellion and disconnection. These realities call into question the parameters of freedom itself, as the biblical understanding of sin reveals how choices misaligned with divine will bring bondage rather than liberty. The tension between autonomy and obedience echoes throughout biblical accounts where the refusal to submit to divine guidance leads to alienation and chaos. Modern secular ideologies that champion limitless freedom without corresponding responsibility potentially echo the folly of humanity's earliest defiance in Eden, illustrating the ongoing relevance of these age-old narratives. In grappling with this tension, believers and seekers alike are invited to rediscover an ethic that transcends cultural whims and grounds moral life in enduring truths.

Sin's impact on mental and emotional health constitutes another significant parallel bridging biblical insights and contemporary challenges. The pervasive sense of guilt, shame, anxiety, and spiritual emptiness that can accompany wrongdoing or estrangement from ethical ideals mirrors the biblical experiences of characters burdened by their transgressions. Biblical narratives do not shy away from depicting the psychological and relational havoc wrought by sin, Cain's anguish after Abel's murder, David's torment over his moral failures, and the collective despair of exile. All illuminate the deep internal consequences of sin.

Today, modern psychology and pastoral care increasingly recognize that unaddressed moral injury disrupts holistic well-being, making the biblical emphasis on confession, forgiveness, and reconciliation profoundly relevant. The transformative journey toward restoration outlined in Scripture offers therapeutic frameworks that integrate spiritual healing with emotional renewal, underscoring the holistic nature of redemption.

Yet, amid these sobering realities, the biblical portrayal of sin is not one of despair but of hope and possibility for redemption. This transformative power emerges as a pivotal thread linking ancient narratives with contemporary lives. The biblical storyline continuously reorients around the possibility of forgiveness, restoration, and new beginnings through repentance and divine grace. In a world where sin's damaging effects often seem relentless and systemic, the ancient gospel message proposes an alternative trajectory, a movement from brokenness to wholeness, from estrangement to reconciliation, from death to life. This hope challenges modern cynicism and fatalism by affirming that no failure is beyond the reach of mercy and renewal. The person and work of Jesus Christ, as the culmination of biblical redemption, provide an anchor for this assurance, inviting individuals and societies to embark on paths of transformation rooted in divine compassion. This redemptive narrative, far from antiquated myth, retains startling relevance for today's fractured world, affirming that the echoes of sin need not define destiny.

Applying these ancient lessons to current societal challenges invites a critical stance toward issues such as systemic injustice, environmental stewardship, and cultural fragmentation. If sin is understood as a pervasive force influencing collective choices and structures, then any authentic moral response must address not only individual behavior but also the socio-political ecosystems that enable or tolerate wrongdoing. Biblical calls for justice, mercy, and humility remain clarion calls to modern communities, urging advocacy for the marginalized, ethical governance, and responsible care for creation. The prophetic voices demanding repentance in the Old Testament challenge contemporary society to vigilance in confronting institutionalized sin. Furthermore, the awareness that human frailty underlies much wrongdoing fosters empathy and patience, discouraging simplistic condemnation and encouraging restorative practices. In this way, the interplay between justice and mercy articulated in Scripture equips society to navigate complex moral landscapes with a balanced, grace-filled approach.

On a personal level, the engagement with biblical sin narratives invites readers into profound self-examination and ethical commitment. The stories compel us to ask pointed questions about how our choices, attitudes, and priorities contribute, however subtly, to broader patterns of harm or healing. They encourage a posture of humility, recognizing the universal susceptibility to error while also affirming the capacity for change through intentional repentance and trust in divine aid. This ethical introspection, grounded in the rich tapestry of biblical wisdom, becomes a foundation for living with greater integrity and grace. It also fosters spiritual awareness, nurturing a sensibility attuned to detecting and resisting harmful impulses that often masquerade as freedom or fulfillment. Here, the ancient lessons offer practical guidance for navigating the complexities of modern moral decision-making, urging vigilance and hope in equal measure.

The challenges posed by sin in a pluralistic and rapidly changing world raise significant questions regarding dialogue, tolerance, and truth. While embracing diversity and respecting differing viewpoints are vital for social harmony, the biblical understanding of sin calls for discernment and courage in confronting moral falsehood and injustice. This balance demands a nuanced engagement, avoiding both relativism that erodes ethical anchors and harsh dogmatism that shuts down compassionate discourse. The ancient narratives demonstrate that righteous living in the face of sin requires both conviction and compassion, a fragile but necessary tension for sustaining communities marked by fragility and grace. In contemporary society, this entails fostering spaces where truth can be honestly confronted and where repentance and restoration are possible, echoing the prophets' call for hearts turned toward renewal.

Importantly, the communal nature of sin depicted throughout Scripture offers vital insight into how modern society understands responsibility. Sin is rarely an isolated act but part of relational and social matrices. Recognizing this fosters a shift from purely individualistic perspectives toward a more comprehensive view that includes community accountability and cooperative transformation. Such awareness challenges privatized ethics and encourages collective efforts to cultivate environments of justice, healing, and peace. It inspires movements dedicated to reconciliation, whether between estranged individuals, divided communities, or humanity and the broader creation, underscoring the biblical vision of shalom as holistic well-being. This paradigm invites each person to see their role not only as a moral agent but as an active participant in the world's restoration, extending the ancient covenantal themes into present-day praxis.

Furthermore, the biblical exploration of sin amidst trials and temptations imparts resilience and hope, reminding us that failure is not the conclusion of the moral journey but an invitation to deeper dependence on divine mercy. Stories of repentance and redemption serve as beacons, illuminating paths forward when societal or personal transgressions seem overwhelming. This perspective reframes sin not as a static condition but as a dynamic reality that can catalyze transformation, growth, and renewed commitment to goodness. In a culture often quick to shame or condemn, the biblical approach fosters restorative justice and compassionate correction, vital for sustaining communities where all members can aspire toward healing and wholeness.

Finally, the persistent relevance of sin's echoes in society underscores the need for ongoing education, reflection, and spiritual nurture to equip individuals and communities to resist and overcome the sway of destructive inclinations. The tradition of biblical storytelling, combined with theological reflection, offers rich resources for cultivating wisdom and moral imagination. Engaging with these ancient narratives invites continual formation, a lifelong journey marked by awareness, repentance, and grace, elements essential for navigating the ethical challenges of any era. As readers ponder the ancient stories intertwined with contemporary realities, they are encouraged to embody the transformative lessons of sin and redemption, becoming beacons of hope and agents of renewal in a world still reverberating with echoes of ancient transgression.

Personal Reflection and Growth

The journey through the echoes of sin, from the dawn of creation to the promise of redemption, is not merely an academic or historical exploration; it is an invitation into a deeply personal conversation with the fabric of our own lives. The stories and struggles that unfold within the pages of Scripture are far from distant relics. They are, in truth, reflections of our own moral landscapes, mirrors casting back the complexities of human choice, weakness, and the relentless yearning for grace. To engage fully with the lessons embedded in these ancient narratives demands that we turn inward, daring to confront the ways sin has shaped not only the world at large but the very contours of our hearts and actions. It requires a profound willingness to translate the symbolism and morality of biblical epochs into the living reality of everyday existence, to inhabit the tension between fallibility and hope in meaningful, transformative ways.

At the core of this personal reflection is the recognition that sin, in its many forms, is not an abstract concept but a living force, one that exerts a subtle yet consequential influence on our decisions, relationships, and self-perceptions. It beckons us to consider not only the grand-scale ramifications of wrongdoing but the quiet, often imperceptible choices that steer the course of our lives. In this light, the biblical narratives serve as a vast tableau of human behavior, illuminating the myriad ways that pride, envy, anger, and disobedience can unravel individuals and communities. Yet, intertwined with these portrayals of failure is the persistent thread of divine mercy and the possibility of renewal. This dialectic invites each reader to embark on a journey not of condemnation but of insight, where understanding sin's grip enables the pursuit of liberation and a deeper alignment with moral truth.

Applying these ancient lessons begins with an honest self-examination. Much like Adam and Eve's initial encounter with disobedience, an event that forever altered humanity's trajectory, we are called to identify where we, too, have yielded to impulses that fracture our relationship with God, others, and ourselves. This process is neither easy nor comfortable, as it requires peeling back layers of denial, justification, and fear to confront vulnerability. It means asking hard questions: Where have I acted out of selfishness or pride? In what ways have I ignored the welfare of others in pursuit of my own desires? How have my decisions contributed to patterns of brokenness or alienation? Yet, amidst these inquiries, there resides the unwavering possibility for repentance, a turning away from destructive pathways toward healing and growth.

This turning is not a momentary gesture but a dynamic, ongoing commitment, an ethical labor of love that colors every facet of our existence. Recognizing the ripple effect of sin compels us to comprehend that our actions, however innocuous they may seem, resonate beyond ourselves. The narrative of Cain and Abel, for instance, is not solely about fratricide but embodies the dangers of unrestrained jealousy and anger, emotions that can corrode the soul and poison community bonds. In our modern context, this calls for vigilance in how we handle conflict, jealousy, and resentment. We become more conscious of the damage that harboring grudges or cultivating envy can inflict upon relationships and social harmony. Such awareness encourages the practice of forgiveness, not merely as a theological ideal but as a practical, transformative act that restores connection and nurtures empathy.

Moreover, these lessons challenge us to consider the systemic and societal implications of sin and injustice. The flood narrative, though centered on divine judgment, also underscores human complicity in perpetuating violence and corruption. It prompts reflection on how our collective actions uphold structures that marginalize, oppress, or harm others. As inheritors of these ancient stories, we bear a responsibility to examine the societal echoes of sin that persist today, in institutions, cultural norms, and economic disparities. This examination is not to cast blame indiscriminately but to awaken a sense of moral accountability and inspire active engagement in fostering justice and compassion within our communities. The biblical witness thus becomes a catalyst for social transformation, urging us to challenge inequities and participate in the restoration of communal well-being.

Integral to this journey of personal and social reflection is the role of humility and the acceptance of imperfection. Biblical figures like King David starkly reveal how even the most anointed and beloved are beset by flaws and failures. Yet, their stories also embody the resilience of repentance and the hope for restoration. Embracing this truth allows us to shed the paralyzing weight of guilt and shame, understanding sin not as a final sentence but as a condition from which redemption is possible. It encourages an attitude of grace toward oneself and others, fostering the capacity to forgive and to seek forgiveness. This relational dynamic is foundational to spiritual growth, cultivating an openness that dismantles barriers of pride and self-righteousness.

Incorporating these lessons into daily life also involves cultivating practices that nurture conscience and spiritual sensitivity. Prayer, meditation on Scripture, and communal worship become crucibles where reflection and transformation coalesce. These spiritual disciplines help attune us to the divine voice of conviction and comfort, balancing the tension between justice and mercy that permeates the biblical narrative. Through sustained engagement, we develop a moral litmus that guides choices with greater wisdom and compassion, shaping attitudes and behaviors in alignment with a higher ethical vision. They create spaces where self-awareness deepens, and the desire to embody love, integrity, and humility finds tangible expression.

Furthermore, the trajectory traced by biblical sin narratives, culminating in the New Testament revelation of Jesus Christ, invites a hopeful reassessment of human possibility. The story of Christ's life, death, and resurrection recontextualizes ancient struggles, introducing a redemptive horizon that surpasses previous limitations. This central message invades the realm of personal reflection with an empowering promise: that no sin is too great to be met with divine grace, no failure beyond the reach of transformative love. It challenges readers to envision a moral and spiritual journey marked by renewal, not resignation, a pilgrimage where setbacks become lessons and grace becomes our compass.

In practical terms, this transformative hope manifests as the courage to make different choices, to cultivate virtues that counteract sin's destructive energies, and to engage in the ongoing work of moral repair. It pushes us to embrace accountability, to seek restoration with those we have wronged, and to participate actively in healing fractured relationships. It sustains perseverance in the face of recurring challenges and setbacks, reminding us that growth is seldom linear but always worthwhile. This sustained commitment reflects the biblical pattern of repentance and renewal, weaving personal narratives into the grand tapestry of divine mercy.

At a deeper level, embracing these lessons transforms our worldview, shifting from seeing sin merely as a list of prohibitions to recognizing it as a pervasive moral reality that calls forth creativity, courage, and compassion. We begin to appreciate the profound interconnectedness of human actions and divine purposes, recognizing our place within a continuum of spiritual struggle that spans generations. This awareness instills a profound respect for the gravity of choice, urging careful cultivation of habits, intentions, and community practices that nurture life and dignity.

Finally, this process of applying biblical lessons to personal life invites an expansive empathy that transcends individual concerns. It nurtures a sensitivity to the shared condition of humanity, recognizing that sin's echoes reverberate in diverse contexts and histories. This empathy becomes a bridge to solidarity and compassion, fueling efforts to embody justice, mercy, and reconciliation in both intimate relationships and wider social spheres. In doing so, it not only honors the legacy of biblical teachings but animates them as living forces that continue to shape our moral imagination and guide our steps through the complexities of the modern world.

Thus, the ancient lessons on sin cease to be distant echoes and instead resonate as clarion calls to transformation, calls that invite us to embrace our brokenness and grace, to confront our shadows with courage, and to walk forward in hope. They compel a lifelong engagement with the tension between human frailty and divine mercy, reminding us that the story of sin is, ultimately, a story of the enduring possibility of redemption and growth. The richness of this reflection offers a path toward deeper authenticity, greater ethical clarity, and a life imbued with purpose and grace amid the challenges and complexities of our own times.

Hope and Redemption

The journey of faith is marked not merely by the recognition of human frailty and the inescapable presence of sin but by the powerful undercurrent of hope and the possibility of redemption that courses through the biblical narrative. As we traverse the ages, from the earliest chapters of Genesis to the transformative revelations of the New Testament, it becomes clear that hope and redemption are not simply abstract ideals but lived realities, dynamic processes that have shaped individuals, communities, and the divine-human relationship itself. This subchapter invites readers to step alongside the ancient pilgrims of faith as they wrestle with sin, stumble through despair, and ultimately find restoration, offering a profound reflection on how these ancient lessons of hope and redemption resonate in our own lives today.

At the heart of biblical history lies a paradox: humanity's propensity to fall short coexists with a divine invitation to rise again. This invitation is neither timid nor conditional in a limited sense; it is an enduring, generous offer that transcends eras, cultures, and personal failings. When we consider figures such as King David, renowned for his courage, leadership, and poetic genius, we also confront his profound moral failings: adultery, deception, and orchestrated violence. Yet, David's story is not confined to his sins; rather, it is enlivened by his contrition and the restorative grace he encounters. His psalms echo with the rawness of repentance and the yearning for renewal, revealing an intimate dialogue with God where hope is kindled even from the depths of guilt and despair. David does not deny his brokenness, but he refuses to be defined by it. Instead, he becomes a beacon of how redemption is woven into the fabric of covenant relationship, a relationship marked by mercy that is neither deserved nor earned but freely offered.

This theme finds powerful expression throughout the prophetic tradition, where voices like Isaiah, Jeremiah, and Hosea solemnly warn of the consequences of sin and social injustice, yet unfailingly hold out hope for restoration. Their oracles often pivot from indictment to consolation, portraying a future where the broken covenant is renewed, sins are forgiven, and harmony is restored between God and His people. The image of a suffering servant in Isaiah, for instance, embodies not simply individual sacrifice but a cosmic act of redemption that reverberates through history. It forecasts a redemption that is transformative and far-reaching, offering healing not just for personal spirits but for fractured communities and nations. Such prophetic visions remind us that hope is not wishful thinking or naïve optimism, but a resolute expectation grounded in divine faithfulness, a promise that human failures will not have the final word.

The journey of faith is also vividly embodied in the Exodus narrative, where the Israelites' deliverance from slavery in Egypt stands as a monumental historical-theological act of redemption. This event is not simply an ancient rescue tale; it is a foundational story that shapes Israel's identity as a people liberated by God's power and love. The wilderness wanderings, with their hardships and tests, reflect the ongoing process through which the Israelites, and by extension all believers, learn to trust God's guiding hand despite setbacks and uncertainties. This journey underscores that redemption is not a singular event but a lifelong pilgrimage. It invites readers today to embrace the reality that liberation from the past, be it personal sin, trauma, or bondage, requires perseverance, faith, and continual reliance on divine grace. The Exodus teaches us that God's redemptive work is patient and persistent, inviting us to move beyond shame and guilt into a future shaped by hope.

In the New Testament, the theme of hope and redemption finds its fullest and most profound expression through the life, death, and resurrection of Jesus Christ. Here, the echoes of ancient Israelite hope resound with new clarity and power. Jesus' ministry confronts human sin head-on but never abandons the sinner to condemnation. Instead, He embodies divine mercy that transforms lives from within, illustrating that redemption is not merely a judicial pardon but the restoration of human dignity and the possibility of new beginnings. The crucifixion, often viewed as the ultimate symbol of suffering and injustice, becomes the pathway to the greatest victory over sin and death, paradoxically, while the resurrection ushers in a new era where hope transcends even the finality of death. Through Christ, biblical hope is reframed not as an uncertain anticipation but as an assured confidence in God's promise to bring renewal to all creation. This hope empowers believers, then and now, to live with courage and purpose amid life's uncertainties, holding fast to the assurance that redemption is both personal and cosmic.

Importantly, the biblical narrative insists that hope and redemption are not passive states but active pursuits, it challenges readers to engage in the work of repentance, reconciliation, and transformation. Redemption calls for honest self-examination, the courage to confront uncomfortable truths, and the willingness to change course. It invokes a community dimension as well, urging restoration not only of individual lives but also of fractured relationships and broken societies. The prophets' calls for justice, mercy, and humility reflect this communal dimension, demanding that faith be expressed through tangible acts of compassion and integrity. Today's readers are thus invited to consider how ancient lessons stir contemporary responsibilities, to seek justice where there is oppression, to extend forgiveness where there is hurt, and to nurture hope in the face of despair. Redemption is a journey that moves outward as much as it moves inward; it is the restoration of wholeness not only for oneself but for the world.

The enduring presence of hope in the midst of human failures serves as a profound encouragement to anyone facing the weight of guilt, regret, or spiritual dryness. Unlike fleeting encouragements rooted in circumstances, biblical hope is anchored in the character of God, the one who is steadfast, compassionate, and eager to restore. This steadfastness challenges our transient human fears, inviting us to embrace a long view that sees beyond immediate failures to the eventual fulfillment of divine promises. The stories of hope set forth in the Bible testify repeatedly that no sin or failure is too great to preclude redemption, that the divine heart is ever open to the contrite. Even the most tragic stories, such as that of Cain's exile or Saul's downfall, are counterbalanced by glimmers of mercy and possibilities for renewal, affirming that hope always kindles amid human darkness.

As readers today grapple with their own moral struggles and seek meaning in a complex world, these ancient biblical lessons offer both a mirror and a beacon. They prompt us to recognize the patterns of sin and consequence in our personal and collective histories, while simultaneously illuminating the pathways that lead to healing and wholeness. The invitation to hope and redemption calls us beyond despair and cynicism toward a faith that transforms sorrow into joy, brokenness into beauty, and exile into homecoming. It urges a refusal to let failures define us and instead to embrace the grace that enables new beginnings. This dynamic interplay between human responsibility and divine initiative crystallizes the essence of faith: a journey marked by the tension between reality and promise, fallibility and grace.

Throughout this exploration of hope and redemption, it becomes evident that they are not endpoints but ongoing movements that ripple through time. Every act of repentance, every moment of forgiveness, every step toward justice echoes through history and propels the journey of faith forward. This ongoing journey invites us to live in a rhythm of grace, acknowledging our shortcomings, accepting forgiveness, and striving toward transformation. It calls us, too, to be vessels of hope in a world replete with pain and brokenness, agents of redemption through acts of love, mercy, and truth.

In embracing hope and redemption, ancient lessons become living truths that sustain, challenge, and inspire. They remind us that amidst the persistent shadows of sin, the light of grace never dims; rather, it beckons us to a deeper understanding of our own stories within the grand tapestry of divine history. We are invited not only to reflect on the solemnity of sin but to celebrate the redemptive possibilities that arise from grace, transforming lives, communities, and the trajectory of history itself. Thus, the ancient echoes of sin become the clarion call to personal transformation and communal renewal, urging each of us to continue the sacred journey of faith with courage, humility, and profound hope.